Presidential Communication and Character

This book traces the evolution of White House news management during America's changing media environment over the past two decades. Comparing and contrasting the communication strategies of Bill Clinton, George W. Bush, Barack Obama, and Donald Trump, it demonstrates the difficulty that all presidents have in controlling their messages despite a seemingly endless array of new media outlets and the great advantages of the office. That difficulty is compounded by new media's amplification of presidential character traits for good or ill. Facebook, Twitter, and YouTube notwithstanding, presidential power still resides in the "power to persuade," and that task remains a steep challenge. More than ever, presidential character matters, and the media presidents now employ report on the messenger as much as the message.

The book also looks at the media strategies of candidates during the 2016 presidential campaign, puts presidential media use in global context, and covers the early phase of the Trump administration, the first true Twitter presidency.

Stephen J. Farnsworth is Professor of Political Science and International Affairs, and Director of the Center for Leadership and Media Studies, at the University of Mary Washington. He is the author or coauthor of six books on the presidency and the mass media, and is a 2017 recipient of the State Council of Higher Education for Virginia's Outstanding Faculty Award.

Presidential Communication and Character

White House News Management
from Clinton and Cable to
Twitter and Trump

Stephen J. Farnsworth

University of Mary Washington

Routledge
Taylor & Francis Group

NEW YORK AND LONDON

Published 2018
by Routledge
711 Third Avenue, New York, NY 10017

and by Routledge
2 Park Square, Milton Park, Abingdon, Oxon, OX14 4RN

Routledge is an imprint of the Taylor & Francis Group, an informa business

Library of Congress Cataloging-in-Publication Data
A catalog record for this book has been requested

ISBN: 978-1-138-21372-2 (hbk)
ISBN: 978-1-138-21223-7 (pbk)
ISBN: 978-1-315-44704-9 (ebk)

Typeset in Sabon
by Apex CoVantage, LLC

To Tanya DeKona, who makes all things possible

Contents

Acknowledgments

This project is the result of support generously offered from many sources. The first debt is to those who have made their surveys available to scholars, including the public opinion and news consumption surveys produced by the Pew Research Center, Gallup and the *Washington Post*. I also thank the Center for Media and Public Affairs of George Mason University and Media Tenor, Inc., for content analysis results. I also am very grateful for my previous research collaborations with Bob Lichter, Roland Schatz, Stuart Soroka, and Diana Owen, who have done much to shape my thoughts about presidential portrayals in the mass media.

Thanks to colleagues Bob Lichter, Emile Lester, and William Wadsworth for reading the entire manuscript and for their helpful suggestions about this project as it took shape. I also wish to express my gratitude to Ben Hermerding, Ellen O'Brien, Emma Valinski, and William Wadsworth, former students of mine who have since gone on to professional careers of their own, for their research assistance on this project over the past few years.

Thanks as well to political communication colleagues who commented on various research papers that are the building blocks of this book. The arguments here were refined in light of the generous advice offered at research panels at the 2016 and 2017 meetings of the American Political Science Association, the 2017 meeting of the Western Political Science Association, the 2016 meeting of the Midwest Political Science Association, and the 2015 Conference on 9/11 and the Academy at Emory and Henry College in Emory, Virginia.

Thanks as well to Jennifer Knerr and her team at Routledge, including Ze'ev Sudry, Kevin Kelsey and Francesca Hearn, for their prompt and professional treatment of this book manuscript and for their patience in my efforts to provide up-to-the-minute discussions of the fast-moving Trump presidency.

I thank the University of Mary Washington and its Center for Leadership and Media Studies for support of this project.

Thanks are also due for the many years of encouragement I have received from my parents and from Tanya DeKona, who in particular has endured my grief as the companion of an anxious academic these many years.

All conclusions in this work, as well as any errors and omissions, are my responsibility.

Stephen J. Farnsworth

1 Presidents Struggle to Shape the News

The first four presidents of the internet age developed markedly different approaches to selling themselves and their policies through the mass media. While the White House has long been the center of American political discourse, the ever-expanding range of media outlets that have emerged over the past two decades have forced recent presidents to redesign their media management strategies repeatedly in the face of frequently changing journalistic and political environments. Consider, for example, the early morning tweet storms of Donald Trump, Barack Obama casually shooting baskets for a viral BuzzFeed video or George W. Bush standing on an aircraft carrier wearing a flight suit. All of these media moments demonstrate that tried-and-true White House strategies of winning the news cycle change to frame different kinds of presidential media presentations in different news environments. Above all, modern presidents emphasize their personal qualities in public communication to maximize their popularity and their effectiveness.

Rapid technology advancements have created new opportunities and challenges for each recent presidential administration, making recent decades a period of extensive White House communication experimentation. This book considers the evolution of presidential news management during the massive changes that have rocked America's mass media over the past quarter century. We examine the differing media strategies of four presidents, starting with Bill Clinton, who used television news (particularly cable outlets) to charm the nation and then to turn the tables on those who would drive him from office. We consider as well the case of George W. Bush, who successfully silenced the critics of the Iraq War early on but subsequently lost control of the narrative nearly everywhere but on Fox News. We then turn to Barack Obama, whose diffident style on social media created a new approach to public communications, and conclude with a study of Donald Trump, whose pugnacious rhetoric and aggressive use of insults and dubious evidence on Twitter marked the greatest departure yet for presidential news-framing efforts during the online age.

Despite their many differences in personality and in the media environments they encountered during their years in office, one theme remains constant: each presidential candidate and later each president had to struggle to shape the news narrative and they fought back against critics and negative media reports by emphasizing presidential character. Rather than concentrating on issues, campaigns often try to win over less partisan and less committed voters by emphasizing the personalities of the men and women who would be president. Bill Clinton ran for president in 1992 by offering a more empathetic approach to the nation's troubles than his predecessor; in 2000 George W. Bush promised a more morally upright approach than Clinton; in 2008 Barack Obama described himself as the personification of a multicultural and culturally tolerant America; and in 2016 Donald Trump presented himself as the voice of white working class voters who felt left behind in a rapidly changing America (Ceaser and Busch 1993, 2001; Ceaser, Busch and Pitney 2009, 2017).

Once in office these candidates-turned-presidents continued to concentrate on character matters, justifying controversial policies on the basis of one's personal toughness, including taking a hard line against the Soviet Union in the 1980s, engaging in the wars in Iraq in 1991 and 2003, or ripping up international trade deals in 2017 (Farnsworth 2009; Schier and Eberly 2017). Even Bill Clinton, whose personal character generated mixed feelings at least when he ran for president in 1992, nevertheless engaged in a moral battle with his accusers during the Clinton-Lewinsky scandal and the impeachment battle of 1998 (Farnsworth and Lichter 2006). The emphasis on character not only helps presidents win battles, it also allows presidents to give citizens general impressions about how presidents will handle problems that emerge during an administration (George and George 1998). And sometimes, the "character" who is the president takes over both the media and the message.

While presidents have a number of media advantages when it comes to getting a hearing in modern Washington's political debates, these factors do not guarantee public relations success. As head of a relatively unified branch of government—particularly when compared to a legislative branch divided by chamber, by party and by factions within parties—presidents usually can at least work their will over the framing of the narratives of the executive branch. Underlings must sing from the White House hymnal, after all. The executive branch also can offer something approaching a united front when it confronts an often deeply divided Congress, helping the president try to become legislator-in-chief as well as communicator-in-chief in the modern political environment. There can be infighting and leaks involving White House aides, particularly when a president's political positions are uncertain. But the president's preferences, once expressed, largely prevail when the executive branch communicates, particularly on high-profile issues.

While the largely unified executive branch makes presidents more capable of dominating the political discourse than any other single political actor, one key challenge all presidents face is the short—and ever-shortening—attention span of both the reporters who produce the news and the citizens who consume it. Ten-second sound bites of quoted material on television, roundly condemned as shallow and insufficiently informative in their day, now seem like soliloquies when compared to a 140-character tweet. While the no-holds-barred coverage found online may provide the president with new and often intensely loyal allies, that environment also amplifies the voices of equally aggressive and relentless enemies who can counter-frame the presidential news narrative in peer-to-peer communication venues like Twitter and Facebook. American public opinion tends to be critical of presidents away from periods of crisis, and there seems to be little that presidents trying to influence the modern media can do to change that, regardless of the structure of the news environment.

What is also new in the Wild West of modern communication is automated deceit, where bots and trolls can spread falsehoods using tweets and posts while the truth struggles to keep pace. During Obama's presidency there were constant online claims aired without evidence by Donald Trump and others that Obama was born in Africa—claims that did not subside even after Obama produced his Hawaii birth certificate (Hohmann 2017b; Shear 2011). President Trump and his supporters have kept up a steady stream of online and offline attacks on defeated rival Hillary Clinton and the health care policies of President Obama in an effort to deflect attention away from Trump's own failure (at least so far) to replace Obamacare and the often-denied but increasingly problematic series of interactions involving the Trump team and the Russians during 2016 and 2017 (Hohmann 2017d).

While personal popularity remains a powerful asset, even popular presidents still have to work aggressively to shape the political discourse in ways that favor their administrations. The aggressive and highly partisan redistricting procedures in nearly every state mean that a president faces a U.S. House comprised of only a few members who represent "swing" districts and who are therefore vulnerable to White House pressure—be it exercised in Washington or in the members' own districts. Senators, with their staggered six-year terms, are experts at wearing down and waiting out presidents when they chose to do so.

In other words, even as the mechanisms continue to change, a president's communication challenges bring us back to where we once began: with the hallowed admonition from Richard Neustadt (1990) that the real power of presidents is mainly "the power to persuade." The creation and expansion of Facebook, Twitter, and YouTube notwithstanding, the limitations on presidential power that Neustadt saw when he served as a junior White House aide decades ago remain—and arguably have intensified—in our current media environment. The Framers' vision of limited power for all politicians (even for presidents) may become blurred during times of emergency or heightened threat—like World War II or the panic-filled days after the attacks of 9/11. Even so, those brief departures from the norm only underscore the general truths that both policymaking in Washington and presidential popularity in the country are mainly about conversation and persuasion, and not about unilateral demands.

This book provides a comprehensive look at modern presidential communication, paying particular attention to the first four presidents of the new media age: Bill Clinton, George W. Bush, Barack Obama, and Donald Trump. All four presidents, including the current one, has or had periods of highly effective political communication efforts. All four also suffered from severe political communication problems during parts of their presidencies—times when the White House endured negative public evaluations and critical media coverage and faced an uncooperative Capitol Hill. While we will examine these connections in detail in the chapters that follow, it is important at the outset to note that the four presidents faced distinct media environments that shaped their political communication efforts. Clinton's media strategy reflected the rise of cable television. Bush's approach centered on the growing prominence of Fox News. Obama took advantage of the increasingly decentralized media environment by orienting his character construction efforts in the direction of social media, including YouTube and BuzzFeed. Trump's combative style and somewhat indifferent approach to evidence and policy details maximized the utility of Twitter, with its 140-character format.

Before looking at those recent presidents, their media environments and their White House marketing efforts in greater detail, one should consider how presidents have used—and been used by—the news media over the years. This is the subject of the next section of this chapter.

Presidents Battle for Media Attention

First, one can offer some good news for the executive branch. Scholarly research into news coverage during the past half-century revealed that reporters pay far more attention to the White House than to Capitol Hill, giving presidents far greater ability to shape the policy discourse than members of Congress possess (Farnsworth and Lichter 2006). With unparalleled access to information—especially material relating to international concerns—presidents can learn about many things sooner and more comprehensively than can other political actors. That gives the White House a vital head start in framing the news, particularly in matters relating to foreign and military policy where information may not be readily available other than via executive branch sources, such as the Pentagon and the CIA. Further, citizens usually view presidents less negatively than they do the legislative branch. As a result, presidents increasingly seek to use their various communication advantages by going public to shape public opinion in ways designed to force greater acquiescence if not agreement from Congress (Kernell 2007). Presidents also engage in a media-friendly "road show" to sell themselves and their policies to the nation and world (Farnsworth et al. 2013; Heith 2013).

Members of Congress and other political actors sometimes try to focus the discourse in a different direction than that favored by the White House, but their ability to shape news coverage in a way contrary to the president on high salience matters is limited (Christenson and Kriner 2017; Entman 2004). While Members of Congress spend a lot of time in their districts during work periods and attract lots of local news attention, modern presidents have a huge advantage with national media: they can get to dominate U.S. political news at just about any time (Cook 1989, 2005; Farnsworth and Lichter 2006).

Presidential efforts to frame a given event in a certain way often depend on some level of agreement with other political actors, including legislators, reporters and the public. That consensus is often present in times of crisis. At such moments, few political actors want to risk challenging a president, particularly if the president's commentary and behavior seem at least somewhat reasonable under the circumstances. If a presidential statement is not widely seen as credible—for example, if a president were to claim that a modest uptick in the unemployment rate is comparable to 9/11—then a political, media, and cultural feedback loop eventually will undermine that official claim in favor of more credible messages (Entman 2004).

One key vehicle to maximize the presence of the president's perspective within news content is by using pseudo-events, stage-managed spectacles designed primarily to attract news coverage and to help advantage a specific perspective relating to an ongoing issue (Boorstin 1961). These marketing efforts can shape public interpretations of an event in ways that may not match the facts surrounding the event itself. An excellent example of this was George W. Bush's 2003 appearance on an aircraft carrier in a *Top Gun*-style flight suit, and then shortly afterwards standing below a "Mission Accomplished" banner. These stage-managed events offered visual images suggesting that the president was a war hero. This pseudo-event on the aircraft carrier, which required the crew to be kept at sea longer than originally planned in order to secure the best images, also was designed to suggest that the war in Iraq was over (Bennett 2012). Americans subsequently learned that, despite the upbeat visuals, the mission remained unaccomplished: the occupation of Iraq would turn out to be far more problematic—and bloody—in the years that followed.

Because few citizens pay close attention to the specifics of public policy concerns, a great deal of presidential marketing focuses on shaping the public views of the president generally, particularly in terms of presidential character (Farnsworth 2009). The theory behind this strategy is that if a citizen likes the president as a person that citizen will be more likely to favor the president's policies. Presidential candidates employ the same focus on character presentations, as the nomination process has become an intensely personal affair as well.

One of the ways candidates first sell themselves in the media is through autobiography. If the public likes what it sees and a candidate becomes a viable contender, then issue preferences may receive more attention. Indeed, part of the reason for Obama's electoral success in 2008 stems from his campaign's effective use of YouTube videos and online peer-to-peer communication efforts emphasizing Obama's personal qualities (Kellner 2009, 2010).

As has been the case at least since the advent of television news, all this public visibility for the president comes with problems. Increasing public expectations of the chief executive often trigger eventual citizen disappointment with a president who can only do so much to keep his promises in a system of separate institutions and overlapping powers (Jones 1994, 1995; Lowi 1985). In the highly partisan and decentralized contemporary media environment, White House teams frequently attempt to use a variety of media outlets, including social media, to enlist public support to give the president greater leverage in his battles with Congress. This strategy involves two steps: presidents sell themselves and their policies to the public; then the citizens who receive these media messages encourage lawmakers to support the president's policy agenda (Kernell 2007).

Although this strategy of going public has generated mixed results at best, presidents devote enormous energies to selling themselves and their policy preferences to the public (Edwards 2003, 2004). Perhaps each new president is optimistic that he possesses skills that previous presidents lacked. Perhaps presidents feel they have little choice: one can rarely make much progress trying to sell a policy based on specifics, which are only marginally interesting to many citizens and therefore of little concern to reporters trying to satisfy public demand for news. So presidents try to manage the news and shape policy by trying to control how the media present them to the public.

Modern social media environments—including YouTube, Facebook and Twitter—allow presidents and their critics to weigh in via a variety of venues—venues, by the way, that often allow a president to emphasize personal character matters. These new media channels also allow citizens to participate in political conversations in a variety of ways, by reposting political content, by commenting upon it, or even offering reformatting of presidential content through mash-ups, GIFs, and memes (Scacco and Coe 2016; Stuckey 2010). In a news environment that features government-to-public, government-to-media-to-public, and peer-to-peer communication pathways, Hopper (2017) developed the concept of "presidential framing resilience" to explain a president's continuing, but arguably diminished, capacity to help shape today's malleable media environment.

In today's short-attention-span politics, politicians do not have much time to discuss their positions on policy matters. Forty years ago, a presidential candidate had roughly 40 seconds to explain himself on the evening news (Adatto 1990). By 2004, the length of time of unmediated candidate commentary—called a sound bite—has shrunk to ten seconds on the evening news (Farnsworth and Lichter 2011a). In today's world of web news, presidents may have even less time than that—originally the 140 and now the 280 characters of a tweet—to be heard. Such an abbreviated opportunity for commentary does not give a politician much time to explain how he or she will fix Social Security or Medicare or deal with inflation, high unemployment, or the trade deficit.

In the modern media environment, there really is little opportunity to express a complicated thought, particularly if you want to hold the attention of an increasingly distracted public. Even the simplest thoughts may take more time to express than the average sound bite and more characters than a tweet. Twitter's format does allow for name-calling and other rapid-fire insults, attacks that can help shape public policy outcomes. Twitter also offers space for slogans of bumper sticker length, like "Hope and Change" or "Make America Great Again," that attract public attention.

While legislating by bumper sticker is hardly optimal, presidents must play the media cards they are dealt. Politicians trying to reach voters these days have to work within the current environment, where extremely brief sound bites are the norm on television and in social media. Such media channels undermine serious discussion of issues. So presidents adapt. Because politicians want voters to hear their views, they have to tailor what they say to the extremely brief formats that are widespread today. Government officials must speak simply and they must provide entertaining snippets of social media content. Otherwise, they are giving up the free airtime or the bandwidth they desperately need to promote their policies and themselves. While a media-challenged politician may win an election now and then because of favorable circumstances, failure to embrace the latest media conventions may doom that politician to a defeat in a future contest.

Framing Presidential Character

Presidents have sought to adapt to these changing media environments, and the efforts by recent presidents to survive and perhaps to thrive in the media environments they faced are the central issues addressed in this book. One key way several recent presidents have tried to adapt has been through emphasizing presidential character: giving the American public the opportunity to gain a sense of who the president is as a person as a means of building public support for a president's policy preferences. While they still talk about policy, of course, personality has become a key component of how presidents sell themselves and how the public evaluates presidents and presidential candidates. Character conversations also are how a president's critics seek to undermine the president and the administration's policy initiatives, as we discuss below.

Successful campaigns and effective modern presidencies employ massive public relations operations to ensure the president comes across as likable and looks to be working diligently to supply the public with popular policy outcomes. These media management efforts frequently involve selective revelations and nondisclosures on a large scale for both candidates and presidents. So the promotion of character continues, as do the character attacks.

Presidential character conversations may create particularly strong expectations for change, perhaps beyond what any president could accomplish regardless of personal characteristics. Campaigns try to turn ordinary mortals into Superman or Wonder Woman. For some citizens, Obama's election in November 2008 represented a transformative event like few presidencies of the past half century. The expectations were extraordinarily high and the dashed public hopes started to emerge rapidly (Campbell 2009; Conley 2009; Harris and Martin 2009). Eight years later, many citizens also viewed the 2016 election of Donald Trump as a transformative event in American politics, a time to "Make America Great Again" by electing an outsider committed to reforming Washington and the world in ways that Trump voters found appealing (Ceaser et al. 2017). Trump's poll numbers, like those of his predecessors, soured as the soaring poetry of campaigning gave way to the prose of governing.

Defining character is a difficult business. U.S. politicians, particularly presidential candidates, need to be likable—or at least to appear less dislikeable than their opponents—to win an election (Barber 1992). Americans have a fondness for presidents who are like them, who have—or at least appear to have—the common touch (Brooks 2006). In recent U.S. presidential elections, character qualities often trumped years of experience in government. People want to like their president, perhaps because television and online news makes the chief executive a regular presence in the nation's living rooms and even, via smart phones, in the palm of one's hand. Reporters, particularly those working in television and online, find it easier and more interesting to write about character than issues. Issues can be complicated, after all, and may require some expertise to discuss matters intelligently. Further, it is not clear how much policy depth the public desires, even when voters are getting to know candidates in advance of an election.

Consequently, many candidates have lost to opponents who were more personable. Jimmy Carter, elected on a smile and an honest demeanor in 1976, lost four years later to Ronald Reagan, a former movie actor and governor of California who was solid gold when the cameras were on (Cannon 1991). Arkansas Gov. Bill Clinton connected with the public in 1992 in a way that George H. W. Bush could only dream about (Ceaser and Busch 1993). In 2008, voters dismissed the lengthy resume of U.S. Sen. John McCain (R-AZ) in favor of a Democratic wunderkind who had been in the U.S. Senate for less than four years before voters elected him president (Ceaser et al. 2009). Indifference if not dislike of greater governmental experience was particularly pronounced in the 2016 election, when voters selected a New York real estate investor without a single day of government service and dismissed a triple threat of political experience: a former First Lady, U.S. Senator, and Secretary of State rolled into one (Ceaser et al. 2017).

Examining Presidential Character: Political Concerns and Scholarly Models

Concerns over presidential character and its relevance to politics did not emerge with the rise of radio or with the television age, technologies that effectively placed presidents in living rooms around the nation. Worries over what sorts of people were likely to arise in the U.S. political system vexed the Founders more than two centuries ago. The creators of our constitutional order were deeply concerned about the characters of people who become presidents. Indeed, in 1787 delegates to the Constitutional Convention developed the Electoral College in part to make sure that people of merit would arise and that the college's members could block any dangerous demagogues from the nation's highest office. As Alexander Hamilton wrote in Federalist 68:

> The process of election affords a moral certainty, that the office of President will never fall to the lot of any man who is not in an eminent degree endowed with the requisite qualifications. Talents for low intrigue, and the little arts of popularity, may alone suffice to elevate a man to the first honors in a single State; but it will require other talents, and a different kind of merit, to establish him in the esteem and confidence of the whole Union, or of so considerable a portion of it as would be necessary to make him a successful candidate for the distinguished office of President of the United States. It will not be too strong to say, that there will be a constant probability of seeing the station filled by characters pre-eminent for ability and virtue.
>
> (Quoted in Carey and McClellan 1990: 354)

Presidents themselves have observed that being president creates a difficult if not impossible situation for maintaining high standards when it comes to one's character. Calvin Coolidge, writing of the White House long before the days of television, suggested as much. "It is difficult for men in high office to avoid the malady of self-delusion. They are always surrounded by worshippers. . . . They live in an artificial atmosphere of adulation and exultation which sooner or later impairs their judgment" (quoted in Dallek 2007: 488).

Despite the fundamental importance of a president's personal characteristics to understanding the president and predicting his behavior in office, political science as an academic discipline has struggled to develop models that effectively capture the personal differences among presidents—and to provide an effective warning system for potentially dangerous outliers.

Some of the research has focused on individual presidents. President Woodrow Wilson's character, for example, has drawn the interest of a number of scholars interested in political psychology. They were particularly interested in Wilson's unwillingness to compromise with the U.S. Senate to secure authorization for the nation to become part of the League of Nations after World War I (cf., Freud and Bullitt 1967). Wilson's rigid insistence on following his conscience, even though this rigidity led to his greatest political defeat, made his character psychologically interesting: "He betrayed the trust of the world as a matter of principle" (Freud and Bullitt 1967: 264). Rather than giving senators key roles at the Versailles peace conference that ended the war, or compromising with them on joining the League afterwards, Wilson rigidly insisted on his sole ability to determine the nation's best interests. Consequently, he rejected any amendments or reservations to the treaty, dooming the pact in the Senate. "Men require ways of expressing their aggressions and of protecting their self-esteem. Wilson's ways of doing both, unhappily, involved demanding his way to the letter and hurling himself against his opponents no matter what the odds, no matter what the cost" (George and George 1964: 291).

Others sought to develop a more general model examining presidents and their personalities. In *Presidential Character*, arguably the most prominent political science work in this area, James David Barber (1992) argued that political science must focus far more extensively than it has on who presidents are as people. "To understand what actual Presidents do and what potential presidents might do, the first need is to know the whole person—not as some abstract embodiment of civic virtue, some scorecard of issue stands or some reflection of a faction, but as a human being like the rest of us" (Barber 1992: 1).

In Barber's model, presidents belong to one of four general character types. His ideal presidents, termed active positives, are very goal-oriented and adaptable politicians, capable of being cooperative and compromising in order to advance their goals. Active negatives, the most problematic type, are in politics in part to compensate for low self-esteem, and their aggressive natures, coupled with their rigidity, make them poor choices for national leadership. Barber (1992) offers Franklin Delano Roosevelt as a key example of an active positive president, and Richard Nixon as a key example of an active negative one.

There are two other categories in Barber's schema, passive positive and passive negative. Passive positive presidents are optimistic and, above all, they want to be liked. Such presidents therefore are highly cooperative and try to avoid alienating others. Passive negative presidents generally are aloof, tending not to get along with others and exhibiting relatively low levels of engagement in the job. These two types do not seem to matter as much in the modern political environment, as few people from those personality types are likely to undertake the immense effort of running for president, nor are they likely to win if they do so (Barber 1992). Barber, who died in 2004, said that Reagan was the only recent chief executive who qualified as a passive president, naming him passive positive, the character type focused on popularity.

Barber argued that character was a fundamental aspect of a person: "the way the President orients himself toward life—not for the moment but enduringly" (Barber 1992: 5). Barber argues that experts can predict likely presidential success or failure by careful study of a person's childhood. In 1972, Barber used his model to warn that Richard Nixon represented a dangerous choice in that year's presidential election. A key piece of evidence Barber offered about Nixon was a letter to his mother that Barber published from Nixon's childhood, a tale of anger and hurt that does not suggest a happy, mentally healthy ten-year-old child. (Nixon was writing to his mother while she was out of state getting medical care for one of the future president's siblings.)

My Dear Master:
    The two boys that you left me with are very bad to me. Their dog, Jim, is very old and he will never talk or play with me.
    One Saturday the boys went hunting. Jim and myself went with them. While going through the woods one of the boys triped and fell on me. I lost my temper and bit him. He kiked me in the side and we started on. While we were walking I saw a black round thing in a tree. I hit it with my paw. A swarm of black thing came out of it. I felt pain all over. I started to run and as both of my eys were swelled shut I fell into a pond. When I got home I was very sore. I wish you would come home right now.
                                            Your good dog, Richard
                                (quoted in Barber 1992: 128, spelling and
                                        grammatical errors in original)

As Barber observed, the letter marked "a tale of hurt, panic and depression. It fits with Richard Nixon's lifelong propensity for feeling sad about himself" (Barber 1992: 128). When Barber's dark predictions about Nixon were borne out during the Watergate scandal, the scholar became a celebrity, with his theories regularly gaining considerable attention in *Time* magazine, among other places (Nelson 2014).

Barber's celebrity in the media did not equal respect among his academic peers. Few political scientists have endorsed Barber's approach; in fact, many have stayed away from it as if to avoid guilt by association. Scholars have offered a number of different objections to the Barber approach, saying that it is not grounded in the scholarly work of psychologists and that those four distinct categories do not represent effectively the range of human character (Nelson 2014). While mental health professionals might be useful additions to this discussion, most hesitate to offer psychological assessments of people they have not treated (Mayer 2017). Psychologists even have a term for this reticence, the "Goldwater Rule," in reference to the intense controversy surrounding a petition signed by 1,000 mental health experts who declared Barry Goldwater, the 1964 Republican presidential nominee, as "psychologically unfit to be president" (Mayer 2017). While some psychologists have offered opinions about Trump, for example, most practitioners prefer to keep silent, worrying about tarnishing the discipline by weighing in on current political figures (Mayer 2017).

While Barber's model has its shortcomings, his arguments demonstrate how important it is for students of the presidency to consider character matters as they consider the activities of the world's most influential unilateral political actor. His model, despite the criticism, offers some key metrics for an examination of presidential character, particularly for the mass public. Since most citizens and most reporters covering politics are not experts in psychology, Barber's general orientations regarding presidential character offer relevant—though admittedly inadequate—guideposts for an analysis that focuses on character communication efforts aimed at a lay audience.

Other political scientists who have tried to develop frameworks that take account of the impact of presidential character on presidencies have also struggled to develop generalizable frameworks that allow the comparison of presidential characters across time. (It is not surprising that the personal dramas of the Clinton years coincided with renewed interest in studying presidential character.)

Many of the most important analyses of presidential character do not try to follow Barber's lead in creating precisely defined boxes into which presidents can be categorized. Alexander George and Juliette George (1998) suggested focusing on three matters relating to presidential character most relevant to White House performance: (1) cognitive style, which relates to ways presidents acquire and utilize information; (2) a president's own sense of efficacy and competence, which relates to decision-making and other political tasks; and (3) a president's general orientation towards political conflict. "These three components of personality combine to influence how a president will structure and manage the policy-making system around him, and how he will define his own role in that system" (George and George 1998: 9).

Stanley Renshon (1998) offered three areas of analysis as well: (1) ambition, which relates to a president's motivation to pursue political goals; (2) integrity, the capacity to remain true to one's ideals; and (3) relatedness, which concerns the interactions with other people, which may be hostile or not, or intimate or not. By looking at these readily available assessments of what presidents do and do not do, one can get a sense of how they are likely to behave as they face the unexpected, a key component of leadership that tests all presidents (Renshon 1998).

Analysts of presidential character, including Barber, have their own doubts about how far one can take these theories. Presidents do not generally speak publicly about their psychological profiles beyond the general talking points they might offer regarding their personal toughness or perhaps their compassion (Wayne 2012). And even if a presidential candidate wished to venture further into discussion of his or her personal mental composition, individuals are not likely to be the best at diagnosing their own anxieties and insecurities nor all that honest in revealing their own elements of conventional human weakness (George and George 1998).

The lack of fully satisfying academic frameworks for the study of presidential character and its impacts on presidents and their policies does not mean that one should not study this vitally important area. Rather, these admittedly imperfect theories offer the best available framework for considering an area that presidents, the media, and the public emphasize as citizens consider who to elect as president and how to evaluate them once they are in office. Considering character seems even more important in an era in which new media serve to magnify and amplify character attributes and defects with variable results.

Presidents from Washington to Reagan and Their Media Challenges

Presidents struggled with news coverage of themselves and their policies long before the creation of television and the internet. Maximizing presidential influence via presidential communication has been a central strategy for many an administration dating back to the creation of the Republic. These early media environments—eras marked by partisan newspapers, and then by the sensationalist "Penny Press" in the nineteenth century and the rise of radio and national communication networks during the early years of the twentieth century—offered their own distinct challenges. Even so, a common pattern emerges. From the nation's start, the presentation of one's character was an important part of marketing presidential candidates and presidents.

As he sought to strengthen the new nation and establish the institution of the presidency, George Washington created an image of the president as a reluctant leader, a person not motivated by ambition but selfless enough to take on the burdens of authority to aid his fellow countrymen. Above all, Washington demonstrated that a president should relinquish power voluntarily, confident that the public would provide a competent successor (Lipset 1963).

Despite the first president's efforts to remain above the political fray, Washington's advisors soon devolved into two combative factions, each seeking to undermine opponents by using character assassination efforts relating to personal financial and sexual scandals that would not have been out of place on Twitter. John Adams, the second president, actually sought to criminalize dissent of the government and its officials through the Alien and Sedition Acts, a law that resulted in the jailing of critical government officials and editors in the new nation (Smith 1977). These censorship efforts lasted only until the contentious election of 1800, won by Thomas Jefferson, the tribune of Adams's critics. The third president came to power in part through nasty attacks on Adams and his allies, amplified by the partisan newspapers backing Jefferson (Smith 1977). Both sides attacked relentlessly without offering evidence in an era of little concern for libel against political figures (Sabato 1993). These attacks were the 200-year-old equivalent of the "Birther" movement's false claim that Barack Obama was born outside the U.S. and therefore ineligible to be president (Shear 2011).

Beyond the founding generation, presidents tended to be less aggressive in building a larger-than-life media or political presence. Most subsequent nineteenth-century presidents—excluding Andrew Jackson and Abraham Lincoln, who governed during tumultuous times—resembled modern city managers executing agreed-upon policy (Landy and Milkis 2014). While these low-key nineteenth-century chief executives demonstrated from time to time that the White House could use the rise of mass-circulation newspapers to emphasize presidential preferences, most deferred to Congress on most things (Skowronek 2014). They rarely tried to dominate the policy process like contemporary presidents do, even though the creation of coast-to-coast newspaper companies and the rapidly expanding telegraph networks of the era offered them greater opportunities to exercise enhanced White House influence as the nineteenth century progressed (Schudson 1978). While Jackson and Lincoln showed how presidential influence expands through aggressive efforts in trying times, few other presidents of the era followed their lead (Schlesinger 1945; Mitgang 1971).

That White House reticence changed as the twentieth century dawned. In the early 1900s, two aggressive presidents took advantage of these mass circulation newspapers—and the rise of national wire services—to shape the policy agenda in way that most previous presidents had declined to do (Cooper 1983). Several years before he became president, Theodore Roosevelt used the mass media to help market an image of himself as a military hero during the Spanish-American War. Thanks to his underlying personal characteristics and his media management skills, Theodore Roosevelt went from serving as a cavalry officer to vice president in just a few years (Morris 1979). Then, after the assassination of President McKinley, Theodore Roosevelt became president and continued to use the media to promote his preferred heroic vision of himself, a "rough rider" who "spoke softly and carried a big stick" (Kinzer 2017).

Roosevelt's emphasis on biography, part of making the political personal, helped explain his successful policy-making role in the White House, when he pushed for consumer safety protections, an expansion of national parks, construction of the Panama Canal, and a breakup of the large national companies that he considered too influential in U.S. politics (Morris 2001). At least in part as a result of his personal force of will, Roosevelt also helped establish the U.S. as a global power, helping mediate distant international disputes—like the Russo-Japanese war—that his predecessors probably would have avoided (Cooper 1983; Skowronek 2014).

A few years later, Woodrow Wilson demonstrated that expanded presidential influence through aggressive media strategies did always not guarantee policy success. Wilson's nationwide media-friendly whistle stop tour at the end of World War I to convince Americans to join the League of Nations failed—and destroyed his health in the process (Smith 1964). Wilson by nature was a far more private person than Roosevelt, who enjoyed the limelight and missed its absence. Even so, the media narrative of Wilson's workaholic personality served the president's purposes: "Many people thought of him as a totally rational, controlled being intent only on his work" (Cooper 1983: 246).

Wilson's policy-making emphasis, coupled with Roosevelt's experiences in the opening years of the twentieth century, helped create a vision of the presidency that made the chief executive central to national policy development—and an important global voice (Cooper 1983). Direct presidential appeals for public support through the mass media became commonplace in the decades that followed—and expositions of presidential character often were a key part of the presidential narrative.

Wilson's disability following his disastrous national tour to secure support for the League of Nations was not widely reported in the media, as matters relating to a president's mental and physical health were generally off-limits to reporters of an earlier era (Sabato 1993; Smith 2001). That past journalistic reticence is in sharp contrast to reporters of more recent decades, where the tell-all stories relating to Bill Clinton, George W. Bush, and Donald Trump demonstrate that White House reporters cover far more in the way of personal matters than they did in the past.

Franklin Delano Roosevelt and the Rise of Radio

In the 1930s, with the U.S. in the middle of the Great Depression, Franklin Roosevelt used the relatively new medium of radio to build public support for the massive expansion of the federal government via the New Deal. With a relatively small number of national radio addresses, Roosevelt convinced a substantial majority of voters to support the president's policies, and helped restore hope to a nation devastated by the worst financial crisis in American history. While he is most well known for his radio addresses, Roosevelt also met with print reporters frequently and routinely used those occasions to charm reporters and to provide grateful journalists with breaking news (Kernell 2007).

Roosevelt used the radio to convey a sense of his personal competence and confidence, trying to convince a Depression-weary nation that he could bring better times (Burns and Dunn 2001). He used direct, personal appeals, as if he were talking to fellow citizens at their dining room tables. During his "fireside chats," Roosevelt described in considerable detail his policy plans to combat the Depression and promised that things would get better. This pattern of intense activity indicated decisive leadership: "a seemingly nonstop flood of actions, some planned and some makeshift—executive orders, proposals to Congress for major bills, statements on pending measures, bill signing ceremonies, [and] press conferences" (Burns and Dunn 2001: 159).

One of the key character challenges Roosevelt faced as president, though, was his patrician background, which made him seem quite distant from ordinary Americans. His Hudson Valley accent added to a potentially negative image of FDR as a plutocrat or at least as an aloof leader (Goodwin 1994). How, a reasonable voter of the 1930s might ask, could someone who came from such wealth understand the misery that ordinary people endured? Since many rich Americans condemned Roosevelt for allegedly turning on his fellow well-to-do citizens, Roosevelt could effectively present himself as a representative of ordinary Americans (Burns and Dunn 2001).

One of the most remembered radio addresses of his career involved FDR's dog, Fala. The president was responding to Republican attacks during the 1944 presidential campaign, which asserted that the U.S. government had sent a ship to the Aleutian Islands at government expense to pick up the Scottie. Roosevelt's vigorous response on behalf of the family dog helped quash rumors that the president was seriously ill and also turned aside claims of government waste (Beschloss 2002, Burns and Dunn 2001).

> These Republican leaders have not been content with attacks on me, or my wife, or on my sons. No, not content with that, they now include my little dog, Fala. Well of course I don't resent attacks,

and my family doesn't resent attacks, but Fala—being Scottish—
does resent them.

(Burns and Dunn 2001: 482, emphasis in original)

In politics, it may never be a mistake to talk about the family dog. Since most people like pets, any warm feelings people have towards their companion animals may brush off onto the president as he refers to his own pet. Perhaps the president has some positive characteristics after all, the thinking goes, since he does have a dog. Several years later, Richard Nixon also invoked another family dog to divert attention from a different political scandal.

Presidents can also benefit from what reporters do *not* say about presidential character and personal circumstances. Had the public known about the true extent of Roosevelt's physical disability from polio he might never have become president.

There was an unspoken code of honor on the part of White House photographers that the president was never to be photographed looking crippled. In twelve years, not a single picture was ever printed of the president in his wheelchair. No newsreel had ever captured him being lifted into or out of his car. When he was shown in public he appeared either standing behind a podium, seated in an ordinary chair, or leaning on the arm of a colleague. If, as occasionally happened, one of the members of the press corps sought to violate the code by sneaking a picture of the president looking helpless, one of the older photographers would "accidentally" block the shot or gently knock the camera to the ground. But such incidents were rare; by and large the "veil of silence" about the extent of Roosevelt's handicap was accepted by everyone—Roosevelt, the press, and the American people.

(Goodwin 1994: 586–587)

The Successful Television Presidency of John F. Kennedy

With the rise of television during the late 1950s, presidents not only could speak to the nation, they also could sell themselves and their policies via a virtual appearance in America's living rooms. This technology rapidly became the main source of news for decades—and television remains highly influential to this day.

During the 1960 presidential election, this new medium provided an exceptional opportunity for launching the presidential campaign of a telegenic young senator from Massachusetts, John F. Kennedy. The question of whether the first loyalty of a Roman Catholic president would be to the U.S. or to the Pope roiled the campaign, as many Democratic operatives believed that few Protestant voters would support a Catholic for president.

As journalist Theodore White observed, television was the key vehicle for candidate Kennedy to introduce himself, as he charmed Americans in places not naturally inclined to support a Catholic for the White House, like heavily Protestant West Virginia. "Over and over again, there was the handsome, open-faced candidate on the TV screen, showing himself, proving that a Catholic has no horns" (White 1961: 108). The doubts quickly disappeared and JFK became the first—and so far the only—Roman Catholic president.

Convinced that television was the key to his rise to the White House, President Kennedy tried to maximize its use as president. He immediately started holding live televised press conferences, which allowed the new president to reach tens of millions of viewers without the editorial filter of journalists who decided what to quote and what not to quote. As he expected, that new technology worked well for him, giving him an opportunity to take advantage of his intelligence and wit, with journalists appearing as sometime foils. An April 1962 Gallup poll found that roughly three-quarters of adults had seen or heard at least one of Kennedy's news conferences and that more than 90 percent of those surveyed had a favorable impression of the new president's performance. "Kennedy's manner—his whole way of speaking, choice of words, inflection, and steady gaze—persuaded listeners to take him at his word. And the public loved it" (Dallek 2003: 336).

Like FDR, Kennedy also benefitted from what the correspondents did not reveal. Before the crisis of confidence in government brought on by the twin deceits of the Vietnam War and Watergate, reporters tended to exclude personal matters from their news coverage, believing that such issues were not relevant to evaluating candidates or presidents (Sabato 1993). As a result, all sorts of physical and mental health issues went unreported in those days. These untold maladies included what modern psychologists consider the profound depression of Abraham Lincoln, the incapacity of Woodrow Wilson following his stroke in 1919, and the severity of Franklin Roosevelt's ill health as he ran for an unprecedented fourth term in 1944 (Goodwin 1994; Sabato 1993). For Kennedy, there were occasional media comments about the president's "bad back," but the variety of his severe health problems—and the powerful medications that he took to treat them—remained largely unreported during his lifetime (Hersh 1997).

The youthful, apparently vigorous president suffered from Addison's disease, a life-threatening adrenal condition, as well as persistent digestive problems and far greater pain than was known at the time (Altman and Purdum 2002). As president, Kennedy sometimes took up to eight medications a day, "painkillers, anti-anxiety agents, stimulants and sleeping pills, as well as hormones to keep him alive, with extra doses in times of stress" (Altman and Purdum 2002). Medical records released decades after the president's assassination revealed nine previously undisclosed hospitalizations between 1955 and 1957, when he was a high-profile Massachusetts senator preparing a presidential bid (Altman and Purdum 2002). If reporters had known about and covered these issues at the time, Kennedy's presidential campaign would have been derailed before it ever started.

Kennedy also benefitted from the so-called west of the Potomac rule, which effectively gave politicians (and the reporters who covered campaigns) a free pass for extramarital activity on the road (Stanley and Dowd 2012). Kennedy's womanizing was exceptionally reckless, even for a time in which such personal misconduct was not likely to make the papers or appear on the evening news. His misbehavior was not all on the road, either. In additions to his liaisons on the campaign trail, others took place at the family home in the Georgetown neighborhood of Washington, as well as in the White House (Hersh 1997). FBI Director J. Edgar Hoover even privately warned the married president that Judith Campbell, one of his girlfriends who frequented the White House, had close ties to a Chicago organized crime boss and therefore represented a substantial security risk (Hersh 1997).

Even after his death, the Kennedy character construction continued. Washington chronicler Teddy White, then working for *Life* magazine, interviewed Jackie Kennedy and produced what became a definitive framing of the assassinated president, the image of the Kennedy White House as a modern Camelot, an evocation of the myths of the English King Arthur that was at the time the subject of a Broadway hit musical (Matthews 2011).

The Challenges of a Televised Presidency: Johnson and Nixon

As much as John F. Kennedy was a natural for television, his successor Lyndon Johnson was not. Johnson was an exceptional legislative tactician: his knowledge of how to persuade, cajole, and threaten fellow lawmakers to get them on board with his legislation was unparalleled (Caro 2002). Johnson's rough appearance and lack of ease before the cameras created a very sharp contrast with his suave, martyred predecessor. The new president sought to be the "faithful agent of Kennedy's intentions. . . . Throughout the transition period, the slain president was invoked in a powerful and decisive fashion" (Goodwin 1991: 173).

At first, the Johnson presidency achieved extraordinary success on Capitol Hill, including passage of major civil rights, social welfare, and voting rights reforms. Johnson's first two years created an exceptional legislative record, but good news can be fleeting. Public opinion regarding the president faded as the news focused more and more on the Vietnam War, as well as on the civil unrest found in several major American cities during the 1960s. As his ratings sank, Johnson raged at how so many of his fellow citizens turned against him despite his legislative success (Goodwin 1991).

Johnson blamed perceived enemies, including journalists who he believed never gave him the credit he deserved. He might have looked inward, however. Johnson's personal characteristics seemed to be part of the problem. His interactions with the press were clumsy, and became clumsier as the war in Vietnam dragged on (Goodwin 1991). After Johnson left office, Goodwin's revealing book helped convince presidential scholars and reporters that character counts for more in understanding presidents than many had appreciated. One key way to understand Johnson, Goodwin observed, was to see how unappreciated he felt, something he expressed throughout his final year in office and in retirement back in Texas. Given how important character is to the way that reporters cover the White House today, and how presidents sell themselves, consider the following complaint of Johnson about how he just did not get any gratitude for his efforts in the White House.

> I tried to make it possible for every child of every color to grow up in a nice house, to eat a solid breakfast, to attend a decent school and to get a good and lasting job. I asked so little in return. Just a little thanks. Just a little appreciation. That's all. But look at what I got instead. Riots in 175 cities. Looting. Burning. Shooting. It ruined everything. Then take the students. I wanted to help them, too. I fought on their behalf for scholarships and loans and grants. I fought for better teachers and better schools. And look what I got back. Young people by the thousands leaving their universities, marching in the streets, chanting that horrible song about how many kids I had killed that day. And the poor, they too turned against me.
>
> (quoted in Goodwin 1991: 340)

With public opinion souring on the war in Vietnam, and as domestic protests for peace and civil rights intensified, Richard Nixon promised to end the national tumult and was able to win the 1968 presidential election on an anti-crime platform. At first, Nixon seemed destined to be a successful television president. He had learned firsthand how television could save a political career, as it did when he gave his famous "Checkers" speech that helped make him vice president. In that nationally televised speech, Nixon lashed out at partisan critics alleging corruption, saying that they would not be happy until his daughter gave up Checkers, a spaniel she had received as a gift (Aitken 1993). After losing the 1960 presidential election to a more media-savvy John Kennedy, Nixon won the White House eight years later partly through an aggressive media management strategy of deliberate, scripted television appearances (McGinniss 1969).

Once in office, Nixon obsessed over ways to generate positive media images of himself, encouraging aides and supporters outside of government to attack critical news via a cascade of letters to newspaper editors and calls to TV stations (Dallek 2007). At first, Washington reporters considered Nixon very effective at public relations, particularly in emphasizing good news and downplaying unfavorable matters, though Nixon often complained that even the favorable coverage was not favorable enough (Dallek 2007). But by the time Nixon began running for re-election, the media reviews of his media management were often unfavorable, particularly as information emerged regarding the president's "enemies list" (Reeves 2001). Reporters also expressed doubts regarding the "Nixon the Man" campaign, a public relations blitz designed to portray the insecure president as "one of the boys" as he sought a second term. As the *Wall Street Journal* wrote regarding the character reconstruction of Nixon:

> The humanizing of Richard Nixon, as it might be called, is not likely to be a fruitful effort. First, it won't work: Mr. Nixon is simply not a very humorous, relaxed, fun-loving man. Second, it will backfire: people resent being told something they know isn't so. Third, it's irrelevant: whether a president is one of the boys or not isn't remotely as important as his policies and ability to lead.
>
> (quoted in Reeves 2001: 312–313)

As the second-term Nixon administration faced the Watergate scandal, Nixon tried all sorts of desperate strategies to divert the investigation. He started freezing out reporters from unfriendly publications, insisting disloyal staffers leaking to reporters be fired, dismissing the Watergate prosecutor (the so-called Saturday Night Massacre), and even threatening to use the government's power to revoke broadcasting licenses for television stations owned by the parent company of the *Washington Post*, which investigated Watergate most effectively (Reeves 2001). None of these efforts worked, and the moody Nixon increasingly kept to himself, drinking heavily, complaining about reporters and perceived betrayals (Reeves 2001; Woodward and Bernstein 1976).

Personality matters helped secure Nixon's ultimate undoing. His paranoia kept him from responding rationally to the growing crisis, imagining that everything could remain under control and distant from public disclosure (Barber 1992). Indeed, historians who have looked at Nixon and his interactions with his staff suggest that Nixon's presidency would have been more successful if his aides had done more to counter his paranoia and his rage (Dallek 2007).

Both Nixon and Johnson before him suffered in deficiencies of a key element of success on television: one's personal appearance. Of course, the good-looking John F. Kennedy was a tough act to follow. Even so, the next two presidents were not particularly comfortable before the camera, nor did their physical appearances inspire confidence or other positive emotions. Their barely concealed rage at journalists did not work to their advantage either, as few journalists were tempted to give these difficult, angry men the benefit of the doubt (Goodwin 1991; Dallek 2007).

Indeed, there was a good deal of concern among reporters that they had not been tough enough on these two presidents. A critical mass of reporters of this era believed that the media's failure to delve more deeply into the character and personal demons of Johnson and Nixon not only allowed them to achieve high office but also kept the public from seeing how dangerous their personality flaws were (cf., Sabato 1993; Sabato et al. 2000). As a result, reporters increasingly emphasized personality matters of the candidates and the presidents who followed Johnson and Nixon (Farnsworth 2009).

Ronald Reagan: Hollywood Meets Network Television News

Ronald Reagan seemed made for television, if television was not in fact made for Ronald Reagan. As an actor, Ronald Reagan had the ability to mold himself to his assigned role, both in Hollywood and in Washington (Cannon 1991). Although Reagan never became a first-rate movie star, he was famously easy to direct and was a diligent, compliant actor who learned his lines, stood where he was supposed to and invariably played the "good guy" (Cannon 1991). His easy-going nature, and his unerring sense of where the camera was, made him highly effective as he moved from acting to politics (Morris 1999). As the anti-communist head of the Screen Actors Guild, as a pitchman for General Electric, and as a candidate for governor of California and later as president, Reagan invariably presented himself as who he was: an unpretentious Midwesterner with Middle American values (Cannon 1991).

At the time of Reagan's 1980 election, television had been the dominant source for news for Americans since the 1960s, and the relaxed, confident presidential candidate was the opposite of the unappealing images offered by the stiff Carter, the bumbling Ford, the devious Nixon, and the kind-of-creepy Lyndon Johnson (Morris 1999). Like Kennedy, another presidential master of television, Reagan was particularly effective at delivering self-deprecating humor, which always tends to humanize the person telling a joke, an important quality in a president's presentation of character (Cannon 1991). Even after being shot, and as his life was in jeopardy, he managed a joke: "I forgot to duck," he said to First Lady Nancy Reagan (Cannon 1991).

> No president in the history of the Republic was as effective at self-ridicule. In public and in private Reagan regularly poked fun at his age, his work habits, his movies, his ideology, his vanities, his memory lapses, his supposed domination by his wife and even the widely held view that he was unintelligent. Reagan was aware that many of his critics thought him a modest man with much to be modest about. But he also realized he could upstage his adversaries by beating them to the punch.
>
> (Cannon 1991: 124)

The legislative successes of the Reagan presidency offer the best evidence among recent presidents for the going-public argument of Kernell (2007). Reagan was popular through much of his presidency, with approval ratings in the 60s after the 1981 assassination attempt, and during much of his second term, until the Iran-Contra scandal (Ceaser 1988). Going public is sort of like a bank shot in pool: the president proposes a policy and focuses on getting the public to support it. The president then encourages citizens to contact their members of Congress to encourage them to support the legislation as well (Kernell 2007). When Reagan asked citizens to write in to their members of Congress about a priority issue, they responded to this likeable president in large numbers. The strategy worked well, for example, in convincing enough Democrats in the House to support Reagan's 1981 tax cut plan, a major early legislative victory for the new president (Jones 1988).

Conservatives sometimes faulted Reagan for not being conservative enough in his deeds. He routinely spoke at pro-life rallies but his Supreme Court appointments (most notably Sandra Day O'Connor and Anthony Kennedy) were centrists who were not about to make abortion illegal (O'Brien 1988). Ever concerned with his public image, Reagan did not want to face the backlash from citizens if he took such a divisive step. Candidate Reagan promised to balance the federal budget, but President Reagan never submitted a balanced budget proposal, once again because he did not want to face the public backlash from the level of cuts in government programs that would have been required to do so (Cannon 1991). Coming across as genial, and maintaining those high approval ratings, mattered more to him than conservative doctrine.

Sometimes Reagan and his team appeared to understand the media better than the reporters themselves did. Lesley Stahl, who covered the Reagan White House for CBS News, worried about the pushback she expected from the White House following the production of a highly critical news report during the 1984 campaign that illustrated the gap between Reagan's upbeat news images and the harsh impacts of his policies on the poor. Instead, she said she received a compliment from an unnamed top White House aide who said, "When you are showing four and a half minutes of great pictures of Ronald Reagan, no one listens to what you say" (quoted in Smith 1988: 409).

Iran-Contra and the Limits of Reagan's Public Relations Presidency

A good public relations presidency, even a very good one, does not always generate good outcomes for a president. For every compelling image of Reagan standing on a Normandy Beach to commemorate the heroes of World War II or before the Statue of Liberty commemorating America's promise, there are images of a confused, disengaged president struggling to come to terms with the Iran-Contra scandal (Cannon 1991).

The flip side of Reagan's heavy reliance on public relations—his inattention to policy details—led to Iran-Contra, his presidency's biggest failure. Making matters worse, Reagan's second term featured an excessive willingness to delegate. Reagan's poor personnel decisions helped create that crisis and made it worse than it should have been (Rockman 1988).

His inattention to detail was a negative aspect of his character, one that undermined his legacy. Iran-Contra was really two crises, and the first one Reagan clearly did know about as it unfolded. The government wanted to get back some hostages held in Lebanon and gave the Iranians weapons in what the president's national security team was an effort to strengthen the moderates in Iran and to help secure the release of the hostages (Ceaser 1988). Reagan had previously promised the country that he would never negotiate with terrorists; during one key White House meeting both Secretary of State George Schultz and Defense Secretary Caspar Weinberger said negotiating with the Iranians was a terrible idea (Cannon 1991). White House staffers who favored the outreach to Iran kept those two top officials out of further meetings on the plan, and targeted Reagan's personal decency by playing tapes of tortured American hostages and having the president meet with family members of those kidnapped (Neustadt 1990). As Schultz and Weinberger predicted, the arms-for-hostages effort was a massive failure. The hostage-takers freed some captives and replaced them with new ones. After the delivery of tens of millions of dollars of weapons to Iran, there were more American hostages in the Middle East than when the initiative started (Neustadt 1990).

The second crisis of Iran-Contra sprang from Reagan's inattention to detail (Benda and Levine 1988). The second crisis, the diversion of the money Iran paid for the weapons to the contras in Nicaragua, was illegal and created conditions for a possible impeachment crisis. The administration's plan—how much Reagan personally knew remains unclear to this day—involved sending old weapons previously provided to Israel to the Iranians through intermediaries (Morris 1999). The U.S. overcharged the Iranians for the weapons and provided the Israelis with new weapons to replace the older ones. The mark-up provided the funds that helped finance the Contras' anti-government rebellion in Nicaragua. Reagan's national security team, most notably Oliver North and John Poindexter, ran the operation (Neustadt 1990).

Reagan later told investigators he did not know about this illegal diversion of funds, which clearly violated expressed Congressional prohibitions on any government efforts to assist the contras under a law known as the Boland Amendment (Destler 1988). Top officials like Poindexter and North said they tried to keep the president from knowing all the details of the operation so that he could deny the existence of contra funding scheme without lying if it ever came to light (Neustadt 1990).

Perhaps Reagan knew about the illegal support for the contras all along and he and his staff lied about his awareness of the diverted funds. Perhaps Reagan did not know about the diversion, as he and his staffers said. If the claimed version of events were true, then Reagan behaved irresponsibly in three ways: in whom he hired, in how he monitored his top aides, and in creating a culture at the White House that would encourage illegal activity conducted without the president's knowledge (cf., Rockman 1988). While Reagan never faced any genuine threat of impeachment, the scandal hurt his approval ratings during his final two years in office and allowed the Democrats to block many GOP policy efforts during Reagan's final years in office (Jones 1988).

One condition of the modern presidency greatly advanced under Reagan: the idea that marketing one's character is a key to successful presidential policy-making. Reagan was very concerned about being popular, and that kept him from pursuing the more divisive parts of the Republican agenda (Cannon 1991). Presidents who governed in the wake of Reagan—more on that in the chapters that follow—sought to use television to create personal narratives that reflected the best of America's perceived self-image. Reagan demonstrated how it could be done. His self-image was less the glamourous Hollywood celebrity and more the brush-clearing cowboy on a ranch.

Reagan's success as a communicator stands in sharp contrast to the media management efforts of his successor. Despite spending eight years as an understudy to a master of the media, President George H. W. Bush often struggled with political communication (Ceaser and Busch 1993). Other candidates learned Reagan's lessons well, however. A dozen years after Reagan's election in 1980, a working class hero from a place called Hope, Arkansas re-created the "up by one's own bootstraps" presidential image that shaped Reagan's character-defining narratives. He used it to win the White House for himself (Berman 2001).

Citizens and Their Changing News Preferences

The four presidents who are the focus of this book—Clinton, G.W. Bush, Obama and Trump—held power during a time of intense changes in the way Americans have obtained their news. In 1992, the year Bill Clinton was first elected president, a Pew Research Center survey of news consumption patterns did not even ask about the internet, as only a tiny sliver of the American population (consisting mostly of military officers and scientists) used it regularly.

As shown in Table 1.1, people mainly learned about the 1992 campaign via television, with 82 percent of those surveyed listing it as one their key sources of news about the election. Newspapers were also a very prominent part of the American media diet, with 57 percent identifying print media as a top source for news (because respondents selected up

Table 1.1 Main Sources of News for U.S. News Consumers, 1992–2016

	Television	Newspaper	Radio	Internet
1992	82%	57%	12%	—%
1996	72%	60%	19%	3%
2000	70%	39%	15%	11%
2004	76%	46%	22%	21%
2008	68%	33%	16%	36%
2012	74%	23%	17%	36%
2016	57%	20%	25%	38%

Note: Respondents identified their top two sources for campaign news, so percentages exceed 100.

Source: Pew 2016a.

to two choices, the percentages exceed 100). Network television news in this era dominated video reporting, although cable television existed and was particularly influential during breaking news stories like the first Iraq War of 1991, which helped put CNN on the media map (Kellner 1992).

Four years later, when Clinton was re-elected, the Pew news consumption survey did include the internet, and only 3 percent of those polled listed it as a top news source, well below the 72 percent who focused on television and the 60 percent who relied heavily on newspapers for their campaign information. In 2000, the news was not much better for online media—only 11 percent listed web outlets as a top source—and television continued to rule the media world, with 70 percent listing it as a top campaign news source. Between Clinton's re-election and the contentious contest of 2000, newspaper use fell sharply. In 2000, 39 percent of those surveyed listed newspapers as one of their top two media sources, a sharp decline from the 60 percent who identified print outlets as one of their key news sources four years earlier.

The enduring importance of television for campaign news is something worth emphasizing, particularly given all the attention paid to new media formats in recent years. Of course, the key role television still plays in political learning may not be as apparent to younger adults, who have distinctly different media consumption patterns than older news consumers. As shown in Table 1.2, in 2016 adults under 30 years of age rely far more on online news than television. Half of those surveyed in that age group listed online news as one of their top two information sources, as compared to 27 percent listing television. Newspapers were only important to five percent of those under-30s surveyed. Television and online news were about equally important to those between 30 and 50 years of age, with newspapers far behind.

Things could hardly be more different for older news consumers. Among those over 65 years of age, 85 percent listed television as their top news source in 2016, and 48 percent identified newspapers. Only 10 percent of these older citizens described online news as a key information

Table 1.2 Age Differences in Sources of News, 2016

Percentages of US adults who often get their news from _____

	Television	Online	Radio	Newspaper
All	57%	38%	25%	20%
18–29	27%	50%	14%	5%
30–49	45%	49%	27%	10%
50–64	72%	27%	29%	23%
65+	85%	10%	24%	48%

Note: Respondents identified their top two sources for campaign news, so percentages exceed 100.

Source: Pew 2016a.

source. For those 50–64, television also ranked first, with 72 percent saying it is one of their top two sources for news, with 29 percent saying radio and 27 percent listing online. Since older adults are far more likely to vote than younger ones (Abramson et al. 2012), the influence of television news reports on election outcomes are even greater than these numbers indicate.

In this survey, Pew asked several questions of online news consumers, including what online sources were most important for news. In further evidence of the continuing importance of traditional media, as seen in Table 1.3, 36 percent said they often turned to news organizations, as compared to 15 percent saying they often turned to people they were close with and 6 percent turning to people who they did not consider close. Another 40 percent said they sometimes turned to news organizations, and 54 percent said they sometimes turned to people they were close with and 28 percent said they sometimes turned to people they did not know well. More than two thirds of those surveyed said that both the traditional news outlets and their close contacts provided new content that matched their interests relatively well.

The survey also found that both local and national news organizations had relatively high levels of trust from news consumers, as did news received from family, friends and acquaintances. Social media, in comparison, received relatively low marks for trustworthiness.

Online news frequently generated an impact with news consumers, according to the Pew survey shown in Table 1.4. Nearly one-third of the time, people spoke with someone about the news they received, with 17 percent of the time news consumers said they searched online for more information. People posted the news on social media or sent it out via email or text in some cases, and still others bookmarked it for later or commented on the story. (Because consumers may do more than one thing related to a story, the percentages here exceed 100 percent).

Taken together, these results from these Pew surveys demonstrate that the media environment has gone through substantial changes since

Table 1.3 Professional News Organizations Remain Major Source for News, 2016

Percentage of online news consumers who get online news from ___ often/ sometimes

	News Organizations	People Close with	People Not Close with
Often	36%	15%	6%
Sometimes	40%	54%	28%
Total	76%	69%	35%

Percentage of U.S. adults who trust the news they get from ___

	Local News	National News	Family/Friends/ Acquaintances	Social Media
A lot	22%	18%	14%	4%
Some	60%	59%	63%	30%
Total	82%	76%	77%	34%

Note: Social media trust measure asked of web-using adults.

Source: Pew 2016a.

Table 1.4 Social Networking and News Consumption, 2016

On average, the percent of the time online news consumers ___ about the news they got online

Did nothing	47%
Spoke with someone	30%
Searched for more information	17%
Posted on social media	11%
Sent via email or text	5%
Bookmarked for later	4%
Commented on story	3%

Source: Pew 2016a.

1992. As the following chapters show, presidential media strategies have evolved along with those changes in news consumption. And while media and character portrayals have always been intertwined, today's options and actions make the communication of presidential character (and its reception) all the more crucial.

What Comes Next?

Chapter 1 focused on the history of presidential communication, both from the experiences of presidents facing different media environments and from the perspectives scholars have employed to examine the nature of presidential communication across time. We examined how presidents (with varying success) tried to turn the media environments they faced to their advantage, often by talking about their own character. We also discussed how media consumption has changed across several recent decades.

In Chapter 2, we examine the political communication efforts of the Bill Clinton presidency. Clinton's years in the White House spanned a range of mass media transitions beyond network television news. As early as when he was a candidate in 1992, Clinton faced a cable news "feeding frenzy" over extramarital affairs and his efforts to avoid service in Vietnam. With Clinton's aggressive efforts to shape his reputation and demonize his critics, the president survived another sex scandal, the resulting House impeachment trial and his eventual acquittal in the Senate. In a final proof of what presidents can do to shape this discourse, Clinton won the public relations battle of 1998: his poll numbers increased and his attackers saw their public opinion ratings sink, despite the president's own deceit and misconduct.

In Chapter 3, we turn to George W. Bush, a presidency strengthened by the terrorist attacks of 2001 but one that sank in the public's estimation following the president's problematic policies relating to the long-running Iraq occupation, the messy response to Hurricane Katrina, and the cratered economy during his final year in office. Like Clinton, George W. Bush subscribed to the Sun King vision of the modern American presidency: the idea that presidents should try to dominate the discourse in all media formats. Like Clinton, Bush generated some victories with that approach, particularly as Fox News became an increasingly important part of the American media diet. Over time, Bush's failure to find weapons of mass destruction in Iraq and the growing insurgency there allowed online critics to undermine his favored presidential narrative and his public support.

Barack Obama is the focus of Chapter 4. In a sharp departure from his two predecessors, Obama offered a much more diffident vision of presidential media management. His much less aggressive public framing of issues as president was also a departure from the forceful "hope and change" narrative he employed during the 2008 campaign. This reticence led to significant problems for the first African American president, including a lengthy debate over whether Obama was really born in the U.S. and whether he really was a Christian. Even so, Obama was able to secure significant legislative successes, most notably passage of the Affordable Care Act, and winning a second term. His interviews with millennial YouTube celebrities (such as the faux talk show *Between Two Ferns*) helped retain a largely supportive base among citizens under 30 years of age. Unfortunately for Democrats, those efforts did not do much to help the party's candidates running for office during the Obama presidency's two midterm elections.

Donald Trump, the forty-fifth president, is the focus of Chapter 5. Trump's campaign for president and the early months of his time in office have suggested a president willing to break strongly from the diffident approach of Obama. He also offered a new twist on the Sun King model of media management employed by George W. Bush and Clinton. Rather than try to dominate the news through media approaches tailored for cable news outlets like CNN or Fox, Trump turned to Twitter. On the newer media format, the forty-fifth president created and promoted a self-image as a populist tribune who channeled his inner reality show brawler. From nasty personal attacks on Twitter to an approach to the truth that earns the condemnation of professional fact checkers, the Trump presidency embarked on a combat-focused strategy of media management. Trump employs the Sun King style discussed above (and pioneered by France's King Louis XIV three centuries ago), albeit with an iron fist. Gone are efforts to cajole reporters, replaced by online attacks on news stories and on individual reporters Trump does not like.

In Chapter 6, we compare these very different presidential media management strategies and consider the future of presidential communication. Is the combative, permanent campaign strategy of Trump the model for presidential media management in the future? How does the personality focus of recent presidential marketing efforts shape political discourse and policy-making? Can experienced politicians hope to prevail in future electoral contests, or has Trump ushered in an era of celebrity newbies in politics? How should White House communication strategies differ for YouTube, Facebook, Twitter, and for traditional media? What lessons can the next president take from the efforts of Clinton, Bush, Obama, and Trump to shape the news and the online discourse about themselves and their policies?

2 The Cable News Presidency of Bill Clinton

The eight years of the Clinton presidency encompass several mass media transitions. When Clinton took office in 1993, network television newscasts continued to dominate the political discourse, as they had for decades. During Clinton's two terms, the number of national news sources grew, with important roles emerging for political talk on cable news, talk radio, online media, and the late night comics (Heith 2013). During the decade Bill Clinton spent as a presidential candidate and as a president, he engaged in unusually aggressive media management efforts, even when compared to other presidents of the modern media-saturated era. Many of these presidential marketing strategies focused on defining, redefining, and eventually defending his character (Farnsworth 2009).

For his accusers, the content of the president's character was a key line of attack as well. From the start of Bill Clinton's role on the national stage, even as he first introduced himself as a relatively unknown presidential aspirant at the outset of the 1992 campaign, Clinton's personality occupied center stage. As the caucuses and primaries of that election year approached, the presidential candidate endured a cable news "feeding frenzy" over allegations of extramarital affairs and his efforts to avoid service in Vietnam, questions of character and of apparent deceit that nearly derailed Clinton's nascent candidacy (Ceaser and Busch 1993). The future president fought back, using daytime and evening talk shows to respond to his critics. He survived the campaign media onslaught, though other crises of chraracter lay ahead.

During his presidency, the media environment changed but the media and public focus on presidential character did not. As soon as most Americans first heard the name of Monica Lewinsky, a White House intern who had a personal liaison with the president, Clinton's character was once again under intense scrutiny. In the months that followed, the embattled chief executive then faced the combined wrath of talk radio hosts, the Drudge Report, and a Republican U.S. House majority determined to drive the president from office. The conservative dream of sending the president packing was not to be, however. Clinton's aggressive efforts to shape his reputation and demonize his critics enabled the second-term president to survive yet another sex scandal as well as the subsequent impeachment efforts pushed by Republicans. In a powerful demonstration of how effectively presidents can shape the national media conversation when they try, Clinton's attackers saw their media narratives crumble despite the president's own deceit and misconduct.

In this chapter, and in the three chapters that follow, we focus on one presidency at a time, considering each administration in light of four key issues. We start by considering the media environment when the president first won the White House, and how the news business changed over the years that followed. We then examine how these candidates and eventual presidents marketed themselves through the lens of character presentation, including challenges by critics who sought to undermine the future president's own character-based narratives. We examine each president's time in office via his news management strategies, including the challenges by critics regarding presidential character and the president's responses to those personal attacks. As befits the modern president's influential role on the global stage, we consider as well the strengths and weaknesses of each president's efforts to sell himself beyond the U.S. Each chapter also includes a focused case study of communication strategies employed in response to a key presidential challenge each administration faced. Each chapter then concludes with a consideration of the president's legacy, with a particular emphasis on the lessons of media management and public character construction (and, as needed, re-construction). This book is an attempt to address presidential messaging and character construction techniques in an objective fashion, though the messaging on behalf of specific policies may raise questions of a more ethical or moral nature that individual readers would do well to consider.

The News Media Environment of the Clinton Era

As the candidates for the 1992 campaign began to organize their efforts, television was at the center of their concerns. Television had been a key information source for Americans for decades, and each evening tens of millions of Americans tuned in to watch the 30-minute flagship evening newscasts on the big three television networks, as they had for a generation or more (see Table 1.1). Those massive nightly news audiences made the television networks essential linkage institutions for members of the public learning about a president or a presidential candidate or the leading policy issues (Cook 2005; Iyengar 1991).

For a national candidate, and for a president, there was little better than getting a positive comment on one of those newscasts. Indeed, the mass media environment during the 1992 presidential campaign looked a lot like the mass media environment during the 1970s or the 1980s, when candidates sought to present themselves to the public in ways designed to minimize critical coverage and maximize favorable coverage on network television newscasts and in the newspapers (Patterson 1994). One thing had changed: the 1992 news coverage included more discussion of presidential scandals and character debates than did news reports from previous contests (Ceaser and Busch 1993).

CNN's Increasing Relevance

Even within the television environment itself, changes were under way. During the 1980s, an upstart news outlet, the Cable News Network (CNN), began broadcasting news at all hours. TV news was no longer available just for 30 minutes at 6:30 p.m. or 7 p.m., or whenever ABC, CBS, or NBC aired the evening newscasts on one's local television stations. This 24/7 outlet—available only to subscribers of cable television packages—often suffered from low ratings. It did offer, though, a steady diet of news content at whatever time was convenient for any viewer (Baum and Kernell 1999; Goldberg and Goldberg 1995).

To succeed as a business, CNN had to offer something different, and it did. With the end of the Cold War, network news offered little foreign news content during Clinton's eight years in the White House. News beyond the U.S. never exceeded 30 percent of those evening broadcasts, as compared to 34 percent international news during 1991, the year of the first U.S.-led invasion of Iraq, and to 43 percent international news during 2003, the year of the second U.S.-led invasion of Iraq (Farnsworth and Lichter 2006: 90). Crime was the most frequently covered topic on network news during four of Clinton's eight years in office. Presidential elections dominated the two presidential election years, and the Clinton-Lewinsky scandal and the related impeachment debate topped the charts in 1998. In only one of Clinton's eight years in office was the top story on network television an international matter: the Serbian/Bosnian war captured more television news attention in 1999 than any other single topic (Farnsworth and Lichter 2006: 67).

In this environment, CNN distinguished itself from conventional evening newscasts through greater coverage of international matters, a wise choice for a television outlet that promised to offer news reports around-the-clock. Fortunately for a 24/7 news provider like CNN, it is always daytime somewhere. (After all, there would be few breaking news stories at 4 a.m. local time anywhere, a problem for overnight news programs concentrated in any single nation). A global news operation likewise could draw on international customers, which could also help the media company's bottom line. In times of crisis before the rise of online news, CNN functioned as a go-to source for up-to-the-minute reports from across the globe. The cable news network first came into its own as a genuine competitor to the broadcast networks during the First Persian Gulf War in 1991, a year before Clinton's election (Goldberg and Goldberg 1995).

Pictures of human suffering, be they from concentration camps in Serbia, of homeless encampments trying to recover from earthquakes and flooding, or of refugees fleeing civil wars, create very powerful images for international news (Robinson 2002). Some scholars have hypothesized that the growing volume of these images on CNN and elsewhere may force politicians to become increasingly responsive to international crises (Brown 2003; Entman 2000). During Clinton's presidency, failure by the U.S. to do more to halt the genocide in Rwanda (along with George W. Bush's limited engagement in Sudan a decade later) did not appear to trigger any public condemnation of U.S. policies, a pattern that undermined the "CNN effect" theory (Kristof 2004; Power 2002). In fact, the pattern may run in the opposite direction. In response to widespread violence in Somalia in 1992, the George H. W. Bush administration sought to draw greater media and public attention to the crisis as a prelude to possible U.S. military action there (Mermin 1997). Arguably the main impact of CNN coverage of international news is about what it decides NOT to cover, since if the cameras are absent there will be little pressure for a president or any other international leader to respond (Hawkins 2002).

Conservative Media Growth

The growing relevance of CNN was one major media development under way as Clinton campaigned for and won the White House. The rise of explicitly conservative news outlets was another. During Clinton's presidency, voices of the ideological right began to become more visible in the media environment, first via increasingly prominent talk radio hosts like Rush Limbaugh and then later via Fox News, which launched during the 1996 presidential election campaign (Davis and Owen 1998; Sella 2001).

The Drudge Report, an iconoclastic online presence, became particularly prominent by breaking the news of the Clinton-Lewinsky scandal. In the two decades since the scandal that made it famous, the Drudge Report has remained a go-to online source for conservatives—and for mainstream media outlets seeking to keep pace with the scandals revealed on Drudge. As journalist John Harris, a co-founder of *Politico*, said of Matt Drudge: "He does one thing and he does it particularly well. The power of it comes from the community of people that read it: operatives, bookers, reporters, producers and politicians" (quoted in Carr 2011).

Drudge and other conservative voices parlayed hostility to Clinton among conservatives into high ratings and solid profits. They did not focus on providing objective news; rather, they concentrated on providing an alternative to the mainstream news outlets that they considered captured by the left. These conservative products were profitable. The commercial success of conservative news outlets represented a sharp contrast to the largely unsuccessful efforts to establish profitable liberal talk radio during the Clinton years (Jensen and Miller 2006; Laufer 1995). Conservative media were not just successful as business enterprises, as they also served a partisan political purpose for the GOP. They offered a support network for Republicans seeking to undermine the Clinton presidency, emphasizing and lending credence to a variety of scandals throughout his time in office (Owen 1996).

Late Night Comics Get More Political

The 1990s also marked a decade of growing prominence for talk shows and late night comics, many of whom turned their opening monologues in a more political direction (Lichter et al. 2015, 2017). Candidate Clinton used these talk shows as way to present his personality to the public, taking advantage of the guest-friendly format by talking in paragraphs rather than in the pithy sentences designed for use as sound bites on the network news (Farnsworth and Lichter 2011a). Clinton's personal foibles also led to considerable attention from the late-night comics, who found in his personal missteps a rich vein of political humor (Farnsworth and Lichter 2006). In addition, the late night comedy shows became a fun-filled way for young people not all that interested in politics to keep up with current events (Jones 2010).

Political humor has been around a long time, since even before the famous parodist Aristophanes, who mocked the Athenian nobles of his day. The iconoclastic nature of American society, present from colonial times onward, created a particularly favorable environment for political humor. Americans have long enjoyed poking fun at people in authority, particularly those who have a relatively high opinion of themselves. Satirists from Benjamin Franklin, famous for the humor found in his *Poor Richard's Almanac*, to Mark Twain and Will Rogers, set the stage for the modern political humor that flourished on late night television programs like *The Tonight Show* and *Saturday Night Live* on NBC and later on *The Daily Show* on Comedy Central (Lichter et al. 2015).

Despite the long history of political humor, Bill Clinton's personal story provided particularly fertile territory for a new generation of political comedians. An exhaustive study of the jokes on late night television reveals that Clinton stands alone: no other political figure—other than perhaps Donald Trump, who may eventually break Clinton's record—has been able to provide more material for the nighttime jokesters (Farnsworth et al. 2017; Lichter et al. 2015). As late night comic Conan O'Brien noted in 2001, the year Clinton left office: "Comedians will soon have to build their own Clinton Presidential Library just to catalogue the thousands upon thousands of joke variations he made possible during his two terms. He made our job so easy it was a challenge not to feel irrelevant" (quoted in Niven et al. 2008: 151).

Embryonic Online Media Gains Attention

In yet another media development that took place during the Clinton presidency, the 1990s marked the start of an online news environment aimed at a mass audience. While few news consumers paid much attention to web-based news outlets during most of the Clinton years, some of the damaging information about Clinton broke online, drawing the attention of mainstream media (Davis 1999). The Drudge Report in particular helped empower the president's critics and galvanized GOP resolve as the House considered how to handle the Clinton-Lewinsky matter, which combined a sex scandal with allegations of perjury and a debate over presidential impeachment (I. Morris 2002). That scandal serves as the media management case study for the Clinton presidency later in this chapter.

As shown in Table 2.1, few people paid much attention to the internet— at least not directly—during much of the Clinton presidency. A 1995 survey, most of the way through Clinton's first term, revealed that only 2 percent of Americans went online for news three or more days a week. By 2000, at the end of Clinton's term, 23 percent of Americans went online

Table 2.1 News Media Use, 1996

Regularly watch, read or listen to ____	
Major News Sources	
Local Television News	65%
Network Evening News	42%
Newspaper yesterday	50%
Network TV News Magazines*	36%
Time/Newsweek/US News	15%
In-Depth News Sources	
National Public Radio	13%
NewsHour (PBS)	4%
C-SPAN	6%
Specialized News	
Business Magazines	5%
Religious Radio	11%
Get News Online 3 or More Days per Week	2%**

Notes: Because many respondents regularly use more than one media source, percentages exceed 100.
*   Includes programs like *60 Minutes* on CBS, as well as *20/20* and *Nightline* on ABC.
** From a June 1995 Pew survey.

Source: Pew 2004a.

regularly for news (Pew 2004a). These figures for 1995 are particularly small when compared to the 62 percent of those surveyed by Pew (2004a) in 1996 who said they regularly watched local television news, the 50 percent who said they had consulted a newspaper the previous day, and the 42 percent who said they regularly watched network television newscasts. In further evidence regarding the importance of television, more than one-third of those surveyed said they regularly watched *60 Minutes* or a comparable news magazine program on network television. Even the audience for C-SPAN, which features gavel-to-gavel coverage of congressional "action" on cable, was three times the size of the 1995 online audience. (Because respondents could identify more than one source, the total of the percentages for these media outlets exceed 100 percent).

While many media scholars anticipated that the 2000 election at the end of Clinton's term would be a watershed election for online news, most predictions went unfulfilled. Campaign web pages were underutilized in 2000, and the audience for election news remained relatively small (Owen 2002). The web was not a total bust that year, though. The 2000 presidential campaigns themselves were able to raise money and provide the relatively small number of web-savvy supporters with repositories of campaign information, speeches, and other information (Ceaser and Busch 2001). As the Clinton presidency drew to its close, the online news environment offered a hint of the amount of influence that it would command in the future.

The online media's early impact resulted mainly from the considerable attention traditional news outlets paid to web content. News outlets followed online reports with great interest and sometimes followed up on claims first heard online, like the Clinton-Lewinsky scandal itself, one of the blockbuster stories of the Clinton presidency (Carr 2011; Isikoff 2000). In many ways, it makes sense to think of the internet media of the Clinton scandal years as representing the first step in a two-step media flow (Lazarsfeld et al. 1944), where information passed from its originator (here online) through an intermediary (traditional media) before reaching the bulk of news consumers through old-style formats like television and newspapers.

For today's readers, nothing demonstrates the very different online environment during the Clinton presidency quite like a peek at the White House website, circa 2000. Figure 2.1 shows what the website looked like near the end of the Clinton presidency. Although we cannot recreate the web product on the printed page, be advised that the flags at the top of the page were waving, the single exception to this otherwise very static White House online portal. Pictures on this page were quite small when compared to pictures loaded on subsequent web sites, a design limitation required by the slower computer speeds of the 1990s.

The Clinton White House web page marketing effort, particularly when compared to subsequent presidents, is quite modest: the picture of

Figure 2.1 White House Website, Clinton Presidency, 2000

the White House is far larger than that of the president and vice president, demonstrating that the first vision of the web page was more about the White House than the nation's chief executive. Some small headlines here provide links to news releases addressing key administration efforts. The text for those links is far smaller than the "Welcome to the White House" banner at the top of the page. The page serves as a useful reminder of how little online communication existed during the Clinton years, even at the top levels of the government. Figure 2.1 also demonstrates how little effort was devoted to the marketing of the president and his policies online in those days.

Given the state of web development during the Clinton presidency, Clinton chose to focus his communication efforts on network television news (ABC, CBS, and NBC) and the increasingly prominent cable news channels like CNN. After all, to modern eyes, the Clinton-era White House website represents neither compelling online content nor compelling online format. The website was not even close on either dimension, one might add. In fairness, though, one should note that the Clinton White House was the first administration that even tried to create a presidential website, and this example demonstrates the wisdom of the old adage that one has to learn to crawl before one can learn to walk.

As noted in Chapter 1, the first people to have access to a technology are not likely to excel at using that technology. Warren Harding was the first president to speak on the radio, but Franklin Delano Roosevelt was the first one to master the medium. Harry Truman was the first president to use television, but John F. Kennedy was the first one to demonstrate its potential for presidential communication (Parry-Giles and Parry-Giles 2002). As Figure 2.1 shows, Clinton's web presence was part of that pattern.

The Character of Bill Clinton

Bill Clinton's emergence as a national political figure in 1992 owes a great deal to the unusually favorable circumstances that benefitted the Arkansas governor. In 1991, President George H. W. Bush stood atop the polls in the wake of the highly successful multination effort to dislodge Iraqi leader Saddam Hussein from Kuwait. Many of the strongest potential Democratic presidential candidates therefore decided to sit out 1992, thinking their prospects would be better in an open seat election four years later (Ceaser and Busch 1993). Sen. Lloyd Bentsen of Texas, the Democratic vice presidential nominee in 1988, chose not to run, as did New York Gov. Mario Cuomo, a nationally prominent figure in the party who also might have been a strong candidate. Sen. Al Gore of Tennessee, who was competitive in the 1988 Democratic primary contest, also declined to campaign for president that year, as he was focused on his son's recuperation from injuries sustained in a car accident (Ceaser and Busch 1993). Clinton later selected Gore for his running mate, a task that involved little campaigning until after the Democratic Party's National Convention that summer.

With those more prominent political figures on the sidelines, the Arkansas governor was part of a field of less nationally recognized candidates seeking the nomination. His main rival was Jerry Brown, at that time a former governor of California (Brown had served as governor from 1975 to 1983. He subsequently won two more terms as the state's chief executive starting in 2011). The 1992 Democratic field also included Sens. Paul Tsongas of Massachusetts, Tom Harkin of Iowa and Bob Kerrey of Nebraska, well-known Washington names but hardly politicians who possessed national reputations comparable to Bentsen or Cuomo. As became apparent relatively quickly, none of the candidates who chose to run in 1992 could match Clinton when it came to winning over Democratic primary voters (Ceaser and Busch 1993),

The Pitch

Clinton sought to portray himself as the personification of the Horatio Alger story of upward mobility thanks to hard work, one of the key tales of optimism that Americans like to tell themselves. Clinton, who empha-sized that he came from a community named Hope, Arkansas, presented himself as the embodiment of the American Dream, a working class kid with a rough upbringing who—through grit and perseverance—became governor of Arkansas (Parry-Giles and Parry-Giles 2002). Clinton cam-paign focus groups revealed that the public often responded positively to accounts of his checkered past, so he emphasized past family struggles with an alcoholic stepfather and with childhood poverty as he sought the presidency (Bennett 1995). To accent his "bubba" bona fides, Clinton de-emphasized the fact that his undergraduate degree was from Georgetown University, his law degree was from Yale, and that he studied at Oxford University as a Rhodes Scholar (Ceaser and Busch 1993).

Above all, Clinton wanted to telegraph the character message that he was empathetic, that he cared deeply about the problems people were facing. The pains felt by Americans were a common part of his pub-lic appeals throughout the 1992 campaign. Clinton most visibly put his concern for the less fortunate on display during a televised presidential debate held in Richmond, Virginia. A questioner asked President George H. W. Bush how the nation's economic troubles had affected him per-sonally, and his stumbling, uncertain response gave Clinton the perfect opportunity to demonstrate the differences between the two men (Glad 1995). When his turn arrived, Clinton figuratively hit the ball out of the park: he responded with a heartfelt discussion of poverty and hardship and vowed that he would turn the economy around as president (Ger-mond and Witcover 1993; Owen 1995).

Another way that Bill Clinton tried to demonstrate his connection with voters, underscoring the argument that he not just another politician, was to appear in a variety of media venues. During the 1992 campaign, Clin-ton found it particularly fruitful to argue his case where few predecessor candidates chose to tread: in a televised conversation with Phil Dona-hue and his studio audience, on an MTV talk show, and even playing the saxophone on Arsenio Hall's late-night television program (Lichter et al. 2015). George H. W. Bush, the incumbent president in 1992, had originally dismissed the idea that he should appear on MTV, calling it a "teeny-bopper network," but the senior Bush eventually relented dur-ing the desperate final days of his flailing re-election campaign (Bennett 1995). Ross Perot, an independent candidate that year, favored novel media approaches like Clinton did: the Texas businessman announced his candidacy on *Larry King Live* and used infomercials for much of his public messaging (Farnsworth and Lichter 2003). Between them, Clinton and Perot made Bush look out-of-touch in his hesitancy to use talk shows and cable news more extensively. If your opponent is demonstrably out-of-touch, it is much easier to argue—as Clinton did—that you are not.

Another character message Clinton sought to emphasize during the 1992 campaign was that he was not a conventional liberal Democrat in terms of his policy preferences. In other words, he wanted to demonstrate he was not simply a slower-talking version of Michael Dukakis. Indeed, the 1988 Democratic nominee's campaign foundered on two key moments. The first was when Dukakis gave a bloodless response about the rule of law when asked in a debate about how he would feel about capital punishment if his wife were raped and murdered. The second incident involved an ad produced by allies of George H. W. Bush that focused on Willie Horton, a convicted felon who attacked a couple while on furlough from a Massachusetts prison (Hershey 1989). The Massachusetts governor did not establish the furlough policy, but Dukakis never really recovered from the soft-on-crime image that intensified existing Republican policy strengths of voters' law-and-order concerns (Pomper 1989).

Clinton sought to change that narrative about the party through two powerful opportunities during the 1992 campaign. Both enabled Clinton to show that he was far tougher on crime than was Michael Dukakis. The first key moment came during the nomination stage, when Clinton made a large media spectacle of suspending his campaign for several days to return to Arkansas to oversee the execution of Ricky Ray Rector, a convicted murderer. Clinton, who was governor of Arkansas at the time, received appeals from many people to stay the execution because of Rector's profound intellectual disabilities. Clinton ignored the liberal outcry, Rector was executed, the media focused on Clinton's commitment to capital punishment, and Republicans were on notice that they couldn't treat Clinton the way they had treated Dukakis four years earlier (Bonner and Rimer 2000).

Clinton sought to demonstrate further to white moderate voters that he was on their side shortly after he became a presidential nominee. With the cameras rolling, Clinton very publicly criticized Sister Souljah, a leading rapper of the time, for what he termed the negative, anti-law-and-order messages in her music (Pareles 1992). By doing so at an event that included Rev. Jesse Jackson, then the nation's most prominent African American leader, Clinton demonstrated to white voters that he was a populist, a "good old boy" who was quite willing to criticize African Americans publicly and to their faces (Ceaser and Busch 1993). Some white southerners, not to put too fine a point on it, could look at the way Clinton insulted his African American hosts that day and see in his character a reassuring reflection of old-time southern values.

The Problem

In a word, Bill Clinton's biggest problem was his infidelity. While this fact may seem strange to younger readers, who may view personal scandals as blasé in the wake of the *Access Hollywood* tape that briefly stalled the Donald Trump 2016 presidential campaign, once upon a time admissions of profound personal misconduct would destroy a presidential campaign.

In fact, it had done so just four years before Bill Clinton's run for the White House. Former Colorado Senator Gary Hart abandoned his 1988 presidential campaign after the *Miami Herald* reported than Donna Rice had been an overnight houseguest of the married Democrat in Washington (Pomper 1989; Sabato 1993). Hart had been ahead in the polls before the scandal broke, but after news reports on his personal life appeared his support promptly collapsed. So when Gennifer Flowers told reporters before the 1992 New Hampshire Primary that she had had a long-term affair with Clinton, many journalists figured they knew how this story would end and started writing the political obituaries of the charming candidate who had been doing so well in the polls (Rosenstiel 1994).

Anticipating a Clinton campaign collapse seemed like a good bet at the time. After all, the candidate's credibility problem did not just involve infidelity. There was also his lack of truthfulness regarding his efforts as a young man to avoid serving in the military during the Vietnam War in the late 1960s (Halberstam 2001). Clinton fought back against these attacks on his character, most effectively when he and Hillary Clinton sat for a *60 Minutes* interview to discuss together the problems in their marriage shortly before the pivotal New Hampshire Primary (Ceaser and Busch 1993). When Clinton finished second in the New Hampshire Primary to a senator from the neighboring state of Massachusetts, he spun his runner-up status as a win. Clinton gleefully declared himself "the Comeback Kid," and went on to win a number of primaries on his way to becoming the Democratic nominee (Farnsworth and Lichter 1999). Because Sen. Tsongas was the favorite to win in New Hampshire, and he did, reporters needed a new angle. So the media readily adopted the "Comeback Kid," story line, offering free media to Clinton at a vital time (Farnsworth and Lichter 2000).

The electoral victories of 1992 did not wash away doubts about Bill Clinton's character. Taken together, his credibility problems fed into the longer-term narrative that Clinton was "Slick Willie," a profoundly untrustworthy character committed mainly to his own personal gratification and political advancement (Bennett 1995). Clinton's marital misconduct did not end with his scandal involving Gennifer Flowers. In fact, worse character problems were yet to come. As discussed later in this chapter, this very lucky presidential candidate did not learn from his brush with political oblivion during early 1992. A few years later the nation and the world would spend months marinating in the details of the president's extramarital interactions with a one-time White House intern named Monica Lewinsky.

Applying Character Models to Bill Clinton

Scholars have found it difficult to classify Clinton according to the traditional Barber (1992) framework of presidential character. While Clinton clearly belongs on the active dimension of the Barber model, the lack of enjoyment Clinton seemed to get as a result of his long work days seemed to suggest the compulsion of an active negative rather than the more favorably regarded active positive (Renshon 1995b). Clinton demonstrated a high level of ambition, a high level of intelligence, and he routinely said he considered his own motives to be genuine. Taken together, these qualities created a high degree of self-idealization in Clinton, according to Renshon (1995b). "Most people wish to think well of themselves. However, Bill Clinton has come to believe the best of himself and to either avoid or discount evidence from his own behavior that all is not as he believes it to be" (Renshon 1995b: 65).

Under the George and George (1998) model, one might pay particular attention to Clinton's high tolerance for conflict, and his profound conviction that he often can get himself out of political jams through his eloquence and his charm. That high level of efficacy and willingness to engage with his critics helps explain why Clinton is prone to react with denial and anger when challenged, as he did in a famous *Rolling Stone* interview early in his first term.

> I have fought more damn battles here for more things than any president in the last twenty years . . . and have not gotten one damn bit of credit for it from the knee-jerk liberal press and I am sick and tired of it and you can put that in the damn article. I have fought and fought and fought and fought. I get up here every day, and I work till late at night on everything from national service to the budget to the crime bill and all this stuff and you guys take it and you say, "Fine, go on to something else, what can I hit him about?" So if you convince them I don't have any conviction that's fine, but it's a damn lie. It's a lie.
> (Wenner and Greider 1993: 81)

The above quote also offers insights into Clinton's personality under the Renshon (1998) approach to presidential character. Clinton's high level of ambition and his ready perception of threats, one might note, made him extremely self-protective, particularly when challenged.

Of course better behavior on the front end might make self-justification less necessary on the back end. Or to put it another way, one wouldn't need to become the "Comeback Kid" so often if one didn't get into so much trouble in the first place (Renshon 1995b). For all his complaints about critical reporters, the media played key roles in Clinton's responses to attacks on his character. Clinton found a ready public audience on talk shows to make his case as a candidate and a president under siege for alleged transgressions that in Clinton's view were trivial. Reporters who covered the Clinton campaign and his presidency were often dismissive of these talk shows as lightweight venues, claiming that the hosts and the audience members who offered questions of public figures tossed softballs, did not follow up on evasive responses, and otherwise failed to hold politicians to account (Kinsley 1992).

> Untrained amateurs are no match for skilled professionals in exposing a candidate's flaws and weaknesses. And second, that semi-journalists like [Phil] Donahue and [Larry] King, not to mention non-journalists like Arsenio [Hall], unhealthily—or at least surrealistically—muddy the distinction between serious politics and trivial show biz.
>
> (Kinsley 1992)

Conversely, Clinton, a leading practitioner of the talk show campaign in 1992, portrayed the mainstream press as the real source of triviality, further evidence of his orientation towards conflict (George and George 1998) and his combative way of relating to journalists (Renshon 1998).

> I think the watchdog function is fine. But it's often carried to extremes in a search for headlines. For instance, the missing pages from my State Department file—here was a deal where *Newsweek* bit on a rumor. So you had these serious reporters who just wanted to grill me about that—when the economy is in the tubes, when 100,000 people a month are losing their health insurance. . . . And I'm supposed to take these people seriously as our sole intermediaries to the voters of this country? Sure, they should do their watchdog function, but anyone who lets himself be interpreted to the American people through these intermediaries alone is nuts.
>
> (quoted in Lichter and Noyes 1995: 261)

News Management & Character Challenges

A key dynamic of Bill Clinton's presidency was one of inconsistency, and an inconsistency relating to more than just his character. His policy-making was also often erratic (Renshon 1995a). Clinton compromised on or abandoned his previous support for conventional Democratic positions on a number of issues to remain popular and to win re-election, including expanded health care, gay rights, and support for lower-income citizens (Campbell 2000).

Clinton's time in office corresponded with the rise of highly sophisticated public opinion strategies employed in the pursuit of presidential popularity and legislative success, where even the words and phrases a candidate might use are pre-tested for maximum impact (Renshon 1995a). But even the cleverest wordsmiths couldn't hide the president's profound character flaws, including "absence of self-discipline, hubristic confidence in his own views and abilities, and difficulty in narrowing his goals" that undermined his ability to succeed at his original policy goals

(Greenstein 1995: 141). Critics faulted Clinton for trying to do too much, legislating too quickly, and for mistakenly believing that campaigning skills transfer seamlessly to the task of governing (Edwards 2000).

Bill Clinton's youth, as discussed above, involved a complicated relationship with the Vietnam War. He opposed the war, but he eventually allowed himself to be subject to the military draft to avoid undermining a future political career (Klein 2002). Clinton, who often benefitted from extraordinary good fortune, subsequently received a high draft number and never had to serve (Isikoff 2000). In other words, military policy was bound to be problematic for Clinton given his personal history. Clinton's vocal opposition to the Vietnam War branded him a radical in the minds of many voters casting ballots in the early 1990s, when veterans comprised a notably larger share of the electorate than they would in the years that followed (Harris 2005).

Electing someone who never served in the military in 1992 represented a sharp departure from the pattern personified by Clinton's eight most recent predecessors, seven of whom served at least briefly in uniform outside the U.S. during World War II or the Korean War. Ronald Reagan, the eighth president who served between Truman (who was himself a World War I veteran) and Clinton, wore a U.S. Army Reserve uniform during World War II, when the actor was assigned stateside to make military films in Hollywood (Cannon 1991). In yet another reminder of the political prominence of the veteran-heavy generation of politicians who came before the Baby Boomers, Clinton defeated two World War II veterans in his two presidential elections: George H. W. Bush in 1992 and Senator Bob Dole of Kansas in 1996 (Ceaser and Busch 1993, 1997). Ross Perot, who finished third in the 1992 and 1996 presidential elections, also had a military background. He was a graduate of the U.S. Naval Academy and served in the Navy during the mid-1950s before building his career as a business executive (Post 1995).

The pattern of youthful military service of the presidents before Clinton is very different from that of recent presidents—not a single president since Clinton has served on active duty in a military theater during wartime. The fact that as a candidate Clinton misled reporters about his efforts to avoid serving in Vietnam made a bad situation worse, also adding to the image of the president as deceitful even about his own biography (Isikoff 2000).

The new president's Vietnam backstory created problems when it came to undertaking a central obligation of a chief executive: sending troops into harm's way. A commander-in-chief who evaded military service in Vietnam as a young man is at risk of appearing, to his critics at least, as a hypocrite when he orders the military into action (Parry-Giles and Parry-Giles 2002). Although we consider this matter more extensively in the international segment of the chapter, it is clear that Clinton faced unusually aggressive challenges from congressional Republicans on international matters. That behavior represented a sharp contrast with the "two presidencies" thesis (cf., Oldfield and Wildavsky 1989; Wildavsky 1966) that provided presidents who served during the Cold War with considerable latitude to conduct foreign and military policy (Sullivan 1991). Perhaps the growing aggressiveness of Capitol Hill regarding foreign policy during the Clinton presidency explains the change, or perhaps it was because Republicans sensed a weak spot for Clinton, the first Democratic president in 12 years. In all likelihood, both factors played a role.

Clinton Struggles with Public Opinion

Clinton's original instincts about trying to work around the mainstream media by holding forth on MTV and at town halls televised on cable television rather quickly proved to be ineffective in framing Washington political discourse, so he warily returned to trying to frame news stories in mainstream media to minimize negative treatment on the television networks. Indeed, he even hired David Gergen, an experienced White House communications expert who had worked for Republican presidents, to help shape his media operations in fashions reminiscent of previous presidents (Kumar 1995).

The difficulties Clinton faced in political communication early on are readily apparent in Table 2.2, which compares public approval throughout his presidency as measured by the Pew Research Center (Pew 2001a). While he started off with public support in the mid-50s, comparable to many other new presidents as they take office, Clinton's numbers quickly plummeted as the new administration struggled to find its footing (Kumar 1995). Early misfires (followed by presidential backtracking) on presidential appointments, gun control, and the question of whether gays should serve in the military undermined the initially positive numbers (Campbell 2000). Six months into Clinton's time in the White House, only 39 percent of the country approved of the new president. While the numbers rebounded briefly after that, the political misfires on Clinton's proposed health care reform bill sent president's approval numbers downward (Skocpol 1997). Only 38 percent of the nation approved of Clinton as voters headed into the 1994 midterms that gave Republicans control of the U.S. House and U.S. Senate (Edwards 2000).

Clinton's difficulty in selling his policies became more challenging because of the effective use of the C-SPAN cameras by Senate Republican leader Bob Dole of Kansas, who provided regular sound bites for television stories on the latest presidential initiative from the floor of the U.S. Senate (Kumar 1995). When the Republicans gained control of the U.S. House after the 1994 midterm elections, House Speaker Newt Gingrich of Georgia likewise used his chamber's proceedings to challenge and question the administration in a variety of ways, including shutting down

Table 2.2 Public Assessment of Clinton Presidential Job Performance

Do you approve or disapprove of the way Bill Clinton is handling his job as president?

	Approve	*Disapprove*
January 2001	61%	30%
July 2000	55%	34%
January 2000	56%	35%
July 1999	58%	31%
January 1999	66%	29%
Late December 1998	71%	27%
Early December 1998	61%	32%
November 1998	65%	29%
September 21–22, 1998	62%	33%
September 19–20, 1998	55%	36%
Early September, 1998	61%	33%
Late August, 1998	62%	32%
Early August, 1998	63%	28%
June 1998	59%	32%
May 1998	62%	28%
April 1998	62%	28%
March 1998	65%	26%
Early February 1998	71%	26%
January 1998	61%	30%
November 1997	58%	31%
August 1997	59%	32%
January 1997	59%	31%
July 1996	54%	38%
January 1996	50%	43%
June 1995	50%	40%
December 1994	41%	47%
Early October 1994	38%	47%
July 1994	45%	46%
January 1994	51%	35%
August 1993	39%	46%
February 1993	56%	25%

Note: Don't Know responses are not reported here, so percentages do not sum to 100.

Source: Pew 2001a.

the federal government over a budget dispute (Campbell 2000). While presidents are far more capable of dominating the discourse than members of Congress are, the modern legislative branch frequently speaks up in national political conversations, particularly on controversial issues where legislative leaders are offering counter-frames that challenge the president's perspective (Farnsworth and Lichter 2005, 2006).

Clinton's poll numbers improved as the new Republican majorities over-reached, offering more conservative policies and more aggressive attacks on the president than public opinion would support (Edwards 2000). Clinton had already learned a powerful lesson about overreaching during his first two years, and his subsequent policies were smaller in scope and more carefully tailored to match middle-class concerns as a result (Campbell 2000). As shown in Table 2.2, that restructuring of Clinton's agenda led to higher poll numbers as his 1996 re-election campaign approached.

Table 2.2 contains the results from a number of polls conducted during 1998, a year that opened with the blockbuster charges about the Clinton-Lewinsky matter and concluded with an impeachment acquittal in the Senate. As the many 1998 surveys reveal, the president approval numbers remained quite strong throughout the year, as Clinton's attackers made him a more popular leader than he had been before they sought to drive him from office. Once the impeachment matter was resolved in Clinton's favor, the president's poll numbers returned to the mid-50s, roughly where Clinton often found himself before the scandal broke.

An effective way to evaluate public opinion relating to presidential character is to place those evaluations into context. In Table 2.3, we compare assessments of President Clinton and Republican presidential nominee Bob Dole in a survey taken during October 1996, weeks before the presidential election that November (Pew 1996). Clinton was particularly

Table 2.3 Character Evaluations, Bill Clinton versus Bob Dole, 1996

As I read a list of phrases tell me if you think this phrase better describes Bill Clinton or if it better describes Bob Dole (candidate names rotated).

	Clinton	Dole	Both (vol).	Neither (vol.)
Would use good judgment in a crisis	46%	37%	8%	3%
Personally likable	66%	20%	7%	4%
Honest and truthful	26%	42%	4%	20%
Has new ideas	51%	28%	3%	12%
Cares about people like me	46%	31%	5%	13%
Keeps his promises	32%	36%	2%	19%
Shares my values	42%	40%	2%	10%
Connects well with ordinary Americans	65%	21%	4%	5%
A strong leader	47%	36%	4%	8%

Which one of the following is most important to you in your overall evaluation of Bill Clinton? (responses rotated)

56%	His record as President
22%	What he has prevented the Republican Congress from doing
18%	The charges that have been made about his personal life and character

Note: Don't Know responses are not reported here, so percentages do not sum to 100.

Source: Pew 1996.

strong where one would expect given his aggressive efforts to present himself as likeable—66 percent considered him more likeable than Dole and 65 percent said that he connected better with ordinary Americans than his Republican rival. Clinton also had double-digit advantages over Dole on the questions of which one of them is a stronger leader, which is most likely to use good judgment in a crisis, and which is most likely to care about ordinary people.

Dole, who would go on to lose the presidential election by more than 200 Electoral College votes and the popular vote by more than six percentage points, had a double-digit advantage in only one of these questions: which candidate is more "honest and truthful." Well before the Clinton-Lewinsky matter became public, Dole had a 42 percent to 26 percent advantage over Clinton on that measure. The candidates scored roughly the same on the questions of which of them most "shares my values" and which one "keeps his promises."

When asked separately about what mattered most in one's evaluation of Clinton leading into the 1996 election, a majority focused on his record as president. Smaller shares of those surveyed said their evaluation of Clinton depended largely on what he had prevented the Republicans from doing or the charges made about his personal life and character. The responses to these questions demonstrate, as would become clearer during the impeachment controversy, that many citizens were quite willing to separate Clinton the president, whom they tended to like, from Clinton the person, about whom they had their doubts (Edwards 2000).

Taken together, the results of Table 2.3 demonstrate that both Clinton and his critics had some success in shaping the character narrative of the forty-second president. He succeeded in convincing a large number of Americans that he was likeable, and his critics were successful in generating doubts about whether the president was being honest.

International Perspectives

President Clinton governed at a pivotal time in U.S. foreign policy. The Cold War had ended during as 1980s drew to a close. Shortly before Clinton's election, the Soviet Union had splintered into more than a dozen nations, many of them at odds with their neighbors. The U.S. victory in the Cold War marked the end of a centrifugal pressure that had long kept Republicans and Democrats largely committed to bi-partisan containment of America's most dangerous adversary (Jacobs and Shapiro 1995). Foreign policy during the Clinton years (and during some of the George H. W. Bush years preceding Clinton's term) involved few certainties. Humanitarian crises that the U.S. often involved itself in to draw a contrast with the USSR faded in importance after the end of the Cold War, particularly if there was a chance of U.S. military casualties (Lebow 1995). Democratization struggles, like in Haiti, likewise received less attention from Washington during the Clinton years than they had when nearly every country on the globe was a possible convert or defection in alliances dominated by the two global powers (Renshon 1995a).

Of course, Clinton was hardly the first president to say one thing and do another in foreign policy. American voters often hear politicians try to win elections by offering foreign policy promises. Candidate Dwight D. Eisenhower, for example, in 1952 promised Eastern Europeans that he would support anti-Soviet liberation efforts, which won him the support of many Eastern European immigrants and their U.S.-born children. Despite that vow, President Eisenhower did not help the rebel movements in East Germany or Hungary that briefly challenged the USSR's domination of Eastern Europe during his presidency (Lebow 1995). In 1968, candidate Richard Nixon promised he had a secret plan to end the war in Vietnam. His secret was that there was no plan, and Nixon aggressively expanded the war into neighboring Laos and Cambodia without congressional authorization—and with catastrophic results (Dallek 2007).

The end of the Cold War marked a significant decline in American military interventions presented as promoting the interests of democracy internationally vis-à-vis communism. With the Soviet Union out of the picture, the pressure to expand the number of allied nations lessened considerably—and the American public knew it. The times that Clinton or George H. W. Bush before him tried to build a case for international humanitarian assistance, as in Somalia, they struggled to win public support in the U.S. for greater international engagement (Jacobs and Shapiro 1995). Indeed, the Clinton years marked the rise of employing national self-interest arguments in the marketing of U.S. foreign policy (Lebow 1995).

International evaluations of the United States during the Clinton presidency were largely positive, according to a series of surveys conducted by the Pew Research Center during 1999 and 2000 (Pew 2003b). Evaluations in many NATO nations, including Great Britain, Germany, Italy, and Canada were all very upbeat: As shown in Table 2.4, more than 70 percent of survey respondents in each nation said they thought positively of the U.S. While people surveyed in France were somewhat less positive, even there more than six out of every ten respondents gave the global superpower a positive evaluation. European leaders had been particularly troubled about Serbia during Clinton's second term, and many leaders in foreign capitals were pleased that Clinton ordered the U.S. to lead NATO airstrikes against Serbia (Berman 2001).

America's Serbia policy likely triggered the relatively negative reaction most Russians had to the U.S., given that Serbia and Russia had friendly relations (Halberstam 2001). Only 37 percent of Russians surveyed had a positive evaluation of the U.S., far smaller than the amount of western Europeans who felt positively about the U.S. Although Clinton courted Russian President Boris Yeltsin during the years both men served in

Table 2.4 International Views of the U.S.
During the Clinton Presidency

Results are those in various national surveys
who hold a positive view of the U.S.

Great Britain	83%
Germany	78%
Morocco	77%
Italy	76%
Indonesia	75%
Canada	71%
France	62%
South Korea	58%
Brazil	56%
Turkey	52%
Spain	50%
Nigeria	46%
Russia	37%
Pakistan	23%
Palestinian Authority	15%

Notes: The results report responses from the most
recent Pew surveys undertaken in the given nation
before the 2000 presidential elections. All surveys
were conducted during either 1999 or 2000.

Source: Pew 2003b.

office, regular bilateral summits and other outreach efforts did not erase decades of public skepticism created during the Cold War and intensified by U.S.-led NATO airstrikes on Serbia (cf., Halberstam 2001). Pakistanis and Palestinians were even more critical than Russians were.

Case Study: Framing and Re-Framing
Sex Scandal and Impeachment

Most Americans first heard the name Monica Lewinsky in January 1998, shortly after the conservative online news outlet the *Drudge Report* dropped a blockbuster story: a *Newsweek* reporter had prepared a story involving numerous liaisons involving the president and his one-time intern and the editors at the magazine were sitting on the story (Isikoff 2000). Hours later, conservative pundit Bill Kristol mentioned the item on an ABC News program, and the yearlong media feeding frenzy began (Powers 1998).

What a feeding frenzy it was. The Clinton-Lewinsky saga was the leading story of 1998, when the sex scandal ripened into a congressional impeachment inquiry. The evening newscasts on ABC, CBS, and NBC provided 1,636 broadcast reports to the matter, or one-seventh of their total airtime (Farnsworth and Lichter 2006). Scandal-related reports on television news outnumbered reports on the pivotal midterms elections of 1998 by a six-to-one margin, and also swamped reports on key international crises like Iraq, Kosovo, the Middle East, nuclear weapons tests in South Asia, and the bombing of U.S. embassies in Africa *combined* (Farnsworth and Lichter 2006).

From the start, Clinton faced immense challenges dealing with the scandal. Numerous White House officials knew of the liaisons, and several concerned administration staffers had transferred Lewinsky to a public relations position at the Pentagon to minimize contacts between the two (I. Morris 2002). Lewinsky herself had been confiding about her involvement with Clinton to a Pentagon co-worker, Linda Tripp, who had been secretly taping those conversations (Morris 2002). Clinton already had a credibility problem regarding an extramarital affair because of the extensive news coverage of Clinton's involvement with Gennifer Flowers during the 1992 campaign. In addition, there was also the story of Paula Jones, a onetime Arkansas state employee who charged that the then-governor crudely propositioned her in an Arkansas hotel room. In 1994, Jones sued Clinton for sexual harassment. The parties settled the case in November 1998, when Clinton agreed to pay Jones $850,000 (Isikoff 2000).

Given that there were still other women not yet in the public eye who also claimed misconduct on Clinton's part, denial might not have been the wisest strategy for the president. Even so, that is precisely the course that Clinton and his team pursued at first. The president forcefully declared: "I did not have sexual relations with that woman," an often-repeated televised sound bite and a claim that White House staffers supported with statements of their own (Isikoff 2000).

In addition to the defense offered via the presidential denial, the Clinton team also played offense. About a week into the scandal, First Lady Hillary Clinton appeared on NBC's *Today Show* to defend her husband's character and attack his accusers.

> There is a great story here, for anybody willing to find it and write about it and explain it, is this vast right-wing conspiracy that has been conspiring against my husband since the day he announced for president . . . Having seen so many of these accusations come and go, having seen people profit, you know, like Jerry Falwell, with videos, accusing my husband of committing murder, of drug running, seeing some of the things that are written and said about him, my attitude is we've been there before and we have seen this before.
>
> (quoted in Blaney and Beniot 2001: 109)

From the start, the counterattacks were effective in shaping news coverage. Less than one-fourth of the news stories about the scandal on the evening newscasts during the first month of the scandal (January 21 through February 20, 1998) implied probable guilt on the part of the president. Nearly three times as many (71 percent) presented the charges in a neutral or balanced fashion. Another 5 percent suggested presidential innocence (Farnsworth and Lichter 2006).

As the scandal intensified throughout the summer, television news stories featuring Lewinsky increased, as did those featuring independent counsel Ken Starr, demonstrating the partial success of the Clinton team in deflecting attention away from the White House and towards the president's accusers. As shown in Table 2.5, the tone of coverage of the leading figures in the Clinton-Lewinsky matter changed considerably over the course of the scandal. Investigator Ken Starr was not in a position to defend his efforts effectively in the media; he had an investigation to run and he would undermine his reputation if he slung mud publicly back at the Clinton team. Not surprisingly, he received overwhelmingly negative notices in the news. Monica Lewinsky, the former intern, also received largely negative comments, as Clinton criticized the former intern and for months denied that there was an affair between the two. During the scandal, Lewinsky mainly sought to avoid the media spotlight, a near-hopeless task given the level of media and congressional interest in the matter.

Table 2.5 Network News Evaluations of Clinton Scandal Figures, Percentage Positive Press

Winter 1998	
Bill Clinton	48%
Hillary Rodham Clinton	71%
Vernon Jordan	58%
Kenneth Starr	23%
Monica Lewinsky	25%
Linda Tripp	30%
Summer 1998	
Bill Clinton	37%
Hillary Rodham Clinton	96%
Clinton's Team	37%
Kenneth Starr and his team	13%
Monica Lewinsky	14%
Congressional Democrats	44%
Congressional Republicans	28%

Notes: The Winter 1998 data cover news reports from January 21 through February 20, 1998. The Summer 1998 data cover evaluations aired on network newscasts from July 27 through September 20, 1998.

Source: Farnsworth and Lichter 2006: 118.

By far the most positive press during this scandal related to Hillary Clinton, which made her a vital, effective defender of her husband. As First Lady, and as the person victimized by Clinton's failure to honor his marital vows, her words carried great weight. She defended her husband, as she often did when he faced trouble for his alleged misconduct, without condoning his poor behavior. Indeed, public sympathy for a wronged spouse amplified her complaints about a "right-wing conspiracy" intent on undermining the voters' decision to put Bill Clinton in the White House in 1992 and keep him there for another four years in 1996. Given the First Lady's pivotal role during this crisis year, one can only wonder whether Bill Clinton's political career could have survived this crisis if his wife had turned on him over his actions.

During the scandal, members of the White House team and the president's lawyers offered much of the president's defense in public. But even they often criticized his personal behavior at the same time, though they emphasized that his actions were personal—not public—acts that did not warrant impeachment. Once Clinton eventually admitted to an improper relationship as the investigators closed in, he too criticized his personal behavior (Farnsworth and Lichter 2006). While television news evaluations of Clinton were more negative during the summer of 1998 than they were when the scandal first broke, coverage of Lewinsky and Starr were notably more negative in tone than news reports that focused on the president.

After Clinton admitted an improper relationship in August 1998, he could no longer plausibly claim he had been fully honest in his previous remarks to the country. (He argued that oral sex did not qualify as "sex" and therefore that he was not guilty of lying in his previous statements.) The investigative report of Kenneth Starr was released in mid-1998 and detailed several instances of Clinton and Lewinsky being alone together at times that Hillary Clinton was away from the White House or out of town (Starr 1998). As his narrative options narrowed, Clinton then claimed he had failed to tell the complete truth in an effort to protect his family and that he was guilty of personal misconduct. He then said nothing he did warranted removal from office. He was a philanderer, in other words, but not a crook. In the end, most citizens agreed and the president remained in office. The House voted to impeach but Clinton emerged from his Senate impeachment trial with an acquittal and with high public approval ratings for his job performance and low public assessments of his personal conduct (Cohen 2002a, 2002b; Newman 2002; Owen 2000).

> People had no trouble believing that Clinton had an affair. But they saw it as a private matter not fit for criminal investigation. . . . The results rolled in: Americans don't prosecute people for having an affair; if Clinton interfered with the legal system, he did so to protect his privacy.
>
> (Schmidt and Weisskopf 2000: 93)

As shown in Table 2.1 and discussed at the opening of the chapter, television news continued to be a key information source for most news consumers during the 1990s. Perhaps the nonstop coverage of the year-long scandal on cable television and elsewhere had made the matter old hat to many by the time that Republicans in Congress tried to drive Clinton from office.

Though Republicans lost the battle, conservative media benefited from the controversy. Conservative media voices were gaining a reputation online, particularly the Drudge Report, which first broke the news of the scandal and remained influential in shaping the news agenda throughout its duration (Isikoff 2000). Talk radio, often conservative in content, helped galvanize opposition to Clinton by GOP lawmakers even before the Clinton-Lewinsky scandal emerged, and helped keep their opposition visible during the year Congress debated impeachment (Laufer 1995; Owen 1996).

Overall, though, Clinton was fortunate that news consumers during his presidency relied largely on traditional media sources like television and newspapers. These legacy news outlets had greater hesitation to publish some of the more salacious or unverified details of the Clinton scandal that often first emerged online. Even though the mainstream media's coverage of the president's misconduct could not fairly be termed "elevated," the reluctance of traditional news organizations to dig too deeply into the political dirt came at a very different time than the culture of untrue, unverified fake news reports that would play an even more significant role in the news environment two decades later.

The Clinton Communication Legacy

Nearly six decades ago, political scientist V. O. Key (1961) urged political leaders to focus on educating and leading the public during their time in office. In light of the experiences of the Clinton presidency, a subsequent generation of political scientists argued that that public education might weaken the health of the democracy if leaders prime public opinion and then respond to the public demands they themselves did much to create. Indeed, if political leaders distract the public from their genuine desires through political marketing, the problems may be severe indeed for what Ginsberg (1986) termed "the captive public."

The media technology available in the 1990s, and the temptation for news outlets to focus on personalities rather than substance, created a circus atmosphere for at least part of Clinton's campaigns and his presidency (Farnsworth and Lichter 2003, 2006). While Clinton bears some responsibility for the trivialized coverage he sometimes endured—after all, he engaged in at least some of the behavior that triggered the soap opera news coverage of his personal life—media norms and consumer preferences were also at work in the news coverage dynamics of those years. There may have been issues galore to cover during the Clinton years, but there were many scandals as well.

These same scandals also became a central part of the Clinton legacy. As shown in Table 2.6, nearly three-quarters of those surveyed (74 percent) at the end of his second term said the scandals were most memorable part of the Clinton presidency. Clinton recorded the first balanced federal budget in decades, but only 14 percent said that the core of his legacy would be his economic policies. Foreign policy was even less relevant, with only 6 percent identifying any foreign policy initiative that rose above scandals as more memorable.

Overall, 44 percent of Americans said in that 2001 survey that Clinton would likely to be remembered as an above average or outstanding president. Eight years earlier, in contrast, 36 percent said that George H. W. Bush would be remembered as an above average or outstanding president. Ronald Reagan, who left office in 1989, had higher end-of-term

Table 2.6 Public Views on Clinton's Legacy, 2001

Thinking ahead, what do you think Bill Clinton will be most remembered for after he has left office? (Topics volunteered by respondent)

74%	Scandals
14%	Economy/Budget deficit
6%	Foreign Policy
5%	Other categories, positive comments
3%	Other categories, negative comments
1%	Domestic policy

In the long run, do you think Bill Clinton will mostly be remembered for his accomplishments as president or for the impeachment and other scandals involving his administration?

28%	Remembered for his accomplishments as president
67%	Remembered for the impeachment and other scandals

How do you think President Bill Clinton will go down in history . . . as an outstanding president, above average, average, below average, or poor?

	Clinton	George H. W. Bush	Reagan
	January 2001	January 1993	January 1989
Outstanding	12%	6%	17%
Above Average	32%	30%	42%
Average	32%	51%	25%
Below Average	10%	8%	9%
Poor	11%	4%	5%

Note: Don't Know responses are not reported here, so percentages do not sum to 100.

Source: Pew 2001a.

evaluations than those two successors, with 59 percent saying that he was an above average or outstanding president.

Even though more respondents evaluated Clinton favorably than George H. W. Bush, Clinton also received more negative notices than did Bush. One out of five respondents (21 percent) said Clinton would be regarded as a below-average or poor president as compared to 12 percent saying the same thing about Bush and 14 percent saying the same thing about Reagan. Clearly, Clinton was a notably more polarizing president than Bush was—and Reagan too—and Clinton governed during a time of increased polarization.

Clinton's presidency, from start to finish, involved an intense focus on presidential communication, a "permanent campaign" featuring nonstop efforts by pollsters and spin-doctors to sustain Clinton's popularity but comparatively little effort devoted to communicating the substance of policy (Edwards 2000). Clinton's use of electronic intimacy, the process of connecting on a personal level with citizens as a way of winning over voters who had their doubts about the president's character, took advantage of the media environment of the Clinton years. In the 1990s, talk shows and town halls had become commonplace and provided a reinforced illusion of intimacy (Bennett 1995). While these media and political trends may have been particularly good news for extroverted politicians like Bill Clinton, it is hardly clear that the country is better off functioning under such a system of candidate and presidential communication.

> In the end, the public is brought no closer to candidates on talk shows or bus trips than on conventional newscasts or meet the press programs; just the opposite may well be true. However, it is the short-term, continually reinforced illusion of intimacy and responsiveness that counts.
>
> (Bennett 1995: 110)

To be fair to Clinton, though, his political survival required him to use the media tools at his disposal—and to use the ones he could manage best. Any politician would have done the same, though personality differences might have suggested different strategies on the way to maximizing one's political success. The combative and scandal-heavy political environment of the Clinton years required aggressive presidential media management push-back efforts as a condition of self-protection in an environment where "the distinctions between reality and representation collapse so as to make them meaningless" (Parry-Giles and Parry-Giles 2002: 1).

Clinton's media approach, critics noted, was particularly useful for a political conversation that emphasizes personality and deemphasizes discussion of issues. Even before Clinton came along, the mass media had a heavy emphasis on episodic coverage of news and struggled to offer thematic coverage of issues that provide a fuller context of existing policies and their alternatives (Iyengar and Kinder 1987; Iyengar 1991).

> The ultimate problem with the constant reinforcement psychology required to sell politicians to ever-wary citizens is that it permits little room for public dialogue about the issues and the programs that politicians are elected to deal with. As the ties between leaders and citizens become ever more illusory, the reality of serious issues seems ever more harsh. It is small wonder that most modern politicians prove better at getting elected than at governing.
>
> (Bennett 1995: 111)

The Clinton years, then, ended in some ways where they began, with a high level of citizen discontent and frustration with the national government's performance (Farnsworth 2001, 2003a, 2003b). Even the constant diet of cynicism was corrosive: "Continually bemoaning the state of American image politics only perpetuates a cynicism and fatalism that corrodes the very substance of democratic governance" (Parry-Giles and Perry Giles 2002: 15).

The contentious election of 2000, which was eventually decided by the Supreme Court, did not exactly reduce America's political tensions. Nor did it reduce public cynicism or anger with the government. This book now turns George W. Bush, the forty-third president.

3   The Fox News Presidency of George W. Bush

The George W. Bush presidency began under exceptionally inauspicious circumstances. His very election was one of the most controversial in decades, as Democrats and Republicans engaged in a titanic political and legal struggle to resolve a variety of ballot counting problems in Florida, where the official margin between George W. Bush and Al Gore was several hundred votes out of millions cast. In the end, a contentious 5–4 Supreme Court ruling ended the ballot counting in Florida and declared Bush the victor.

For reporters, the 2000 campaign and the month of post-campaign wrangling that followed Election Day was a news story for the ages. Since the dawn of television, never had a presidential election turned into such a dramatic month of news: with near daily charges and counter charges of electoral misconduct, bombshell court rulings, and lawyers, lots and lots of lawyers. The story was a ratings bonanza for established media like the television networks, for upstart cable news outlets like CNN and Fox, and for the ever-growing online news outlets clawing their way into the public's field of vision. In the ever-expanding media environment, there was plenty of news, and news consumers, for everyone during election and post-election 2000.

Once George W. Bush took office, the new president continued to face some of the same challenges he endured as a candidate. Foremost among them involved public concerns about his character: was this genial southern governor sufficiently disciplined and prepared to be an effective president? To try to dispel the doubts over himself and his election, the new president had to continue to sell his personality to the public long after he settled in at 1600 Pennsylvania Avenue, or at least until the tragic morning of September 11, 2001, when all but the president's most skeptical critics looked to Washington and saw a genuine leader. Unfortunately for Bush, those questions of character—particularly public uncertainty regarding his competence—resurfaced during his second term. As the occupation of Iraq turned increasingly bloody and as the president struggled to demonstrate that his team could respond effectively to a massive hurricane in New Orleans (Bennett et al. 2007), growing numbers of

Americans once again began to wonder if this president really could handle the job of being president.

The News Media Environment of the George W. Bush Era

When George Bush and Al Gore squared off in the 2000 presidential election, they faced a news environment far different than the one Bill Clinton faced when he first ran for president eight years earlier. Some things were similar, of course. The evening news reports on network television remained the most effective means of communicating with the public, particularly those likely to vote, as had been the case for decades (Pew 2000a, 2000b, 2000c, 2000d). But other factors changed a great deal. The rise of cable news and the internet during the 1990s created the need to shape one's media strategy differently (Owen 2002). Even within the world of cable news, one size would not fit all. CNN's 24-hour news cycle, which became particularly prominent during the Persian Gulf War of 1991 and during the Clinton impeachment year of 1998, meant that one had to win one news cycle after another—even over the course of a single day! The 2000 campaigns and the president who took office in January 2001 also had to take account of Fox News, an aggressive conservative media voice that had won the support of many Republicans troubled by traditional news outlets (Ladd 2013).

To make matters worse, any campaign operating in 2000 could never know what trouble might strike and then be broadcast worldwide almost immediately. Indeed, the salacious news coverage of the Clinton-Lewinsky scandal a few years earlier meant virtually nothing would be off-limits for reporters; even dubious rumors would quickly make their way to the public (Sabato et al. 2000). After all, if one news outlet did not bite when offered a juicy news tidbit, another certainly would.

The Continued Dominance of Television News

As shown in Table 3.1, television news remained the dominant news source for news consumers seeking election information during the George W. Bush years. In 2000, the year Bush was elected, 70 percent of those surveyed said that television was either their first or second most important source for news, far ahead of newspapers, with 39 percent listing those outlets as a key media source. The internet was a major source for only 11 percent of news consumers in 2000, ranking fourth behind television, newspapers and radio. (Because respondents could select up to two news sources, the percentages exceed 100). The media environment of 2000 was quite different from that of subsequent presidential elections, in other words.

Four years later, when Bush sought re-election against John Kerry, television continued to dominate the news environment. While the percentage of

Table 3.1 News Media Use, 2000–2008

How did you get most of your news about the presidential election campaign? From television, from newspapers, from radio, from magazines, or from the Internet? [randomize options, accept up to two answers]

	2008	2004	2000
Television	68%	76%	70%
Newspapers	33%	46%	39%
Radio	16%	22%	15%
Magazines	3%	6%	4%
Internet	36%	21%	11%

On television, did you get most of your campaign news from [randomize options] *

	2008	2004
Television (total)	68%	76%
Local news programming	10%	12%
ABC Network News	7%	11%
CBS Network News	6%	9%
NBC Network News	8%	13%
CNN Cable news	21%	15%
MSNBC Cable news	9%	6%
Fox News Cable Channel	22%	21%

Did you happen to get any news or information about the 2008 elections from the Internet, or not? **

	2008	2004	2000	1996
Yes	56%	41%	30%	10%
No	44%	59%	70%	90%

Notes: Because respondents were allowed to list more than one influential news source, the percentages do not sum to 100.
* Asked if respondent listed television in the previous question as a top media source. Results in percentage of total sample.
** Yes response includes those who already listed the internet as a major news source in a previous question.

Source: Pew 2008a.

internet-reliant news consumers increased dramatically—up to 21 percent in 2004 from 11 percent four years earlier, as seen in Table 3.1—television news also increased (albeit slightly), with more than three-quarters saying those broadcasts were a major source of campaign information. Despite its gains, the internet ranked far behind television, and well behind newspapers, which 46 percent identified as a major news source. Even in 2008, at the end of Bush's second term, television remained highly influential. Notably, newspapers fell sharply and the internet gained considerably in importance between 2000 and 2008.

Content analysis, the careful line-by-line scientific study of news content, of the big three evening newscasts during George W. Bush's first term revealed the same problems identified in studies of news coverage of previous presidencies. News coverage of those years provided a very administration-focused orientation towards Washington that undermined the ability of Congress to compete effectively in shaping the policy agenda, and a heavy focus on domestic news apart from nations where the U.S. military were actively engaged (Farnsworth et al. 2013).

In addition, content analysis revealed that the 2001 terrorist attacks marked a pivot in news coverage of international matters on network television. During the part of 2001 before the terrorist attacks of 9/11, the evening newscasts of the three broadcast networks spent 21 percent of their time talking about international matters, increasing to 36 percent during the remainder of 2001 (Farnsworth and Lichter 2004, 2006: 90). Coverage of international news also increased in 2003, the year of the second U.S.-led invasion of Iraq by the second President Bush. Coverage of international news that year reached 43 percent, a higher proportion of international news coverage than during any year of the Clinton presidency. By itself, news from the U.S.-led occupation of Iraq accounted for 24 percent of all news coverage on the big three networks that year, while international news from every other country except Iraq accounted for only 19 percent of the evening newscasts during 2003 (Farnsworth and Lichter 2006: 90). During the four years of George W. Bush's first term, terrorism was the single largest story during 2001 and 2002 and Iraq was the largest story during 2003 and 2004 (Farnsworth and Lichter 2006: 67). Domestic matters increased in importance as Bush's second term wound down, with domestic economic concerns like a burst real estate bubble, a near-collapse of the banking system, and a major recession receiving far greater media attention during 2008 (Farnsworth and Lichter 2011a).

A group called the Swift Boat Veterans for Truth revealed the continuing influence of television news during this era. The group claimed that John Kerry, the 2004 Democratic nominee for president, did not deserve the medals he received as a naval officer in the Vietnam War (Bumiller 2004; Rutenberg 2004b). The group bought a relatively limited number of television ads in three battleground states, Iowa, Wisconsin, and Ohio and marketed their message online (Geer 2012). Mainstream media reporters were primed to cover the ads in that contentious race: television networks gave the story extensive coverage, airing 89 sound bites on the scandal between June 2 and September 2, 2004, when the controversy was most prominent in the news (Farnsworth and Lichter 2011a). A fellow veteran even campaigned with Kerry to attest to his heroism, recalling that the future presidential candidate had pulled him out of a river in Vietnam while under enemy fire (Rasmussen 2004). While it may seem strange that Kerry, a decorated Vietnam veteran, would lose a legacy battle over the 1960s to a man who stayed safe in America during the war—that is exactly what happened. The considerable media attention to the Swift Boat attacks, particularly on Fox News and other conservative media, undermined Kerry's support among veterans and may have been one of the decisive factors in Bush's narrow victory that year (Easton et al. 2004; Nagourney 2004; Wilgoren 2004).

The Rise of Fox News

The late 1990s, the years just before George W. Bush's election, had been very good to Fox News, an upstart cable news outlet that began broadcasting its conservative media voice in the midst of the 1996 presidential campaign. For conservatives frustrated by the relative absence of a right-facing message on television comparable to that found on talk radio, Fox News filled a gap in the marketplace, and was rewarded with a growing audience during the Bush presidency (Pew 2008a). Fox News started drawing larger audiences than CNN by 2002, as its strategy of building a loyal, conservative audience began to pay off (Cohen 2008).

Indeed, content analysis of network news coverage of the 1996 presidential campaign offered some evidence to explain the conservative frustration that gave rise to Fox News. The evening news broadcasts of ABC, CBS, and NBC were particularly critical of Republican challenger Bob Dole. Content analysis of the three evening newscasts during the two months before the 1996 election revealed that reports on Clinton were 50 percent positive, as compared to 37 percent positive for Dole, a 17 percentage point gap (Farnsworth and Lichter 2011a: 99). Republicans angry at Bill Clinton's ability to remain in office despite misconduct relating to the Clinton-Lewinsky matter also might have found Fox News a welcome respite from the mainstream media criticism of Clinton's accusers (Farnsworth and Lichter 2006).

What's more, Fox News provided George W. Bush with an unexpected gift on Election Night 2000. At 2 a.m. the cable network prematurely declared that Bush had won Florida and therefore the election. It turned out that a cousin of George W. Bush was working as a vote counter for Fox News (Fritz et al. 2004). Other networks quickly followed the Fox News announcement that Bush won with victory announcements of their own, since they did not wish to lag behind on the biggest news story of the year (Sabato 2002). Al Gore called Bush to accept defeat, but on the way to the campaign rally the vote counters realized that Bush had not won after all; Gore then retracted his concession call and the month of litigation and recounts began (Owen 2002).

Earlier on election night, the networks had announced, and then retracted, their statements that Gore had won Florida. But the premature reports hours later that Bush had won the presidency—coupled with the Bush team's own marketing of finishing ahead of Gore in the early re-counting—helped create an environment where Gore seemed (at least to some) to be trying to undo the actual outcome in Florida via the recount process (Fritz et al. 2004).

Conservatives sought out Fox News for a sympathetic portrayal of their political views, and they were not disappointed, as content analysis of the 2004 presidential election reveals. A content analysis of the first half hour of Fox News' *Special Report* during the two months before the election revealed a powerful pro-Bush tilt more pronounced than network television's less critical treatment of John Kerry. (The first half-hour of that Fox News program most closely resembles a network newscast in structure, while the second half hour contains panel discussions, a departure from the format of network evening newscasts.) Coverage of Bush was 37 percent positive on network television during the two months before the 2004 election, as compared to 53 percent positive reports on Fox News. Coverage of Kerry was 59 percent positive on network news, as compared to 21 percent positive on Fox. These comparisons provided a 22 point advantage for Kerry on network television, as compared to a 31 point advantage for Bush on Fox News (Farnsworth and Lichter 2011a: 143).

Fox News and the networks also split on news coverage that related to the leadership qualities of the candidates, with Fox News providing a 63 percent positive coverage in this area for Bush, as compared to 34 percent positive coverage of Kerry's leadership qualities. Network television reversed the pattern: Kerry's leadership qualities received positive notices 68 percent of the time on network news, as compared to 47 percent of the time for Bush. Once again Fox News had the wider comparative coverage gap, with reports on leadership qualities providing a 29 percentage point advantage for Bush on Fox News and a 21 point advantage for Kerry on network television (Farnsworth and Lichter 2011a: 143).

While Fox News did not qualify as a ratings powerhouse during these years, it performed relatively well when compared with other television outlets. As shown in Table 3.1, 21 percent of those surveyed by Pew (2008a) said they used Fox News as a major information source during the 2004 campaign and 22 percent said the same in 2008. The numbers were about as good as the results for CNN during both election cycles, and by 2008, Fox News did about as well with the public as the three broadcast networks combined. In addition, Fox News has a loyal audience that watches for a longer period of time than do CNN viewers, making Fox News a very effective way to reach Republican voters and encourage their support for Bush (Geidner and Holbert 2011; Pew 2006).

A Growing Public Appetite for Online News

Never had the up-to-the-minute potential of online news seemed more important than during the key late-breaking crises of this era: the Clinton impeachment controversy of 1998, the recount-from-hell election of 2000 or the terrorist attacks of 2001. In all three of these cases, citizens became insatiable news consumers who could not wait for the evening news and sought to get the latest reports online. As revealed in Table 3.1 above, online news became steadily more important to news consumers between 2000 and 2008. Around the time Bush finished his second term, more than one person in three described online news as one of their major information sources (Pew 2008a).

In addition to those heavy consumers of online news, there were also people who used the web to get information now and then. In the final question presented in Table 3.1, we see that 10 percent of respondents in a survey used any online news in 1996, rising to 30 percent in 2000. Four years later, 41 percent said they used online news at least some of the time, and that figure rose to 56 percent by 2008.

The web played a particularly influential role in the 2004 campaign, starting with the insurgent candidacy of former Vermont Gov. Howard Dean, a Democrat who generated strong feelings among party activists. During the second half of 2003, Dean signed up hundreds of thousands of supporters, raised a significant amount of money, and drew huge crowds via a vigorous online presence (Burden 2005). For a while, it looked like Dean would become the nominee, thanks in part to the campaign's savvy use of the internet (Ceaser and Busch 2005). But conventional media marked his downfall, particularly through aggressive attack ads on television (West 2014). Increasingly critical coverage of the apparent front-runner on network television, including coverage of the candidate's boisterous "scream," triggered a rapid decline in Dean's support and cleared the way for John Kerry to win the Democratic nomination (Farnsworth and Lichter 2011a). Dean's strategy of building his campaign by connecting and thereby empowering activists online made him a credible candidate for the nomination, but his innovative use of online tools fell short (Trippi 2004). In the end, Dean's online approach turned out to be a beta version of the online-focused strategies that subsequent presidential candidates employed in the 2008 election and beyond (Farnsworth 2009).

The power of the web to challenge traditional media became particularly visible in 2004, when George W. Bush faced a series of highly critical reports regarding what he did and did not do while he was stateside during the Vietnam War years. Pre-election stories in the *New York Times* examined whether Bush used family connections to secure a coveted spot in the Texas Air National Guard to avoid serving in combat in Southeast Asia (Rimer et al. 2004). The *New York Times* also reported that Bush failed to undergo a required physical or show up for required training during his time in the Guard (Seelye and Blumenthal 2004). No one came forward to vouch that Bush had served his time in the Guard as required, but the spotty records that survived show that Bush left military service with an honorable discharge (Rimer et al. 2004).

Bush's less than heroic behavior was a sharp contrast to the many previous presidents who had served in uniform during the years of World War II and the Korean War and was potentially devastating to voters with such a long history of electing veterans to high office (excepting Bill Clinton, who also evaded service in Vietnam). Subsequently, CBS News reported erroneously on *60 Minutes II* that it had obtained records from Bush's guard service that contained instructions to the military to "sugar coat" the young man's record (Rutenberg 2004a). The internet and its bloggers swung into action: they demonstrated that the memos were fake, since typewriters of that era did not use the font used in the document (Rutenberg and Zernike 2004). In the end, CBS retracted the story, apologized to Bush and fired three top news executives over the matter (Kurtz 2005). The incident demonstrated that the upstart online world could bring evidence to bear that could challenge and ultimately destroy erroneous news reports offered by one of the nation's top traditional news outlets. As was the case with the Clinton-Lewinsky matter, online voices were powerful ones when it came to focusing media and public attention about matters of value to conservatives, in this case the erroneous reporting of CBS News (Drudge 2000; Rutenberg 2004a).

An examination of the White House website during the Bush years illustrates the uncertain early beginnings and evaluation of the federal government's internet presence, seen in Figure 3.1. This illustration from a typical day from Bush's second term looks more familiar to modern-day users of the web than did the Clinton page offered in Chapter 2. Part of the reason the Bush page is more sophisticated is because of improving technology: faster download speeds enable greater use of pictures and links when compared to a 1990s web page. The page contains links to the president's most recent weekly radio address and photos of the president's activities that the administration wants to emphasize. This page shows the evolution of presidential marketing online as well: this page is far more about the president, and far less about the White House, than was the Clinton page. In an effort to maximize the page's marketing potential, visitors could enter their email addresses to receive updates from the White House, and the page itself contains a handy search function to make sure that visitors get information on the issues of greatest interest promptly. The Bush White House web presence, in other words, seems familiar to modern eyes, though the home page is relatively thin on photos and illustrations when compared to many of today's online offerings.

The Character of George W. Bush

As a presidential candidate, George W. Bush had a rare—and unusual— advantage: he was the son of a former president. Bush watched at close range his father's political rise and even assisted in it (Minutaglio 1999).

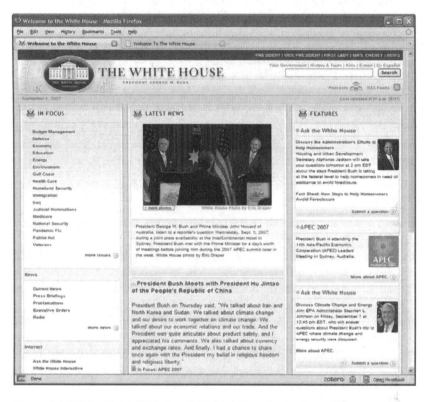

Figure 3.1 White House Website, G.W. Bush Presidency, Second Term

After George W. Bush became a candidate in his own right, first for governor of Texas and then for president, the son could and did call upon his father's vast network of policy aides and donors. These were not last-minute introductions to influential Republicans. During 1988 and in the years that followed, the younger Bush served as a conduit to conservative Christians, starting with his father's successful campaign and then during his father's presidency (Minutaglio 1999). As the younger Bush built his own 2000 campaign organization, donors donated. His Bush family pedigree convinced many Republicans than he would be a sound, reliable choice (Rockman 2004).

There was more to Bush's success than the family advantages of money and contacts. There was also the character of George W. Bush, widely perceived as a decent man in the rough-and-tumble world of politics (Ceaser and Busch 2001). In the wake of conservative Republican attacks on the Clinton presidency throughout the 1990s, the Texas governor used the Bush family legacy of political optimism to help paint a congenial portrait of the family's next presidential aspirant (Ceaser and Busch 2001; Sinclair

2000a). So father Bush's "thousand points of light" in the early 1990s became the son's "compassionate conservatism" in 2000 (Sinclair 2004).

Bush's use of the term "compassionate conservatism" suggests the possibility that not all conservatism was compassionate. Seeking to distinguish oneself from the extremists in one's own party was a key strategy that Bill Clinton used to present himself as a different kind of Democratic politician in 1992, and that so-called Third Way approach offered opportunities for George W. Bush as well (Rockman 2004). In a powerful rebuke to the Democratic-versus-Republican trench warfare that marked the 1990s, the younger Bush declared repeatedly throughout the campaign that he was "a uniter not a divider" (Dimock 2004).

The Pitch

Americans have conflicting desires when it comes to presidents, and successful presidential candidates usually are able to combine a common touch with establishment credentials and relevant experience that voters think will demonstrate they are up to the job (Cronin and Genovese 2013). In a strategy that borrowed from the folksiness of the Clinton 1992 campaign that defeated his father, George W. Bush sought to portray himself above all as someone who was very likeable on a personal level. His jocular public demeanor and his well-known penchant for giving his aides nicknames suggested that Bush was a hard man not to like, at least on a personal level (Rockman 2004). For many voters, turned off by the partisan bickering and by the numbing complexity of policy issues like health care, Bush the person seemed like a breath of fresh air (Ceaser and Busch 2001).

The Bush campaign's decision to emphasize character rather than policy clearly played to Bush's strengths and minimized his weaknesses. The Texas governor would never prevail on policy specifics in the presidential debates with Vice President Al Gore, long recognized as a policy wonk of the first order (Ceaser and Busch 2001). Bush, unlike Gore, seemed during those high-profile campaign events to be comfortable in his own skin, offering a solid contrast to Vice President Gore's inconsistent presentations of his own personality across those debates (Rockman 2004).

There was another reason for the 2000 GOP campaign to emphasize personality over policy. Many Bush II campaign insiders long believed that the first President Bush lost his re-election in 1992 because of concerns that he lacked a sense of how to connect with ordinary Americans (Ceaser and Busch 2001). As a result of the bitter lessons the Bush family learned in 1992, the George W. Bush campaign wisely decided to emphasize the prairie folksiness presented by the Connecticut-born, Yale- and Harvard-educated Texas governor (Ceaser and Busch 2001). Clinton's 1992 efforts to deemphasize his elite credentials offered clear evidence of the utility of this approach for a presidential candidate.

The re-creation of the Clinton "bubba" character strategy from 1992 clearly worked in shaping public views of George W. Bush's personality during the campaign and beyond. Polls showed that the younger Bush scored very high in surveys that asked about his character: he took office with more than 60 percent saying that he was tough enough for the job, and that he was honest. More than 55 percent agreed with statements that the new president "shares your values," "inspires confidence," and "cares about the needs of people like you"—all particularly strong numbers, given the intense divisions generated in the nation because of the recount mess that had played out on Bush's way to the White House (Edwards 2004).

There was yet another reason for the Bush campaign to emphasize character conversations and to deemphasize policy specifics: Republican conservatives. Another factor in the elder Bush's loss in 1992 involved his limited ability to work well with conservatives in his own party. Anger on the right in 1992 gave rise to the renegade campaign of Pat Buchanan during the primaries and created an opening for independent candidate Ross Perot to peel off some Republicans lukewarm about Bush that year (Ceaser and Busch 1993). By emphasizing personal matters, Bush publicized his born-again values and indicated he would govern in a more conservative direction than the mantra of "compassionate conservative" would have suggested. Bush used character conversations to make his pitch to evangelical Christians, without having to face a backlash from swing voters in the razor-thin contest of 2000 (Ceaser and Busch 2001; Sinclair 2004).

Like Clinton, Bush's public character presentation came with a side order of toughness. Like Reagan, Bush's direct public speaking style fits the mold of the straight-talking, uncomplicated western sheriff or even a Texas Ranger, a popular role in the American imagination (Scott 2000). This law and order role suited the younger Bush. Like Clinton, George W. Bush had demonstrated no public qualms about capital punishment. As governor of Texas, he oversaw a number of executions in the Lone Star State, most notably the high-profile execution of Karla Faye Tucker in 1998 (Minutaglio 1999). In a manner reminiscent of Gov. Clinton's handling of the Ricky Ray Rector matter in 1992 (Bonner and Rimer 2000), yet another southern governor with presidential ambitions rejected a wave of appeals to spare the life of a convicted murderer, using an international death penalty controversy to demonstrate that he was not "squishy" on law and order concerns (Minutaglio 1999).

Bush's image of personal toughness presaged what many expected would be a muscular approach to foreign policy. They were not disappointed. When crises arrived, and they did before his first year in office was through, Bush consistently favored an aggressive response. Indeed, Bush's promise of quick military action in Afghanistan following the terrorist attacks of September 2001 captured the public desire for revenge (Campbell 2004b;

Frum 2003). When Bush decided to invade Iraq, and justified doing so on the basis of what he said was a weapons of mass destruction (WMD) program, as well as links between Saddam Hussein and Osama bin Laden, a majority of the U.S. public supported Bush (Edwards 2003).

Toughness may be appealing to the public, but that quality is not always an asset in a president. Bush proudly declared that he was "the decider," and that he would not second-guess or otherwise agonize over—or some might say learn from—tough decisions (Stolberg 2006). When Bush made a decision, he stuck to it—not apologizing for mistakes, nor even admitting that he made any (Kinsley 2003). When voter sentiment turned against the Iraq War in a particularly strong way in 2006, Bush ignored the political setbacks and vowed to escalate the war. Ever confident, at least before the cameras, he said his unpopular approach would be justified by future historians (Farnsworth 2009).

The Problem

From the time George W. Bush first burst on the national stage, reporters and some citizens wondered whether the Texas governor was temperamentally up to the job of being president. Bush was not a strong student in college, and he sometimes was unusually inarticulate for a politician (Minutaglio 1999). Before entering politics, Bush had failed in the oil business (Minutaglio 1999). It was not an auspicious professional beginning for this presidential son.

As a candidate in his own right, Bush did not always impress with his command of the facts. During the campaign, Bush endured a media narrative that he was not all that bright (Jamieson and Waldman 2003). During their first debate, the candidate mistakenly claimed that Gore had outspent him, a basic campaign fact that should not have taxed him to recall (Hershey 2001). Bush, though, received largely a free pass from the media that night, as reporters preferred to focus on Gore's audible sighs and aggressive demeanor (Farnsworth and Lichter 2003). Bush also made a significant mistake in the second debate when he said that Texas was going to execute three people over a high-profile murder (Actually, only two men were to be executed for the crime). One might have expected the governor to know more about such an exceptional case, a horrific incident where the murderers tied the victim to a pickup truck and drove down the road until his body broke apart. Fortunately for Bush, once again he received less media attention for his factual errors than Gore's misstatements about the price of canine medications and the length of time a student had to stand up in a crowded Florida classroom (Ceaser and Busch 2001; Sabato 2002). Reporters' generally low assessment of Bush's capacities served to insulate him from the greater media scrutiny Gore received for his own arguably less significant missteps during those debates (Farnsworth and Lichter 2003).

For the late-night comics, though, both candidates proved fertile sources of humor, with the advantage, if you can call it that, going to George W. Bush. Tabulations by the Center for Media and Public Affairs of the candidate jokes told about the two candidates on the *Late Show with David Letterman* and the *Tonight Show with Jay Leno* revealed that Bush was the subject of 254 jokes during the general election campaign and Gore was the subject of 165 (Media Monitor 2000). Many of the jokes fit into the "Bush as dim bulb" frame. As Conan O'Brien offered: "At a Washington museum, a new exhibit is about to open that features a first-grade report card of President Bush's where he received straight A's. That sounds impressive, but President Bush was 23 at the time" (quoted in Lichter et al. 2015: 59)

To some observers, the life story of the younger Bush seemed reminiscent of the biblical tale of the prodigal son, albeit with a youthful history of extensive alcohol use and a fondness for pranks that were more at home in a fraternity house than in the offices of government (Phillips 2004). Of course, prodigal sons do find their way home, and to adulthood, eventually. Following conversations with evangelist Bill Graham during his father's years as vice president, the younger Bush started studying the Bible, and eventually he gave up alcohol and began describing himself as "born again" (Phillips 2004).

Youthful indiscretions do not always stay hidden, particularly for a presidential candidate in the modern media environment. Questions about the suitability of Bush's character reappeared in the final week before the 2000 election. With the vote just days away, media reports revealed that Bush was convicted of driving under the influence of alcohol in Maine when he was in his 20s, providing a media peg for a new round of stories about Bush's wild youth (McClellan 2008).

Bush sought to manage the story about his character by addressing the matter personally, rather than leaving the issue to a public relations staffer, and by stressing that the event took place decades earlier. "I've oftentimes said that years ago I made some mistakes. I occasionally drank too much. I did on that night. I was pulled over. I admitted to the policeman that I had been drinking. I paid the fine. I regretted that it happened. I learned my lesson" (quoted in McClellan 2008: 52). While the last-minute disclosure of past misconduct may have cost Bush some undecided votes, the candidate's straightforward, direct response limited the damage (Ceaser and Busch 2001).

Taken together, these personality conversations led to a mixed result for the new president.

> George W. Bush, too, came to office with an already established image. On the plus side, he was seen as personable, honorable and decisive, and straightforward. On the negative side, there were frequent jabs and jokes about his intelligence. To no small extent, these

images can be attributed to the campaigns themselves; in 2000 the Bush campaign emphasized the president's personal character over his political agenda.

(Dimock 2004: 70–71)

Bush's forthright apology demonstrated what he hoped to present regarding the nature of his character. Admitting the error of one's ways is a decent thing to do. By way of perspective, imagine if Bill Clinton's first response to the Clinton-Lewinksky matter had been to apologize to all concerned and beg the public for forgiveness over his personal misconduct.

Applying Character Models to George W. Bush

As discussed in Chapter 2, one of the challenges of employing the Barber (1992) model of presidential character is a question of utility. Since most modern presidents seem more active-positive than anything else, the model may not be a particularly valuable vehicle for distinguishing among most recent presidents. Given the immense work involved in running for president, only the most aggressive and upbeat politicians are likely to undertake the task and to be successful at it. Only a few candidates are likely to fall into one of the other three categories, though if a modern president does not qualify as active-positive they may be more likely to be active-negative than the two passive categories.

George W. Bush does seem to be more an active-positive president than anything else under the Barber (1992) framework. As Barber suggests, one key factor to consider is a future president's personality development as a young adult. One defining quality of the younger Bush was the extent to which he sought to distinguish his character from that of his father, particularly in terms of un-seriousness of purpose.

> From a fairly early age, he was more of a rascal and less of an Ivy League gentleman in training, a Texas cut-up with a Texas drawl. At Andover, he could manage to become a big man on campus only by rowdy wit—his nickname was "the Lip"—and by postures like making himself "Stickball Commissioner" . . . As president of the DKE [fraternity] house at Yale, he got into trouble for lifting a Christmas wreath from a store and for branding pledges as an initiation.
>
> (Phillips 2004: 48)

When he was the same age as a father who served his country with distinction in World War II, the son reveled in the bacchanal that was fraternity house life at an elite college in the 1960s. George W. Bush clearly sought to enjoy himself, as a confident active-positive type would.

This personable nature is also highly relevant to the relatedness component of the Renshon (1998) model of presidential character. Bush's personal interactions discussed across this chapter demonstrate someone who was very comfortable interacting with other people.

The differences between father and son also relate to the younger Bush's high level of confidence in his own competence, a key issue in the George and George (1998) model. Bush's self-confidence may be seen to undermine his curiosity, a cognitive style shortcoming that can lead making decisions without sufficient collection of and consideration of evidence, a pattern that can lead to both error and rigidity, as seen in President Wilson's inflexibility over the League of Nations (George and George (1964).

While he underwent numerous personal changes as an adult, including an embrace of evangelical Christianity and a rejection of alcohol, George W. Bush continued to present the upbeat, sunny temperament of an active-positive across his adult life (Barber 1992). This component of his character speaks as well to his emphasis on maintaining consistency with his own ideals, the "integrity" of the Renshon model (1998) of presidential character.

> In all, Bush seemed to be conveying what might be called a presidency of "dignified authenticity." His would not have the routine grandeur of formal East Room press conferences, nor would he strive for the elegance of the poet in his speeches, but neither would he display the informality of appearances on pop television programs or distractions of recurring personal scandals. Though there was one president, we seemed to have two Bushes: one displayed understated dignity and formality at the White House, while the other reveled in playing the gritty cowboy at the ranch in Crawford.
>
> (Gregg 2004: 92)

When you compare George W. Bush's highly optimistic approach to the presidency with that of the paranoia seen in the presidencies of Richard Nixon and Lyndon Johnson, as examples, the extent to which Bush belongs in the active-positive category becomes clear (Barber 1992). Indeed, he seems like a better fit for the Barber model's preferred category than does Bill Clinton, his immediate predecessor (Renshon 1995b).

News Management and Character Challenges

One of the ways that the new president sought to respond to the character challenge that he was not up to the job of being president was to fill the administration with highly experienced Washington hands from previous Republican administrations, providing the equivalent of "adult supervision" for the relatively inexperienced younger Bush (Hersh 2006).

The problematic nature of Bush's 2000 election, with chads hanging from outdated ballots and partisan decisions relating to the vote-counting in Florida, created a significant media challenge for this new president (Tapper 2001, 2002; Toobin 2001). Or so it appeared at first. A Gallup poll taken shortly before Bush took office revealed that only 45 percent of Americans thought Bush won "fair and square," while 31 percent thought he won "on a technicality" and another 24 percent believed he "stole the election" (Edwards 2004).

George W. Bush would fully become president when his first true crisis hit, according to Richard Neustadt, the leading presidential scholar of the past half century. "If he can manage graciousness during the transition period, and if he can get two or three events that permit him to look very presidential, then by summer he'll be president and it won't matter how he got there" (Neustadt, quoted in Campbell 2004a: 3).

Of course, Bush's early situation was less than dire, even given lingering concerns over the Florida recount. Despite those public misgivings, many Americans were optimistic that Bush would be successful, with 81 percent in a January 2001 CNN/USA Today/Gallup poll believing the incoming president would "set a good moral example" and 78 percent expecting he would "use military force wisely." In addition, many citizens told pollsters they respected Bush as a person (Edwards 2004).

Some politicians might choose to tread cautiously if they had become president after the highly controversial circumstances of Election 2000. But not Bush, who responded to questions of legitimacy with toughness. He became highly responsive to conservative voices in the Republican Party—more so than his "compassionate conservative" pre-election messaging might have suggested (Campbell 2004a). Bush also engaged in a heavy rotation of presidential travel to promote himself and his policies in a nation where most citizens voted for someone else (Heith 2013).

While Bush did work with Democrats in Congress to craft a bipartisan education reform measure known as No Child Left Behind, most of his domestic and international policies during his first months in office were conservative (Sinclair 2004). In response to this rightward turn, a Republican member of the Senate, James Jeffords of Vermont, left the party in mid-2001, handing control of the Senate to the Democrats until Republicans regained control in the 2002 midterm elections (Jeffords 2003; Tenpas and Hess 2002).

September 11, 2001, marked the deadliest day on American soil since Pearl Harbor, the surprise 1941 Japanese attack on Hawaii that launched American involvement in World War II. When two hijacked planes hit the two towers of the World Trade Center in New York City on the morning of 9/11, Bush was reading to children in a Florida classroom. The president was quickly hustled onto Air Force One and spent much of the day in the air or on military bases as Americans learned the magnitude of the terrorist attack. One additional hijacked plane hit the Pentagon; passengers brought down a fourth plane to stop hijackers from using it as another weapon.

Experts thought that Bush's speech to the nation that night was not particularly effective, but the new president found his presidential voice a few days later when he addressed firefighters near the rubble of Lower Manhattan. "I can hear you," Bush said to rescue workers gathering around a wrecked fire truck that a few days earlier had rushed to the World Trade Center. "The rest of the world hears you. And the people who knocked these buildings down will hear all of us soon" (quoted in Frum 2003: 140). The roars of the crowd—chanting "USA! USA!"— were televised globally in an instant.

The crowd's support was an early manifestation of an extraordinary increase in favorable public opinion. Bush's approval rating went from 51 percent to 86 percent in less than a week, and Congress rapidly passed the anti-terrorism legislation Bush requested, including the Patriot Act (Dimock 2004; Nelson 2004). The newly popular Bush continued to press Congress to pass other measures, including a 2002 authorization to wage war in Iraq. The measure passed easily; even though some parts of the national security community and international weapons inspectors doubted Bush's arguments that Iraq helped Al Qaeda chief Osama bin Laden and that Iraq was developing weapons of mass destruction (Clarke 2004; Fisher 2004; Pollack 2004).

Military threats tend to trigger three political responses in the U.S.: increased legislative deference to the executive branch, an increase in public approval for the president, and more positive media coverage for the White House (Entman 2004; Lindsay 2003; Pew 2001b). All three were present in the wake of the 2001 terrorist attacks. On the big three television networks, the tone of coverage of Bush jumped: reports on ABC, CBS, and NBC were positive 64 percent of the time in the two months after the attack, a sharp contrast from the 36 percent positive news of Bush during the part of 2001 before the terrorist attacks (Farnsworth and Lichter 2006: 117).

Despite these responses, concerns over whether Bush was capable of being president did not entirely evaporate after 9/11. Paul O'Neill, Bush's first Treasury Secretary, said many of Bush's problems stemmed from the president's own lack of intellectual curiosity (Suskind 2004). Richard Clarke, a former top National Security Council official, criticized the Bush team for its unwillingness to take the Al-Qaeda threat seriously until after 9/11 (Clarke 2004). Particularly as violence in occupied Iraq worsened, Bush's war management seemed increasingly incompetent (Bennett et al. 2007; Woodward 2006). The Iraq War is the case study of this chapter, and is examined more extensively below.

Arguments about the Bush team's competence also came ashore in New Orleans with gale-force winds in 2005. FEMA fumbled its response to the devastation wrought by Hurricane Katrina, thanks to governmental misjudgments and staffing mistakes (Bennett et al. 2007). Pictures of bodies floating in bogs, angry crowds standing on freeway overpasses, and the horrific conditions inside the Superdome created a major public health crisis and a public relations nightmare for the Bush administration (Nagourney 2006; Shane and Lipton 2005). To make matters worse for Bush, his appointed head of the FEMA had no professional experience in emergency management. Michael ("Brownie") Brown had been a Republican loyalist and a horse show official before Bush appointed him to run the nation's chief disaster response agency (Dowd 2005; Krugman 2006). Bush then compounded the problem by appearing to be shockingly ill-informed, telling "Brownie" before the television cameras that he was doing "a heckuva job" (Dowd 2005).

Public Opinion

As noted above, public opinion started out in a relatively good place for President George W. Bush despite the extraordinary controversy over the 2000 election. As shown in Table 3.2, within a few months of Bush's inauguration, 56 percent of the country said they approved of the job Bush was doing. The number skyrocketed as the nation reeled from the 9/11 attacks later in 2001, and remained high for a year afterwards.

Bush's approval numbers revived at the time of the U.S.-led invasion of Iraq in March 2003. As questions of competence arose for Bush in subsequent months, his approval numbers sank. The administration's stumbling response to Hurricane Katrina made the president's sinking numbers even worse (Bennett et al. 2007). By January of 2006, as the violence against the U.S.-led occupation of Iraq continued and the devastation triggered by Katrina continued to roil domestic politics, only 38 percent of Americans said they approved of the president. By July 2007, when Democratic majorities in Congress had begun to challenge Bush more extensively, only 29 percent of the nation approved of Bush. When he prepared to leave office in December 2008, his approval rating dropped to only 24 percent, an unusually low figure and one comparable to Nixon's ratings in the depths of Watergate.

Assessments of Bush as a person also trended downward during his second term, as shown in Table 3.3. By January 2007, 40 percent of those surveyed said they would describe Bush as "honest and trustworthy," far below the 71 percent who said those words described Bush in a July 2002 survey. Even as late as May 2004, 53 percent said they would apply those terms to Bush.

Longstanding efforts by the White House to present President Bush as someone with a common touch were less successful post-Katrina. In a January 2007 survey, only 32 percent agreed with the statement that Bush "understands the problems of people like you." Nearly six out of ten respondents (57 percent) believe Bush understood their problems in a July 2002 survey—less than a year after 9/11. Other presidential character questions were also less than encouraging for the Bush team. Only

Table 3.2 Presidential Approval Ratings for George W. Bush

Do you approve or disapprove of the way George W. Bush is handling his job as president?

	Approve	*Disapprove*
December 2008	24%	68%
July 2008	27%	68%
January 2008	31%	59%
July 2007	29%	61%
December 2006	32%	57%
July 2006	36%	57%
January 2006	38%	54%
July 2005	44%	48%
January 2005	50%	43%
October 2004	44%	48%
July 2004	46%	46%
January 2004	56%	34%
July 2003	60%	29%
May 2003	65%	27%
April 2003	74%	20%
March 20–24, 2003	67%	26%
March 13–16, 2003	55%	34%
January 2003	58%	32%
September 2002	67%	22%
July 2002	67%	21%
January 2002	80%	11%
Early October 2001	84%	8%
Late September 2001	86%	7%
Mid-September 2001	80%	9%
Early September 2001	51%	34%
July 2001	51%	32%
April 2001	56%	27%
February 2001	53%	21%

Note: Don't Know responses are not reported here, so percentages do not sum to 100.

Source: Pew 2008b.

42 percent of those surveyed in January 2007 thought Bush could "be trusted in a crisis," as compared to 60 percent who said he was trustworthy in a July 2001 survey. Citizens also increasingly saw Bush as stubborn: 36 percent said in January 2007 that they thought the president was "willing to listen to different points of view," as compared to 49 percent who thought that was true in May 2004.

The powerful decline in public assessments of Bush across his presidency demonstrated that first impressions, or even second ones, do not last forever. Despite continuing White House efforts to enhance the president's image, media marketing can take one only so far. The longer someone serves as president the more actual events color public assessments.

Table 3.3 U.S. Public Opinion on Character Traits of President George W. Bush

---

Please tell me whether the following statement applies to George W. Bush or not.
He is a strong leader.

	Yes	No
January 2007	45%	54%
May 2004	62%	37%
July 2002	75%	24%
July 2001	55%	43%

He can be trusted in a crisis.

	Yes	No
January 2007	42%	56%
May 2004	60%	39%
July 2001	60%	37%

He understands the problems of people like you.

	Yes	No
January 2007	32%	67%
May 2004	42%	57%
July 2002	57%	41%
July 2001	45%	54%

He is willing to listen to different points of view.

	Yes	No
January 2007	36%	63%
May 2004	49%	50%

He is honest and trustworthy.

	Yes	No
January 2007	40%	57%
May 2004	53%	45%
July 2002	71%	26%
July 20001	63%	34%

Note: Don't Know responses are not reported here, so percentages do not sum to 100.

Source: Balz and Cohen 2007.

Putting a shine on a candidate's character during the "getting to know you" phase of a presidential campaign or a first year in office is one thing; retaining the president's reputation as the years go by—and the policy frustrations pile up—is quite another.

One of the key reasons that presidents seek to maximize news reports that include matters of character and personality is that the coverage of such topics tends to be more positive than most presidential news coverage. A Media Tenor content analysis of news reports that related to Bush's personality during the first 18 months of his second term revealed that the president's overall coverage on ABC, CBS and NBC was more negative than the subset of stories that focused on personality and character matters. Both categories, though, were more negative than positive during 2005 and the first half of 2006 (Farnsworth et al. 2013: 105).

International Perspectives

During the 2000 presidential campaign, candidate George W. Bush had little to say about international matters. For Bush and for many Americans, the end of the Cold War and the dissolution of the Soviet Union reduced the attention devoted to international concerns. Network newscasts said almost nothing about international matters during the 2000 campaign: during the two months before Election Day, ABC, CBS, and NBC devoted 10 stories to any foreign policy topic—less than the 16 network news stories devoted just to the late-breaking reports of Bush's drunk driving conviction decades earlier (Farnsworth and Lichter 2003). A Media Tenor study of television news broadcasts during the Bush presidency in more than a dozen nations notes revealed that even after 9/11 and the Iraq invasion, U.S. broadcasts were notably more focused on domestic news than were comparable news reports in Europe and the Middle East (Farnsworth et al. 2013: 46).

Bush's early forays into international matters were not particularly impressive. As a candidate, he mocked a reporter who challenged him to name the president of Pakistan, an important U.S. ally (Dowd 1999; Quirk and Matheson 2001). At Bush's first official meeting with U.K. Prime Minister Tony Blair, the new president offered an odd remark that the two men use the same brand of toothpaste (Sanger 2001). (In case readers are wondering, the toothpaste brand favored by the two world leaders was Colgate.) When he met Russian President Vladimir Putin, an ex-KGB officer, Bush observed that he had a sense of his soul and found the former Soviet intelligence operative to be "honest and straightforward" (Friedman 2001). None of these comments would encourage global audiences to respect this new American president's judgment and wisdom (Pew 2003a, 2003b).

Global views regarding George W. Bush were consistently more critical than U.S. views about Bush's capacity to "do the right thing regarding world affairs." In Table 3.4, we compare evaluations of Bush in a variety of nations in both 2003 and 2008. Of the 19 nations examined here, only the residents of one nation—Israel—were more positively disposed towards Bush than Americans were in 2003. In 2008, residents of

Table 3.4 International Evaluations of George W. Bush, 2003–2008

For each, tell me how much confidence you have in each leader to do the right thing regarding world affairs a lot of confidence, some confidence, not too much confidence, or no confidence at all . . . U.S. President George W. Bush.
(Results are percentage of survey population answering first two categories.)

	2003	2005	2008	Change 2003 v. 2008
US	78%	62%	37%	−41
Israel	83%	—	57%	−26
Canada	59%	40%	28%*	−31
UK	51%	38%	16%	−35
Poland	—	47%	41%	−6****
South Korea	36%	22%	30%	−6
China	—	34%	30%	—
Germany	33%	30%	14%	−19
Italy	33%	—	30%*	−3
Japan	—	33%**	25%	−7***
Spain	25%	19%	8%	−17
France	20%	25%	13%	−7
Lebanon	17%	23%	33%	16
Brazil	13%	—	16%	3
Mexico	—	—	16%	—
Turkey	8%	8%	2%	−6
Russia	8%	28%	22%	14
Pakistan	5%	—	7%	2
Palestinian Terr.	1%	—	8%	7
Jordan	1%	1%	7%	6

Notes: Dashes signify that Pew did not ask the question in that country in that year.
*   Results from 2007 survey.
**   Results from 2006 survey.
***   Comparison is 2006 versus 2008
**** Comparison is 2005 versus 2008.

Source: Pew 2015.

only two nations listed here—Israel and Poland—liked Bush more than Americans did.

In most of the nations in Table 3.4, the results in 2003 were far more positive for Bush than were the results for 2008. In the U.S., the percentage of the population that believed Bush would do the right thing in world affairs fell from 78 percent to 37 percent, a 41-point drop over those five years. A variety of other nations recorded double-digit drops over those years, including several close allies. The surveys revealed declines of 35 points in the assessment of Bush in the U.K., 31 points in Canada, 26 points in Israel, 19 points in Germany, and 17 points in Spain.

Several nations registered views that are more positive for Bush as his presidency concluded, but all these nations started out overwhelmingly critical of Bush: support for Bush in Lebanon increased from 17 percent to 33 percent, support in Russia went from 8 percent to 22 percent and support in Jordan rose from 1 percent to 7 percent.

News outlets broadcasting in many of these nations provided critical media assessments of Bush as president, according to a Media Tenor analysis across his second term. News reports in key television news programs in Germany, the U.K., and in two leading Arabic language outlets—Al-Jazeera and Al-Arabiyah—were net negative in their assessment of Bush for each year of his second term (Farnsworth et al. 2013: 99).

Case Study: The Iraq War and Occupation Raise Questions of Competence

Above all, the Bush Administration's media management style, post 9/11, focused on presenting the president as a wartime commander-in-chief. Bush took World War II as his media image for the war on terror. Bush described the terrorist attacks as the Pearl Harbor of a new generation, and Bush's term "axis of evil" recalls the Axis powers of World War II. With this comparison, Bush hoped to recreate a time when Americans came together in rare unity to defeat their enemies. In addition, the administration routinely portrayed Bush's goals as crises in order to maximize both media attention and the chances that Bush's preferences would be followed (VandeHei 2005).

As discussed above, there was widespread support in the nation, and among America's allies, for a forceful response in Afghanistan following the 2001 terrorist attacks. The administration's efforts to link Iraq to 9/11 to justify additional military action in the region were more problematic. Top officials who served under the first President Bush, including former National Security Adviser Brent Scowcroft, argued that there was little evidence to link Iraqi leader Saddam Hussein to terrorists, much less the 9/11 operation (Pfiffner 2004a). While there was little doubt the U.S. would prevail relatively quickly in a military engagement against Saddam's army, James Baker, Secretary of State for the first President Bush, predicted that if the U.S. waged war with Iraq it would end up occupying the country for quite some time and risk antagonizing other nations in the region (Pfiffner 2004b). Army Chief of Staff General Eric Shinseki told Congress before the war started that the occupation of Iraq would require nearly twice as many troops as the White House claimed (Shane 2007). For his honest assessment—required by law in congressional testimony—Shinseki was "permitted" to retire early (Shanker 2007).

The administration said the pivotal issue of the 2002 midterm elections was the looming war in Iraq. Congress must, Bush insisted in speeches on behalf of Republican candidates, make a decision on whether to authorize force before the election. Because the Pentagon and the Central Intelligence Agency (CIA) are part of the executive branch, little official information emerged to undermine the president's story—even though the nation later learned many experts inside the government disagreed with Bush's conclusions at the time (Entman 2004).

Presidential administrations reward reporters who produce stories that placed the president in a good light and punish critical reporters by denying them information (Kurtz 1994, 1998). The Bush White House was no different. The wide range of media outlets found online during the twenty-first century made it even easier for an administration to play favorites and provide ideal vehicles for attacking mainstream media outlets as reflexively anti-Bush (Mooney 2004). Fox News often was a favored vehicle for promoting the administration line on Iraq and attacking Bush's critics (Bennett et al. 2007).

Media favoritism is a key presidential advantage in a low-information environment like the national security arena, and the Bush administration traded access for favorable news reports. Judith Miller, then a national security correspondent for the *New York Times*, became a favored conduit for information that the Bush team wanted to make public to help build the case for the Iraq War. After the combat operations concluded, a subsequent internal *Times* investigation condemned the paper's performance, saying it did not scrutinize the Bush administration's pre-war claims carefully enough (Kurtz 2007c; Okrent 2004).

The president used his media advantages to play hardball with elected officials as well. Because the 2002 elections occurred fourteen months after 9/11, public anxiety over possible terrorist attacks enabled Republicans to attack as soft on defense those Democrats who objected or even hesitated to pass Bush's resolution to authorize military force (Fisher 2004). U.S. Senator Max Cleland (D-GA), a skeptic of Bush's war plans, was defeated in 2002 in a campaign marked by advertising that featured Cleland's face morphing into that of 9/11 mastermind Osama bin Laden (Halbfinger 2002). For years, Cleland's 2002 defeat haunted Democrats. Even after public sentiment shifted against Bush, critics hesitated to mount a coherent legislative challenge to the unpopular president's unpopular foreign policies (Risen and Lichtblau 2007).

As the president's self-imposed deadline for action approach, Bush employed a rosy scenario to quell public doubts. The Bush team predicted that the benefits of the Iraq War would be great and the costs would be minimal, and that the costs of the war would be paid back by future Iraqi oil revenues (Gordon 2003). Bush predicted Iraq would undergo a brief occupation and that it rapidly would become a peaceful, stable democracy, even serving as a model for other nations in the region (Rieff 2003). Presidents sometimes exaggerate to try to get what they want. More than two decades before the Iraq War of 2003, Ronald Reagan sold his tax cuts to Congress and to the country based on estimates of economic growth and revenue expansion that turned out to be false (Quirk 2006).

At first, news coverage of the 2003 Iraq War largely mirrored the administration's frames, and the administration's efforts enjoyed general public approval (Pew 2004b) and more positive news coverage, particularly while the war was under way. As shown in Table 3.5, content analysis of network television evening newscasts during the combat phase of the Iraq War of 2003 showed coverage of the president that was

Table 3.5 Tone of Network News Coverage of Presidents in Wartime

Percentages shown are percent positive coverage	
George W. Bush (2003 Iraq, early occupation phase)	
All Networks	32%
ABC	33%
CBS	23%
NBC	38%
George W. Bush (2003 Iraq, combat phase)	
All Networks	49%
ABC	39%
CBS	55%
NBC	56%
George W. Bush (2001 Terrorist Attack)	
All Networks	64%
ABC	64%
CBS	65%
NBC	69%
Bill Clinton (1999 Kosovo Crisis)	
All Networks	62%
ABC	62%
CBS	70%
NBC	57%
George H. W. Bush (1991 Persian Gulf War)	
All Networks	56%
ABC	44%
CBS	63%
NBC	58%

Notes: The 2003 Iraq early occupation phase content analysis data are from evening newscasts from May 1 through October 31; the 2003 Iraq combat phase data are from March 19 through April 30; the 2001 data are from evening newscasts from September 11 through November 19; the 1999 data are from evening newscasts from March 24 through May 25; the 1991 data are from evening newscasts from January 17 through February 27.

Source: Farnsworth and Lichter 2006: 94.

56 percent positive on NBC, 55 percent positive on CBS and 39 percent positive on ABC. Comparative data of television reporting of previous combat operations showed comparable results: the first Persian Gulf War in 1991 also showed relatively positive news coverage of the president, in this case George H. W. Bush. The same goes for coverage of Bill Clinton during the U.S.-led bombing of Kosovo in 1999. Coverage was even more positive during the immediate aftermath of 9/11, when there was less disagreement about how to respond to Al-Queda.

Fox News provided extensive and highly supportive coverage of the war, particularly the pyrotechnics of the initial assault on Baghdad, with one anchor gushing it is "hard to believe things could go much more successfully" and another Fox commentator calling its media competition "weenies" for dwelling on casualties (quoted in Rich 2006: 75). When a mob toppled a statue of Saddam Hussein, a Fox News reporter said, "my goose bumps have never been higher than they are right now" (quoted in Rich 2006: 83).

While network television also provided relatively positive reports during the combat phase of the war, that positive news was short-lived. Once President George W. Bush declared major combat operations in Iraq concluded on May 1, 2003, critical news coverage returned. Content analysis of the first six months of the U.S.-led occupation of Iraq was roughly two-thirds negative, somewhat more critical than the average tone of coverage of presidents on network television and far more critical than the wartime reports (Farnsworth and Lichter 2006).

One of the bright areas for Bush regarding news coverage of the problematic occupation of Iraq came from Fox News. A study by the Project for Excellence in Journalism, part of the Pew Research Center, found Fox News was consistently more positive about the war than network television or CNN, its key cable rival. Fox News was positive about the Iraq War 38 percent of the time as compared to 20 percent of the time on CNN (Pew 2005). The administration was grateful for the relatively positive reports on Fox News. Vice President Cheney provided a testimonial for the cable outfit, saying that its coverage of Iraq was "more accurate" than other news outlets (Rich 2006: 128).

In addition, Fox News was also helpful to Bush when it mattered most in terms of his re-election. During the two months before the 2004 election, a content analysis of the first half-hour of *Special Report* found that coverage of Bush's Iraq policies was 54 percent positive in tone, as compared to 5 percent positive for Democratic rival John Kerry. On network television, the direction reversed: Kerry received 21 percent positive reports relating to Iraq, as compared to 11 percent positive reports on Bush's Iraq policy. Once again the gaps were greater on Fox News, where Bush had a tonal advantage of 49 percentage points, as compared to a 10 percentage point deficit on network television (Farnsworth and Lichter 2011a: 143).

As the occupation turned steadily more problematic, Bush's team worked diligently to control what the legislative branch, reporters, and the public knew by refusing to release information requested by Congress. At first, Republican legislative majorities generally blocked Democratic efforts to obtain information. Despite these defensive efforts, there are limits to presidential spin, particularly over time. The undeniable problems of the Iraq occupation made the war a negative factor for Republicans in the midterm elections two years later (Broder 2006; Milkis 2006). Then the Democratic majorities that took power in 2007 were routinely ignored by an administration making expansive claims of executive privilege (Lichtblau and Johnston 2007; Mann and Ornstein 2006).

As trouble mounted, the Bush administration relied on a variety of media management approaches previously employed by recent presidents. While no administration would volunteer a full disclosure of its own shortcomings, consistently unrealistic portrayals of policies undermine the believability of the White House spin, creating a troubling credibility gap between actual conditions and what the government maintains is the reality.

During the 2006 midterm elections Bush claimed the administration was committed to "staying the course" in Iraq, but after the midterms Bush revealed that the administration actually had been planning a major troop escalation, called a "surge" (Burns et al. 2007; Rutenberg and Cloud 2006). After leaving office, former Bush press secretary Scott McClellan (2008) lamented the aggressive political propaganda campaign that he said he helped engineer to promote the Iraq War.

One problematic area of presidential Iraq rhetoric involved the debate over whether the U.S. was employing torture to solicit information from its prisoners. When Congress passed a law banning torture, Bush signed it and said the U.S. government would not torture—but only as he defined the word (Shane and Liptak 2006; Zernike 2006). The administration repeatedly refused to state publicly what it believed constituted torture, and even key allies such as the United Kingdom faulted the United States for continuing to torture suspects (Bonner and Perlez 2007).

Over at Fox News, the viewers did not get to see the full range of critical news coverage that others provided about the Iraq occupation. The cable network chose not to show the most vivid images of the occupation, including the mutilated corpses of Americans strung up on a bridge over the Euphrates River (Rich 2006). Bill O'Reilly of Fox News worried that efforts by other media outlets to "exploit casualties in a time of war" could undermine the national resolve (Rich 2006). When Cindy Sheehan, the mother of a soldier killed in Iraq, started asking questions about why her son died, the Bush administration sought to undermine her credibility. Fox News was happy to assist, calling Sheehan a "crackpot" (Rich 2006: 194). A mother's genuine grief was hard for the public to dismiss, and Sheehan's voice was yet another one emerging as the problems in

Iraq mounted and public doubts grew that the war had been worth the price families like hers had paid (Rich 2006).

Following the 2006 midterm election, George W. Bush faced very negative public approval numbers and highly critical reviews of his Iraq policy, as shown in Table 3.6. By January 2007, despite all of the Bush team's public relations efforts, the public turned thumbs down on all

Table 3.6 Public Opinion on President Bush's Iraq Policy: January 2007

Do you approve or disapprove of the way Bush is handling the situation in Iraq?

Approve	Disapprove
29%	70%

Do you support or oppose Bush's proposal to send approximately 22,000 additional U.S. military forces to Iraq?

Support	Oppose
34%	65%

Do you think Congress should or should not try to block Bush's plan to send more troops to Iraq?

Should	Should not
59%	39%

Do you think the war with Iraq has or has not ___?

	---------- *Has* ----------		*Has not*
	NET	*Great deal*	*Somewhat*	
a. Contributed to long-term peace and stability in the Mideast	28%	9%	19%	68%
b. Encouraged democracy in other Arab nations	36%	13%	23%	59%
c. Helped to improve the lives of the Iraqi people	48%	18%	30%	48%

Which of these do you think is the better way to address the problems in Iraq— through diplomatic and political efforts, or through military efforts?

Diplomatic/ Political	Military	Both (vol.)	Neither (vol.)
63%	25%	8%	2%

Note: Don't Know responses are not reported here, so percentages do not sum to 100.

Source: Balz and Cohen 2007.

major aspects of the president's plan to increase the number of troops in Iraq. Overall, fewer than three people in ten in the United States—29 percent—approved of Bush's handling of the situation there (Balz and Cohen 2007), a sharp drop from the roughly two-thirds who supported the Iraq War before it started (Entman 2004).

Bush's plan to increase the number of troops in Iraq also generated little public support. Barely more than one out of every four people surveyed—28 percent—believed that the war in Iraq "contributed to the long-term peace and stability in the Middle East," one of the Bush administration's key justifications for the war. Just over one-third of those surveyed—36 percent—believed that the Iraq War encouraged democracy elsewhere in the region, another key pre-war justification (Balz and Cohen 2007).

These results show the limits of Bush's ability to persuade the public by the seventh year of his presidency. Bush's strongly pro-war appeals and the shaping of the pre-war discourse helped him win the political debate in 2002, but subsequent events took a heavy toll on the president's credibility. Overpromising and under-delivering may help win short-term political debates, but a president who follows that course is likely to lose in the longer term, when the extent of White House deception and spin become clear (Fiorina 2008).

The Bush Communication Legacy

The Iraq case study, like the case study of the Clinton-Lewinsky scandal in Chapter 2, demonstrates the limits of presidential news management. Presidents have powerful communication advantages, to be sure, particularly when it comes to winning the daily news cycle. Congress cannot easily communicate collectively, and even in those rare cases when they do so, the senators and representatives always find it difficult to maintain a united front against the executive branch for long (Entman 2004). Despite the lack of convincing evidence of the utility of going public, presidents continue to do so. Bush's public relations victories, particularly in his first term, helped make going public a staple of presidential media management. In fact, the more positive media treatment a president receives during periods of international instability may encourage future presidents to emphasize the military policy part of the White House portfolio to the public and to Congress whenever they can.

When asked to consider Bush's presidential legacy, the public reviews as he left office were highly critical. As shown in Table 3.7, Bush's wars in Afghanistan and Iraq poisoned public assessments of his presidency, with fully half the respondents listing those international engagements as key to their assessments of the president. Only one respondent in four (24 percent) said that Bush's accomplishments were likely to outweigh

Table 3.7 Public Opinion on President Bush's Legacy: December 2008

Thinking ahead, what do you think George W. Bush will be most remembered for after he has left office? (accept up to three responses)

Wars	51%
Other negative assessments (net)	17%
September 11/Foreign Policy	13%
Economic issues (net)	12%
Other Positive assessments (net)	4%

In the long run, do you think the accomplishments of the Bush Administration will outweigh its failures, or will the failures outweigh the accomplishments?

	Bush	Bush	Clinton
	2008	2004	2001
Accomplishments will outweigh failures	24%	49%	60%
Failures will outweigh accomplishments	64%	36%	27%

How do you think President George W. Bush will go down in history . . . as an outstanding president, above average, average, below average, or poor?

	G.W. Bush	Clinton	G.H.W. Bush	Reagan
	2008	2001	1993	1989
Outstanding	3%	12%	6%	17%
Above average	8%	32%	30%	42%
Average	28%	32%	51%	25%
Below average	24%	10%	8%	9%
Poor	34%	11%	4%	5%

Note: Don't Know responses are not reported here, so percentages do not sum to 100.

Source: Pew 2008b.

his failures, a sharp contrast from the overall positive reviews offered for Bill Clinton eight years earlier, when 60 percent said his accomplishments would outweigh his failures. Indeed, the assessments of George W. Bush at the end of his first term were far more positive than they were at the end of his second.

Only 11 percent of those surveyed considered George W. Bush an above-average or an outstanding president, as compared to 42 percent saying that about Bill Clinton, 36 percent saying that about George H. W. Bush and 59 percent saying that about Ronald Reagan at the end of their terms of office. The poor numbers for George W. Bush might discourage future presidents from following his lead in truth-challenged media management.

Bush demonstrated that presidents can limit what the public learns about foreign and military policy in the short term, but keeping information secret over the longer term is often an impossible challenge. Bush may have limited what the public knew about expert doubts regarding the evidence that the administration used to link Saddam Hussein to Al Qaeda before the start of the Iraq War, but the failure to find weapons of mass destruction or a program to build such weapons eventually became common knowledge for all but committed Republicans (Jacobson 2008). Far more Americans believed that Saddam Hussein was personally involved in September 11 when the Bush administration was making the case for war in 2002 than continued to believe the administration's claim in 2008 (Jacobson 2008).

At its bleakest, the news from Iraq as reported by Fox News was not as troubling to the administration as that offered by other media outlets. Over the Bush years, Fox News viewers increasingly developed alternative perspectives on news from viewers of other newscasts, including greater support for Bush. Fox News viewers knew less about the facts relating to Iraq, and their mistakes were primarily in the direction that favored the Republican president (Bennett et al. 2007). Taken together, these findings suggest that Fox News can be of great value for Republican presidents, as the skepticism about mainstream media—and relatively uncritical acceptance of false claims offered by Republicans—makes Fox News a very effective place to argue that conservative values and conservative politicians are under attack.

Even the best media management strategies may fall victim to outside events that presidents cannot control. As Bush sought to divert attention away from bin Laden and toward Saddam Hussein in 2002 and 2003, bin Laden frequently returned to the public eye with new videotapes warning of future attacks. Although those commentaries generally became only brief snippets on U.S. television news, they undermined the administration's efforts to get the public to concentrate on Iraq. Bush's intense focus on Iraq, and his "Mission Accomplished" appearance on an aircraft carrier in mid-2003, backfired when the occupation proved far more violent than promised (Chandrasekaran 2006; Milbank 2004). Even though the "surge" of increased U.S. military involvement in Iraq seemed to improve conditions in Iraq during 2008, Bush's poll numbers did not improve (Farnsworth 2009). Instead, public attention turned towards the domestic policy matters that bedeviled the Bush administration's final year in office, including bank failures, stock market declines, and the near-collapse of the U.S. housing market.

Presidents have a far greater ability to shape the county's political discussion than any other single actor does, but that relative influence does not guarantee positive news coverage unless circumstances have created an international crisis. The temptation therefore exists for an unscrupulous subsequent president to manufacture a crisis or intensify its severity to maximize the political advantage possessed by the White House. When citizens believe there is an international crisis, the White House does well: the news reports are less critical, more citizens support the White House, and even the number of late-night jokes about the president declines (Farnsworth 2009; Lichter et al. 2015).

As Bush's experiences show us, a short-term media win may presage a long-term public loss. Bush left office with exceptionally weak public opinion numbers, and his final years in office featured investigations by Democratic legislative majorities that fed into the deep public disenchantment with his presidency. Absent partisan majorities, future presidents may find it difficult, though, to convince Congress to be as docile as it was during the Bush years. Republicans did little investigating of the Bush administration during their years in the majority, and the Democrats remained sufficiently scared of being attacked as soft on terrorism that they kept funding the wars as well. The legislative branch has a history of asserting itself against subsequent presidents after wartime presidents dominate Congress—and a revived legislative branch may be more assertive against future presidents (Woodward 1999).

Bush's overall media strategy, not unlike Bill Clinton's, might be considered the Sun King vision of White House media management. Like France's legendary King Louis XIV, who considered himself the personification of the nation, both presidents believed the White House should be very aggressive in shaping the political discourse by being very visible and by attacking enemies as they emerged. While few issues are more different in content than are a sex scandal and a war, the media approach was the same: both presidents prevailed at least temporarily by dominating the discourse. In other words, the media management strategies of Bush and Clinton were more similar than partisans of either might expect. The two similar approaches could not be more different from what followed—the understated, diffident media strategy of Barack Obama, the "Cool Hand Luke" of presidential media management.

4 The Social Media Presidency of Barack Obama

Barack Obama's rise to the presidency was quite rapid, though not as rapid as that of his successor. Many Americans first learned of Obama when he gave a keynote speech at the 2004 Democratic National Convention that focused on seeking bipartisan cooperation, with the theme that there was not a Red America or a Blue America. It was an exceptional opportunity for Obama, who at the time was a state senator in Illinois and a candidate for a U.S. Senate seat. Four years later, he accepted his party's nomination for president. Four years after he won a U.S. Senate election, Obama was president-elect.

Obama's 2004 speech on inclusion was a compelling introduction to his character. Negotiating personal and cultural differences had a powerful internal dimension for the future president. In *Dreams from My Father* (2004), Obama recounted his personal struggle to figure out who he was, with an absent African father and a mixed-race background that was a source of tension. As others have observed, Obama's personal journey for identity and meaning in life involved a challenging negotiation of the many somewhat difficult aspects of his childhood, and led to a president whose personal experiences made him highly sympathetic to the concerns of other nations (Lester, forthcoming).

As he stood before the Democratic Party's 2004 Convention, Obama seized the moment, introducing himself to the nation as the personification of an America that was inclusive and optimistic about its future.

> My parents shared not only an improbable love; they shared an abiding faith in the possibilities of this nation. They would give me an African name, Barack, or "blessed," believing that in a tolerant America your name is no barrier to success. They imagined me going to the best schools in the land, even though they weren't rich, because in a generous America you don't have to be rich to achieve your potential. They are both passed away now. Yet I know that, on this night, they look down on me with pride.
>
> (quoted in Elahi and Cos 2012: 79)

That stirring autobiographical summary, together with Obama's rejection of the "politics of cynicism" in favor of the "the politics of hope," turned the Senate aspirant into a global celebrity and perhaps a potential president (Heilemann and Halperin 2010). Many national reporters soon descended on the new senator's Washington office to try to figure out who he was, a challenge given that Obama was a more complex, if not enigmatic, figure than previous presidents such as George W. Bush or Bill Clinton (Renshon 2012).

During his time as a state senator, Obama frequently worked with Republicans in the Illinois legislature, where the Harvard Law graduate turned Chicago community organizer turned elected official found opportunities to practice bipartisan cooperation in Springfield. Obama's confidence in his persuasiveness grew as he negotiated the highly competitive world of fellow law students—who named him the first African-American president of the *Harvard Law Review*—and through his negotiations in the rough world of community politics in Chicago and state politics in Illinois (Scheiber 2012; Wayne 2012).

The News Media Environment of the Obama Era

Barack Obama's 2008 campaign focused more on social media than any previous effort, though even more emphasis on social media communication would take place in subsequent elections. Media use data collected by Pew (2016a), presented in Table 4.1, illustrates that throughout that campaign and during Obama's eight years as president, the media environment qualified as a mixed one. Television remained a highly influential source of news, far outpacing the percentage of people saying they relied on newspapers, radio, or online content. Between 2008 and 2016, television was consistently named as a leading new source by at least half the respondents in surveys, with a high of 74 percent using that traditional media source during 2012, the year of Obama's reelection. The internet is a consistent runner-up, with between 36 percent and 38 percent using online information as a leading news source in the presidential elections of 2008, 2012, and 2016.

Those television viewers who tuned in to the big three network evening newscasts of ABC, CBS and NBC saw consistently positive treatments for Obama. Coverage on those three newscasts were 68 percent positive for Obama and 33 percent positive for McCain in the two months before the 2008 election (Farnsworth and Lichter 2011a: 99). That 35-percentage point tonal difference is by far the largest tonal gap found in the six presidential elections between 1988 and 2008 (Farnsworth and Lichter 2011a: 99).

The bottom portion of Table 4.1 illustrates the changes in news consumption across Obama's second term. Some patterns, like those of news consumption of local television reports, network television offerings and

Table 4.1 Main Sources of News by U.S. News Consumers, Obama years

How did you get most of your news about the presidential election campaign? From television, from newspapers, from radio, or from the internet? [randomize options, accept up to two answers]

	2016	2012	2008
Television	57%	74%	68%
Newspapers	20%	23%	33%
Radio	25%	17%	16%
Internet	38%	36%	36%

How often do you . . . [randomize options]

	Often	Sometimes	Hardly ever	Never

Watch local television news?

	Often	Sometimes	Hardly ever	Never
2016	46%	27%	17%	10%
2013	46%	26%	17%	11%

Watch national evening network television news (such as ABC World New CBS Evening News, or NBC Nightly News)?

	Often	Sometimes	Hardly ever	Never
2016	30%	27%	25%	17%
2013	31%	28%	24%	18%

Watch cable television news (such as CNN, The Fox News cable channel, or MSBNC)?

	Often	Sometimes	Hardly ever	Never
2016	31%	27%	24%	18%
2013	24%	28%	26%	21%

Read any newspapers in print?

	Often	Sometimes	Hardly ever	Never
2016	20%	28%	31%	21%
2013	27%	27%	27%	19%

Listen to news on the radio?

	Often	Sometimes	Hardly ever	Never
2016	25%	34%	24%	17%
2013	26%	30%	27%	18%

Get news from a social networking site (such as Facebook or Twitter)?

	Often	Sometimes	Hardly ever	Never
2016	18%	26%	18%	38%

Get news from a website or app?

	Often	Sometimes	Hardly ever	Never
2016	28%	28%	18%	26%

Note: Don't Know responses are not reported here, so percentages do not sum to 100.

Source: Pew 2016a.

cable news channels, did not change much over the three-year period. Others, particularly newspaper use, declined considerably.

Table 4.1 also allows us to compare the public's use of key social media vehicles like Facebook and Twitter with that of other web news sources and with traditional media. (The social media question was only included in the 2016 survey, so we do not have comparable 2013 data.) For 2016, we see that use of social media for news was below all the other media outlets, while web news was comparable in utility to that of traditional media outlets.

The Rising Influence of Social Media

By 2008, the news media environment had "evolved into a hybrid arrangement where traditional and new sources co-exist, complement, compete and conflict with each other" (Owen 2009: 9). The 2008 campaign was notable for the high level of public online activity, far greater than that seen in previous elections (Copeland and Bimber 2015). That increased use of social media may have been a result of the particular enthusiasm Obama generated among young people and in using online media to participate in political discussions (Owen 2009).

Whatever the reason, the 2008 election represented a watershed year for online news. As shown in Table 4.2, 56 percent of those surveyed by Pew (2016a) said they used the internet for news and information about the 2008 election, when Obama defeated McCain. Four years earlier, only 41 percent used online news for information about the election.

Of course, many of those who go online to obtain information end up using traditional media content posted online. Among those who said they used the web for campaign news in 2008, 27 percent said they used CNN, as compared to 17 percent who said they used Yahoo, 13 percent who said they used MSNBC and 13 percent using presidential campaign websites. Fox News ranked fifth on this list, with 11 percent of those going online naming it as a key news source, followed by 9 percent using MSN/Microsoft for news, and 7 percent using Google. The *New York Times* ranked eighth at 6 percent.

A Project for Excellence in Journalism content analysis examined online news coverage of the 2008 presidential election, a study that included 1,264 stories found on sites that created their own content (like CNN. com) and on sites that provided material wholly or largely generated by others (like Google News). The study period included the early weeks of the financial crisis (September 8 through October 16, 2008) and found that Obama had a significant double-digit tonal advantage over McCain online, comparable to that found on network television (Farnsworth and Lichter 2011a: 109).

As the media environment changed, the campaigns changed along with it. From the start, the Obama 2008 team appreciated the importance of

Table 4.2 Online News Media Use, 2008

Did you happen to get any news or information about the 2008 elections from the internet, or not? [Yes response includes those listing the internet as a major news source in Table 4.1]

	2008	2004	2000	1996
Yes	56%	41%	30%	10%
No	44%	59%	70%	90%

What web sites did you use to get information about the election? Just name a few of the web sites that you went to most often. [accept up to three responses] *

CNN	27%
Yahoo	17%
MSNBC/NBC	13%
Presidential candidate websites	13%
Fox News	11%
MSN/Microsoft	9%
Google	7%
New York Times	6%
Local news (TV/newspaper/radio)	5%
AOL	5%
Other conservative blogs/websites	5%
Parties/interest groups/527 websites	4%
Drudge Report	4%
Polling websites and aggregators (e.g., Real Clear Politics)	3%
Washington Post	3%
You Tube	2%
Huffington Post	2%
Other liberal blogs/websites	2%
BBC	2%
ABC	2%
Other blogs	2%
Politico	2%
Cable or internet service provider	2%
Wall Street Journal	1%
Political magazine websites (e.g., National Review, The Nation)	1%
Factchecking websites (e.g., factcheck.org)	1%
Social networking websites (Facebook or MySpace)	1%
USA Today	1%
Financial news websites	1%
CBS	1%
Other international news websites (Economist or Guardian)	1%
Online magazines (Slate or Salon)	1%
Newsmagazines (Time, US News or Newsweek)	1%
NPR/public radio	1%
Wire services (AP/Reuters)	1%

Notes: Because many respondents regularly use more than one media source, percentages do not sum to 100.

* Asked if respondent said s/he received any information online. Results expressed as percentage of total sample.

Source: Pew 2008a.

new media for presenting character issues, connecting with younger voters in particular via Facebook and YouTube (Owen 2009). In particular, the campaign emphasized the candidate's youth and optimism, and the vague theme of "change" allowed people to imagine in the candidate the change they personally wished to see (Ceaser et al. 2009).

Indeed, part of the reason for Obama's electoral success in 2008 stems from his campaign's effective use of YouTube videos and online peer-to-peer communication efforts to create a personal connection (Kellner 2009, 2010). The 2008 campaign social networking website, MyBarackObama.com, enabled users to contribute and to build personal profiles, interact with other supporters and learn about area campaign events, all designed to maximize opportunities for individuals to connect with the campaign (Aaker and Smith 2010). By November 2008, the Obama campaign had 2.5 million Facebook followers, and 50 million online visitors watched Obama-related videos on YouTube (Aaker and Smith 2010).

In a time of social media mash-ups, YouTube videos, and the like, presidents have to be a good deal more inventive to reach citizens than was the case during the days when tens of millions of Americans tuned in to watch the evening news. To reach audiences that may have little interest in politics, presidents have to be informal, and be able "not only to make a joke but in some cases to be in on the joke" (Scacco and Coe 2016).

Obama's past history as a community organizer may have made him particularly sensitive to the opportunities social media provided. A campaign event was no longer just a politician giving a speech, followed by news reports. Now it was also an interactive activity: a crowd of people reacting to the candidate, and to each other, in real time via Facebook, emails, and text messages (Gupta-Carlson 2016). McCain consistently lagged far behind Obama in the social media space, though he scored significant hits online, including an ad that described Obama as a celebrity candidate, perhaps comparable to Britney Spears (Kenski et al. 2010).

Presidential candidates also have to deal with campaign ads from supporters, including more than 100,000 of them posted online about Obama and 64,000 about McCain (Owen 2009). These independent contributions may or may not focus on the messages the campaign wants to emphasize, and may not be helpful. One of the more famous independently produced ads starred a model confessing: "I got a crush . . . on Obama," which generated more than 11 million hits on YouTube and spawned numerous comparable tributes to other politicians (Owen 2009).

The same pattern of intense citizen involvement online seen in 2008 did not return with comparable intensity in 2012, even though the Obama team kept a highly visible social media presence online during the re-election cycle (Conway et al. 2013; Copeland and Bimber 2015). Mitt Romney's team consistently struggled to keep up with the Obama organization online, as the McCain team did four years earlier (Ceaser et al. 2015).

In Figure 4.1 we see how the White House web page changed when the forty-fourth president took office. This page was from the first month of the Obama presidency, when the new president was focused on passing an economic stimulus package. In comparison to other web pages seen in previous chapters, we see how much the White House web page has mutated into a personal presidential web page. This page features not one but two images of Obama, an image of Obama in the background, apparently delivering a presidential statement, and a large Obama image in the foreground that focuses on Obama's use of the mass media.

Of course some aspects of the previous pages have been retained. There is a search function for citizens to find the information most interesting to

Figure 4.1 White House Website, Obama Presidency, 2009

them, as well as a few headlines of key issues that the new administration wants to emphasize. Even so, this page is more Obama-centered than were the pages for George W. Bush and Bill Clinton presented in earlier chapters.

Fox News and the Rising Influence of Conservative Media

Conservatives had been turning to Fox News for a less liberal perspective on the news for more than a decade before Obama and McCain faced off in 2008. The audience for Fox News continued to grow during Obama's two terms. Fox News helped establish and promote the Tea Party movement, which arose in response to Obama's policies regarding the economy and health care. The network also advanced the argument that Obama may not have been born in America, and therefore was not eligible to be president (Chadwick 2013; Williamson et al. 2011). Throughout the Obama years, Fox News and its personalities also served as agenda-setters of sorts within the world of conservative media, priming bloggers and conservative voices on talk radio with a range of conservative conversation topics (Dreier and Martin 2010).

As shown in Table 4.2, conservative news organizations were popular online. In addition to the 11 percent who relied on Fox News's online content, 5 percent regularly turned to conservative blogs and websites, and 4 percent turned to the Drudge Report, one of the oldest names in conservative online news. In contrast, liberal news organizations were less popular, with 2 percent checking in regularly with the Huffington Post and 2 percent relying on liberal blogs and websites.

A Project for Excellence in Journalism content analysis looked at Fox News reports of the 2008 campaign during the early weeks of the financial crisis (September 8 through October 16, 2008). The PEJ study found that the tone of coverage between Obama and McCain on Fox News was roughly comparable, with Obama having an advantage of a few percentage points (Farnsworth and Lichter 2011a: 109). In other words, Fox News was less critical of McCain than network television was, but the evening newscast on Fox News was not all helpful to the Republican either.

The Character of Barack Obama

Obama's campaign call for "change" resonated with a nation reeling from the continuing wars in Iraq and Afghanistan and rendered breathless by the financial collapse of September 2008. Obama's election in November 2008 was heralded as a transformative event like few presidencies of the past half century, and the expectations for the new president were extraordinarily if not impossibly high (Campbell 2009; Conley 2009; Ceaser et al. 2009; Harris and Martin 2009). Even before Obama emerged victorious, he was the political equivalent of a rock star. His 2008 convention acceptance speech took place at an outdoor arena to accommodate his enthusiastic mass following. A public rally in Berlin during the summer of 2008 drew hundreds of thousands of adoring Europeans. French President Sarkozy gushed over the Democratic candidate at a Paris press conference to a degree that bordered on the unseemly for a successor of de Gaulle. Obama filled stadiums and arenas across the country that fall, and his Inauguration brought one of the largest crowds ever to the Washington Mall.

The Pitch

At the core of the Obama campaign was the theme that Obama himself was both the messenger calling for "hope and change" and the personification of that mantra. Obama, the first African-American major party presidential nominee, was a highly visible representative of change. His election marked a significant departure from the unbroken line of white male presidents who served before him. Many people believed his victory said something very positive about this country and the open-mindedness of its citizens (Edge 2010).

In other words, Obama's mixed racial heritage may have had its advantages, particularly with African-American and liberal voters who vote in Democratic primaries and caucuses. But it also had its potential disadvantages. During the general election campaign, he navigated this potential minefield with caution. Obama was very careful to present himself as a candidate who was an African-American rather than as an African-American candidate (Wayne 2012). As Obama said, "I'm rooted in the African-American community, but not limited by it" (quoted in Remnick 2010: 382).

During the campaign, Obama frequently embraced the legacy of another son of Illinois: Abraham Lincoln (though neither president was born in the state). This connection established a link between the candidate and one of the nation's most respected presidents, and one known for far-sighted leadership, involving both civil rights and a plan for healing a divided nation after the Civil War (Renshon 2012). Linking oneself to such an extraordinary president could minimize the concerns of some voters that Obama might be *too* different.

> He, like America, was a nation divided, a nation in need of healing, health that could be accomplished by the American people's electing him. From the decision to launch his 2008 campaign from the Old State Capitol in Springfield, Illinois where Lincoln had declared that a "nation divided could not stand" to his declaration at this 2013 inaugural address that the rebuilding of the nation was not yet complete, Obama built a compelling story rich with historical referent.
> (Gupta-Carlson 2016: 72)

Obama was also careful to keep his anger in check in public, as a means of keeping persuadable but skeptical white voters from rejecting his campaign. A relatively mild-mannered African American candidate is likely to do better with white voters than a visibly angry one, after all (Edge 2010).

Obama sought to present himself as part of what a multirace America has become, a personal symbol of the political and economic opportunities no longer foreclosed by the color of one's skin (Wayne 2012).

> Obama evidences little anger in public life today. In fact, he seems to repress his emotions. He is amazingly self-disciplined and self-confident. He needs to be in control, keeps his grandiosity, which he retains, under wraps and displays a cool rationality. The Obama running for elected office seemed comfortable with his mixed racial heritage; he wore that heritage as a mantra, a badge of social acceptance.
> (Wayne 2012: 16)

Obama's most effective personal skill may be in making himself comfortable, or at least appearing so, in whatever environment he finds himself: a single-parent home, Indonesia, an elite high school in Hawaii, Occidental College, Columbia University, Harvard Law School, Southside Chicago, the Illinois Senate, and then Washington, D.C. (Wayne 2012). He adjusted even the cadence of his speech to connect with his audiences, using different voices in a black church and at a political meeting in the suburbs (Remnick 2010).

The Problem

Obama may have been born in extremely modest circumstances—his father was nearly always a continent away, his mother faced professional struggles, and his grandparents ended up playing a key role in raising the future president—but nevertheless critics attacked Barack Obama as a child of privilege. Obama's opponents ignored his modest childhood circumstances and his years of community organizing, emphasizing instead his elite credentials, including degrees from Columbia and Harvard Law. Once he entered the national political arena, Obama consistently faced suspicions, fueled by conservative media and activists (including Donald Trump), that he was not born in America and that he was a Muslim, not a Christian (Abramowitz 2017; Kurtz 2007a, 2007b).

Those character destruction efforts, amplified online, had a significant impact. The racially oriented strategy was deliberate: "If the Republicans succeeded in persuading voters that Obama's calm demeanor masked seething anger, they could not only elicit race-tied fears but also undercut the disposition of non-blacks to get to know and like him" (Kenski et al. 2010: 82).

Some of Obama's rookie mistakes as a presidential candidate practically played into Republicans' hands. During the 2008 nomination campaign, Obama briefly refused to wear a pin featuring the U.S. flag. Although he said it was a matter of principle, it was even more profoundly a matter of politics. In the end, his advisors convinced him that the controversy over not wearing the pin, as so many other politicians do, distracted the public from his policy messages. Obama relented, but the controversy left some with a sense that he might not be sufficiently patriotic. After a stunningly poor performance in a bowling alley, Americans had further opportunities to claim that this candidate was not a "real" American (Heilemann and Halperin 2010).

The most damaging evidence of disdain or perhaps arrogance was the secretly recorded comments candidate Obama made at a private California fundraiser. He remarked that some Americans were bitter and were "clinging to guns and religion" during these hard times (Owen 2009). Taken together, some might have suspected that Obama did not have much in common with the people he sought to serve as president—and he had little respect for them!

Another use of social media to emphasize the character of Obama in a negative way can be seen through the rise to celebrity of "Joe the Plumber" during the 2008 campaign. Republicans regularly presented him as the everyman objecting to Obama's plans to raise taxes on small businesses (Owen 2009). The conservative effort to reframe Obama as just another tax-and-spend liberal generated considerable attention during the campaign, even though Joe made too little money to be subject to Obama's proposed tax increase, nor was he a plumber, nor was his first name Joe (Kellner 2009). As the polls discussed later in this chapter show, the argument that Obama somehow was not an ordinary American influenced the views of many citizens during his presidency.

One final area of criticism of Obama's character concerned his relative inexperience. He won election to the Senate in 2004, and he spent much of his first term running for president rather than learning the particulars of national and international policies. Both Hillary Clinton and John McCain sought to portray Obama's optimism about the level of change he could accomplish to be naïve at least. "He's the biggest celebrity in the world, but is he ready to lead?" asked one announcer in a McCain campaign ad that juxtaposed photos of Obama's rallies with those of singer Britney Spears and pop culture celebrity Paris Hilton (quoted in Kenski et al. 2010: 77).

Character counts because it can give a president some wiggle room when he needs it. When policies disappoint, as the half-hearted economic recovery did for many voters in 2010, skepticism about a president's character makes it very hard for any administration to shape the public discourse to their liking. That is why character definition efforts are so important for a president, as a likeable president often gets "the benefit of the doubt" in tough times. If people had felt better about Obama in 2010, maybe Democrats would have retained more seats in Congress.

Applying Character Models to Barack Obama

As journalists John Heilemann and Mark Halperin (2010: 25) noted, Obama "could come off as cocky, that was for sure—and not just to people outside his circle. He was smarter than the average bear, not to mention the average politician, and he not only knew it but wanted to make sure that everyone else knew it too."

Taking a page from the Renshon (1998) model of presidential character, Wayne (2012) focuses on Obama's ambition. Wayne (2012) notes, for example, that it takes a strong sense of self-regard, after all, to write the first version of one's life story at the age of 33. But that same self-confidence is required for a successful career in politics, particularly as a presidential candidate. Notably, though, Obama's goals were not simply about winning the office, but in doing something with that office, the integrity component of the Renshon (1998) model that forces some leaders in public life to strive to live up to their ideals.

> He has been captured by the passion of his own message—unifying America, renewing its spirit and providing greater and better opportunities for more people. He saw in his inauguration a powerful affirmation of the opportunities in America for everyone. He thinks of his triumphs in symbolic terms and sees great opportunities to improve conditions for everyone, particularly those who need it the most and have the least capacity to help themselves.
>
> (Wayne 2012: 22)

A candidate who imagines accomplishing great things along these lines is the very definition of an active-positive leader (Barber 1992).

For Renshon (1998), another key measure of a president's character involves relatedness, the ways in which a politician is shaped by his or her interactions with other people. As the titanic struggle over health care during his presidency reveals, Obama had considerable interest in helping others deal with their problems, and had a high level of confidence in his own efficacy and capacity to deliver change in policy areas where presidents usually fail (George and George 1998, Skocpol 1997). Note in particular Obama's very deep commitment to reaching out to the public to explain policy challenges and initiatives, a sharp contrast from the limited information released during the George W. Bush administration, particularly over the divisions within the government about whether Saddam Hussein was developing weapons of mass destruction (Entman 2004). As Obama said in an interview with correspondent Steve Kroft on the CBS News program *60 Minutes*:

> One of the things that I do think is important to be able to explain to the American people what you're doing and why you're doing it. That is something that I think every great president has been able to do from FDR to Lincoln to John Kennedy to Eisenhower.
>
> (quoted in Wayne 2012: 63)

News Management and Character Challenges

While the Affordable Care Act is the case study of this chapter, the first major issue Obama addressed as president was the financial crisis that exploded shortly before the 2008 presidential election. Bush, McCain and Obama all quickly lined up behind an emergency plan to ramp up federal spending to restore the shaky credit markets. A few weeks after taking office in January 2009 Obama convinced Congress to pass a major stimulus package designed to accelerate the pace of a hoped-for recovery. As Obama would go on to do with respect to his health care bill, he avoided the aggressive rhetoric that might have made him popular with the Democratic left (Alter 2010). By taking a somewhat reticent approach to jawboning in the early going, Obama maximized the chances that the stimulus bill and related regulatory reforms would become law relatively quickly (Alter 2013).

Focusing on the economy was an essential response to political conditions in January 2009 (Campbell 2012). Economic concerns routinely trump other matters as a source of public anxiety about governmental policies (Farnsworth 2015). A 2010 Pew Public opinion survey (Pew 2010a), taken after conditions had improved somewhat, revealed that the American public still wanted an activist government in a number of policy areas, particularly when it came to strengthening the nation's economy and improving the job situation. These goals were each rated as a top or important priority for government action by more than 95 percent of those surveyed, demonstrating that the new president faced intense public demands. Also high on the public's list were protecting the country against a terrorist attack, saving Social Security and Medicare, fixing the public schools and reducing the deficit (Pew 2010a).

For Barack Obama, the magnitude of government activities became a major public opinion problem very quickly. The near-collapse of the U.S. financial system left the nation mired in the worst economic downturn in a generation. As a result, Americans continued to express deep skepticism of government's capacity to manage the economy. In April 2009, shortly after Congress passed a major economic stimulus bill, 54 percent of Americans agreed with the statement that "government regulation of business does more harm than good," about the same as the 57 percent who agreed with that statement in a 2007 survey conducted more than a year before the crisis hit (Farnsworth 2015).

Although his 2008 campaign masterfully focused on "change," the administration's rhetoric of governing was quite prosaic. Perhaps it had to be so. Leaving the details of the health care bill to Congress may have been smart politics—Clinton tried and failed to pass a health care bill in 1994 the administration designed—but that deference did not enhance Obama's leadership credentials. Efforts by endangered

Congressional Democrats to campaign at some distance from the president—and the health care bill—made it difficult for Obama to trumpet its accomplishments. In addition, the uncertain pace of economic recovery did not give the administration much to talk about along those lines either. "It could have been worse" is not a message that generates voter enthusiasm.

Modern social media environments—including YouTube, Facebook and Twitter—can empower critics who attack Obama or any other president. They also allow citizens to participate in the conversation in a variety of ways, by reposting political content, by commenting upon it, or even offering reformatted presidential content through mash-ups, GIFs, and memes (Scacco and Coe 2016; Stuckey 2010).

Obama's social media efforts involved reaching out in a number of ways and via a number of media venues. Obama reached a distinctly less-politically obsessed audience on ESPN, where he offered his college basketball tournament picks during "March Madness" (Scacco and Coe 2016). The lack of political content in that arena was precisely the point—the appearance demonstrated that Obama was something of a regular person (Scacco and Coe 2016). The White House website during Obama's tenure likewise offered opportunities for citizens to obtain email updates and provided clickable opportunities to engage with and otherwise participate in ongoing administration political activities. White House tweets also emphasized direct interaction with the White House and with Obama through popular hashtags like #whchat and #whtweetup (Scacco and Coe 2016). While these efforts did not always focus on selling a particular policy, and may not have involved talking about politics at all, a presidential administration employs social media outreach in the hopes of making citizens more likely to support the president generally as well as in regard to his policy priorities (Heith 2013).

Public Opinion

President Obama started with relatively high public approval ratings, as shown in a series of Pew Research Center surveys reported in Table 4.3. The early results demonstrate how effective presidents can be in selling themselves to the public, particularly in the early going. Following Obama's January 2009 inauguration, more than 60 percent of the country approved of Obama's job performance. In January 2010, after more than a year of high unemployment, sluggish growth, and pummeling from congressional Republicans regarding the economic stimulus package, the health care reform bill, and the bailouts of the banking and auto industries, roughly half the country approved of Obama's job performance. Support dipped around the time of the 2010 midterm elections, when Republicans took control of the House, but quickly rebounded. It peaked

Table 4.3 Obama Presidential Approval

Do you approve or disapprove of the way Barack Obama is handling his job as president?

	Approve	Disapprove
January 2017	55%	40%
October 2016	54%	42%
August 2016	53%	42%
June 2016	50%	44%
January 2016	46%	48%
July 2015	48%	45%
January 2015	47%	48%
November 2014	43%	52%
July 2014	44%	49%
January 2014	43%	49%
July 2013	46%	46%
January 2013	52%	40%
December 2012	55%	39%
June 2012	47%	45%
January 2012	44%	48%
July 2011	44%	48%
May 2011	50%	39%
April 2011	47%	45%
January 2011	46%	44%
June 2010	48%	43%
March 2010	46%	43%
January 2010	49%	42%
July 2009	54%	34%
June 2009	61%	30%
April 2009	63%	26%
March 2009	59%	26%
February 2009	64%	17%

Note: Don't Know responses are not reported here, so percentages do not sum to 100.

Source: Pew 2017b.

again around the time Obama was re-elected in November 2012, and fell again in late 2013. Public approval of Obama then rebounded during his final year in office.

The relatively narrow range of approval ratings across those eight years serve as a useful reminder of the challenges presidents face when they try to go public on policy items: public appeals generally have little impact on presidential ratings. Policy frustrations may undermine public approval of a president, as was the case for Obama and health care (Jacobson 2011). Apart from times of crisis, and even sometimes during those periods, Americans worry about governmental overreach. As the support for health care reform coalesced, so too did its opposition. The president's Tea Party critics tapped into a traditional

American skepticism of big government that would serve the movement well as the 2010 midterms approached (Williamson et al. 2011). As Table 4.3 demonstrates, even the U.S. military's raid in Pakistan that killed Osama bin Laden, the mastermind of the 9/11 terrorist attacks, during April 2011 had little lasting impact on the president's public opinion standings.

National public opinion surveys conducted for Gallup during Obama's first year showed considerable public respect for the president's character. As shown in Table 4.4, evaluations of Obama as a person were consistently high during his months as a presidential candidate and as a new president. In April 2009, around the 100-day mark of his new presidency,

Table 4.4 U.S. Public Opinion on Character Traits of President Obama

Thinking about the following characteristics and qualities, please say whether you think each applies or doesn't apply to Barack Obama. How about ___?

Is a strong and decisive leader

	Applies	Doesn't
June 2014	45%	53%
November 2013	47%	51%
September 2013	53%	46%
June 2013	53%	47%
June 2012	53%	47%
March 2011	52%	47%
March 2010	60%	39%
September 2009	66%	33%
July 2009	67%	31%
April 2009	73%	25%
October 2008	61%	37%
April 2008	55%	39%
March 2008	56%	37%

Understands the problems Americans face in their daily lives

	Applies	Doesn't
June 2014	48%	50%
November 2013	54%	45%
September 2013	56%	43%
June 2013	56%	42%
June 2012	58%	41%
March 2011	57%	42%
March 2010	56%	43%
September 2009	64%	36%
July 2009	66%	33%
April 2009	72%	27%
October 2008	73%	26%
April 2008	63%	34%
March 2008	67%	30%

Has a clear plan for solving the country's problems

	Applies	Doesn't
June 2014	34%	65%
November 2013	38%	60%
September 2013	38%	59%
June 2013	38%	60%
June 2012	40%	59%
March 2011	36%	60%
October 2008	51%	46%
April 2008	40%	53%
March 2008	41%	53%

Is honest and trustworthy

	Applies	Doesn't
June 2014	47%	51%
November 2013	50%	47%
September 2013	55%	42%
June 2013	55%	44%
June 2012	60%	38%
March 2011	61%	36%
April 2008	60%	32%
March 2008	63%	29%

Can manage the government effectively

	Applies	Doesn't
June 2014	39%	60%
November 2013	42%	57%
September 2013	47%	52%
June 2013	44%	54%
June 2012	45%	54%
March 2010	49%	49%
September 2009	55%	43%
July 2009	59%	39%
July 2009	66%	29%
October 2008	55%	41%
April 2008	48%	45%
March 2008	48%	45%

Shares your values

	Applies	Doesn't
June 2014	43%	56%
June 2013	48%	50%
June 2012	53%	46%
March 2011	51%	47%
March 2010	48%	50%
September 2009	52%	46%
July 2009	55%	43%
April 2009	60%	37%
October 2008	58%	40%
April 2008	51%	44%
March 2008	51%	44%

Note: Don't Know responses are not reported here, so percentages do not sum to 100.

Source: Jones 2014.

about three-quarters of Americans considered Obama "honest and trust-worthy" and that he "is a strong and decisive leader." Solid majorities said that Obama "understands the problems of people like you" and that he "can be trusted in a crisis." The highest score of all was reserved for agreement with the following statement, "He is willing to listen to different points of view."

.   All four of those categories were notably lower one year later, around the time he signed Affordable Care Act into law. While solid majorities continued to believe that Obama understood the problems of ordinary people and considered him decisive, only roughly half thought he could manage the government effectively or that he shared the public's values. By 2014, when citizens were getting some sense of how the ACA would work in practice, personal evaluations of Obama's temperament and competence were even lower.

One key factor that distinguished the Obama media strategy from those of Bush and Clinton is a greater hesitancy to try to dominate the discourse in the mass media (Farnsworth 2009, 2015). Despite the powerful presidential advantages in the shaping of domestic news content, Obama's team tended to be relatively deferential in policy matters, leaving the many health care legislative details to Capitol Hill and giving Congress considerable authority to shape the economic stimulus package and other key bills. As the only president of the four examined here to come to the White House from the Senate (and one who named one of the most senior senators as a running mate), Obama understood that Congress often chafes at presidential demands to fall in line, something the other three presidents examined here were not so quick to grasp.

Is Obama a Muslim?

This same diffidence drove other debates regarding Obama's personality. Nowhere are the consequences of failing to drive the narrative of one's own identity clearer than in the large numbers of Americans who wondered whether the forty-fourth president was a Christian.

Obama's identity as a practicing Christian became quite visible during one of the major religious issues of the 2008 campaign, the controversy over the sermons of Obama's outspoken pastor, Rev. Jeremiah Wright (Denton 2009). Even so, the president's critics were able to reshape the Obama religious narrative away from Christianity for many, particularly online (Kellner 2009). Conservative blogs were key early voices in spreading the myth that Obama was not a Christian before the 2008 election, and Fox News subsequently amplified the lies (Chadwick 2013). While mainstream media quickly debunked the claims and Obama's supporters fought back online with contrary evidence, the continuing conversation about this matter on social media and elsewhere—even after the election—kept Obama's religious status from being fully resolved in the minds of many voters (Kenski et al. 2010).

While feelings about race may have had some role in generating negative evaluations of the first African-American president, polls show there was far more to public opinion on this point than that. As shown in Table 4.5, only 34 percent of Americans were convinced in August 2010 that Obama is a Christian, down 14 percentage points from a March 2009 survey. While less than one in five Americans believed at that time that Obama was a Muslim, a surprising 43 percent said they did not know Obama's religion. The declining percentages of people saying that Obama is a Christian appeared even among supportive groups, with increased numbers of even Democrats and African-Americans saying that they were uncertain about Obama's religious preference.

Obama could have done more to combat this perception, which was not helpful to his public approval ratings. (Although the U.S. Constitution prohibits the establishment of any religious qualification for public office, the U.S. population is largely Christian and every president in American history has been a Christian.) Had Obama chosen to do so, the president could have spoken more about his Christian faith during his many public statements and made more family church appearances to resolve the lingering public doubts about Obama the person. (Although biblical teachings suggest one should not make too public a demonstration of one's religious devotion, U.S. elections demonstrate that public expressions of deep piety can generate electoral rewards.)

One of the key reasons that presidents seek to maximize news reports that include matters of character and personality is that the coverage of such topics tends to be more positive than most presidential news

Table 4.5 Many Uncertain about Obama's Religion

	Obama is a Christian		Obama is a Muslim		Don't Know	
	Aug 2010	Change from 3/09	Aug 2010	Change from 3/09	Aug 2010	Change from 3/09
Total	34%	−14	18%	+7	43%	+9
White	35%	−15	21%	+10	40%	+8
Black	43%	−13	7%	+1	46%	+10
Republican	27%	−20	31%	+14	39%	+11
Independent	34%	−11	18%	+8	44%	+6
Democrat	46%	−9	10%	+3	41%	+9
White Evangelical	27%	−12	29%	+9	42%	+9
White Mainline Protestant	36%	−15	22%	+12	40%	+8
White Catholic	32%	−19	18%	+8	46%	+10
Unaffiliated	38%	−9	13%	+7	44%	+7

Source: Pew 2010b.

coverage. A Media Tenor content analysis of news reports that related to Obama's personality during his first 18 months as president revealed that coverage on ABC, CBS and NBC was more positive than negative, as compared to net negative coverage overall of Obama and his presidency at the same time on those networks. While coverage of character matters relating to Obama was also negative on balance on Fox News, those reports were less negative than Obama's overall coverage on Fox News during his first 18 months in office (Farnsworth et al. 2013: 84).

International Perspectives

The profound unpopularity of George W. Bush in many global capitals and among most global publics created an environment tailor-made for Barack Obama, who even as a candidate aggressively engaged international populations and global leaders. His presidency triggered high levels of optimism in many parts of the world as he sought to rebuild international relationships that many viewed as weakened during the Bush years (Sinclair 2012; Singh 2012).

Obama's foreign policy approach reflected his conviction that past aggressive military responses, like the U.S.-led invasion of Iraq in 2003 and subsequent occupation, undermined America's long-term interests (Goldberg 2016).

> The president believes that Churchillian rhetoric and, more to the point, Churchillian habits of thought, helped bring his predecessor, George W. Bush, to ruinous war in Iraq. Obama entered the White House bent on getting out of Iraq and Afghanistan; he was not seeking new dragons to slay. And he was particularly mindful of promising victory in conflicts he believed to be unwinnable.
>
> (Goldberg 2016)

As president, Obama continued to distinguish between the conflicts in Afghanistan and Iraq, noting that the former was a "war of necessity" with an enemy that would try to attack the U.S. again (Mann 2013). Even though he felt more positively about the U.S. military presence in Afghanistan, the new president routinely challenged his generals, who favored longer-term commitments and higher troop levels than did Obama (Woodward 2013). Obama saw the nation he led as one with a more limited ability to impose political and military outcomes upon other nations at a reasonable cost than Bush believed (Woodward 2013). "Once the dogs of war are unleashed, you don't know where it is going to lead," Obama said (quoted in Woodward 2013: 375).

Obama applied that lesson of studied reluctance on whether to engage militarily in Syria as the chaos there mounted. "Dropping bombs on someone to prove that you're willing to drop bombs on someone is just about the worst reason to use force," Obama said (quoted in Goldberg 2016).

Of course, Obama's reluctance to follow through on his vow to protect civilians in Syria may mark one of the larger foreign policy missteps of his presidency (White 2016). Obama warned Syrian President Bashar al-Assad not to use chemical weapons on his own people. When the Syrian leader did so, Obama dithered and in the end did not launch air strikes to demonstrate American resolve on this matter (White 2016).

Global public opinion of the U.S. president became far more favorable when Obama took office, and remained so even as his term was winding down, as shown in Table 4.6. Many close allies examined in

Table 4.6 International Evaluations of George W. Bush and Barack Obama, 2008–2015

For each, tell me how much confidence you have in each leader to do the right thing regarding world affairs: a lot of confidence, some confidence, not too much confidence, or no confidence at all [George W. Bush / Barack Obama].

	Bush 2008	Obama 2009	Obama 2015	Change 2008 v. 2015
US	37%	74%	58%	21
South Korea	30%	81%	88%	58
France	13%	91%	83%	70
Italy	43%*	—	77%	34**
South Africa	32%	—	77%	45
UK	16%	86%	76%	60
Canada	28%*	88%	76%	48**
India	55%	—	74%	19
Germany	14%	93%	73%	59
Japan	25%	85%	66%	41
Poland	41%	62%	64%	23
Brazil	17%	—	63%	46
Spain	8%	72%	58%	50
Mexico	16%	55%	49%	33
Israel	57%	56%	49%	-8
Turkey	2%	33%	45%	43
China	30%	62%	44%	14
Lebanon	33%	33%	46%	36
Palestinian Terr.	8%	23%	15%	7
Pakistan	7%	7%	13%	14
Jordan	7%	31%	14%	7
Russia	22%	37%	11%	-11

Notes:
Percentages combine the first two categories.
Dashes signify that the question was not asked by Pew in that country in that year.
*   Results from 2007 survey.
** Comparison is with 2007 survey results.

Source: Pew 2015.

these international surveys by Pew (2015) saw massive jumps in popular approval as Obama replaced Bush, with increases of more than 60 percentage points between 2008 and 2009 in France, Germany, the U.K., and Spain, among others. When considering how these international audiences felt about Obama in 2015 compared with Bush in 2008, the differences remained remarkable: the margins in many nations for the forty-fourth president remained 45 points or more above the comparable levels for Bush, including in South Korea, France, the U.K., Canada, South Africa, and Germany.

Americans were also more positive about Obama in the foreign policy arena, and remained so across his presidency. In the U.S., Obama's selection brought a 37-point increase in Americans thinking the president would "do the right thing regarding world affairs" between 2008 and 2009. In 2015, Obama continued to outpoll Bush on the question, albeit by a narrower 21-point margin.

Of the more than 20 nations examined in these surveys, only two were more negative regarding Obama in 2015 than they were of Bush in 2008. Among Russians, only 11 percent thought Obama would do the right thing in world affairs; 22 percent of Russians said the same about Bush. In Israel, 57 percent thought in 2008 that Bush would do the right thing in world affairs, as compared to 49 percent who said the same thing about Obama seven years later.

Case Study: Selling the Affordable Care Act in an Angry, Anxious Nation

Improving health care in the U.S. has long been a domestic policy priority, with debates over health care reform initiatives going back to the 1940s (Skocpol 1997). More recently, Bill Clinton sought to pass a comprehensive health care bill, but doubts over its workability and concerns over its cost led to abandonment of the bill and to Democratic defeats in the 1994 midterm elections (Sinclair 2000b). While George W. Bush shied away from comprehensive health care reform packages, he did secure passage of a significant expansion of Medicare through a prescription drug benefit program (Foreman 2008). As a presidential candidate in 2008, Barack Obama repeatedly emphasized that he would focus on health care reform if elected (Abramson et al. 2012; Kenski et al. 2010).

Obama took office facing profound partisan divides that had deepened across the 16 years that Bill Clinton and George W. Bush had served as president (Campbell 2016; Fiorina 2008). While the 2008 election secured relatively large Democratic majorities in Congress, Obama's health care reform plan moved slowly on Capitol Hill. At first, more pressing matters—particularly an economic crisis and repairing frayed relations with allies that developed during the last years of

George W. Bush's presidency—commanded Washington's attention (Sinclair 2012; Singh 2012).

When he turned to health care, Obama offered general policy preferences and bill-drafting assistance, but left much of the heavy lifting to Capitol Hill (Sinclair 2011). Obama and congressional Democrats trod carefully, working with health care business to build a plan that corporate interests considered acceptable (Jacobs and Skocpol 2010). Had the president railed against hospitals, pharmaceutical companies and insurance firms, as a more impulsive president might have done, opposition from those well-funded industries would likely have doomed Obama's health care plans just as they killed the Clinton health care plan more than a dozen years earlier (Alter 2010; Skocpol 1997).

Public criticism of the Obama health reform plan increased as it was being prepared. A rising anti-government movement dubbed itself the Tea Party and spread its criticisms of Obama and his health care bill through social media and through many contentious congressional district meetings that debated health care changes (Skocpol and Williamson 2012). Powerful anti-reform themes, like the false claim that the bill contained provisions for government "death panels," emerged on social media and received considerable attention from more traditional news outlets as well (Hopper 2017). In terms of the legislation itself, the administration preferred to engage with policy specifics only in the final stages, believing that members who took leading roles in drafting the bill would care more about its success than if they were moving a White House bill (Sinclair 2011). Passage of the Affordable Care Act proved to be a legislative marathon as well, with back-and-forth struggles between the Democratic House and Senate majorities, made doubly difficult when the Democrats lost their 60-seat majority following a Republican victory in a Senate special election in Massachusetts in early 2010 (Hulse and Palmer 2009; Sinclair 2011).

After Obama signed the Affordable Care Act, another round of presidential political communication struggles began. Republican lawmakers, who gained control of the House after the 2010 midterm elections, challenged the president over many aspects of the legislation, as did Republican activists who employed pro-Republican news outlets and social media to make their case to the public. Opponents of the law first sought to have the federal courts declare the measure unconstitutional, and when that failed, critics sought to undermine it by reducing the law's scope and effectiveness through additional court action (Busch 2016). Several states under at least partial Republican legislative control refused to expand eligibility for Medicaid, which was part of the Obamacare reform package. By choosing not to do so, those states limited the ability of millions of Americans to obtain affordable insurance coverage and undermined the reform program itself (Snell 2016).

The Tea Party movement that arose in the wake of Obama's victory was particularly valuable to the Republican Party given the widespread Democratic gains in the 2006 and 2008 elections. The movement was particularly effective at attacking government programs that it alleged were giving too much to "unworthy" people, a useful line of attack for reviving the Republican Party. This more-than-implicit racial appeal undercut the Obama presidency among many white working class voters (Williamson et al. 2011). Opposition to allegedly too-generous immigration policies and too lax enforcement of the U.S. border helped fuel the resentment against a Washington allegedly too friendly to minorities (Brader et al. 2008). A group of national Republican elites helped build the movement by organizing and funding local and regional efforts by the movement (Mayer 2010).

This largely white populist movement rapidly became very influential in the Republican Party, holding rallies to protest liberal government policies and high taxes as well as helping the party challenge Democrats up and down the ballot. The 2010 midterm elections were particularly good news for the Tea Party movement. Tea Party-linked candidates won 39 of 129 races for the House with a linked candidate; five of nine Senate candidates backed by the movement won election to that chamber (Williamson et al. 2011).

In the contemporary mixed media environment, presidents tend to emphasize the personal and the informal. As examples, President Obama sought to increase health care enrollment by joining late night comic Jimmy Fallon to "slow jam the news," by wielding a selfie stick on a BuzzFeed video and by trading insults with Zach Galifianakis on *Between Two Ferns* (Scacco and Coe 2016).

There are limits to what these sorts of public relations efforts can accomplish, however. When the health care enrollment website crashed, the administration mishandled the problems by trying to frame the startup as "just glitches" and arguing that the president's staff, not the president, was responsible for the screw-ups (Hopper 2017). This framing misstep provided critics with further ammunition to claim that the ACA was unworkable (Hopper 2017).

There were also specific efforts to employ social media in support of the Affordable Care Act. The Obama administration was particularly adept at educating social media consumers about the key factors of the health care bill (Katz et al. 2013). As early as November 2009, the health care bill had its own Twitter account (@HealthCareGov), and when the law was signed in March 2010 the administration put Facebook and Google+ pages online to help promote the Affordable Care Act (Leonhardt 2015). The administration also produced YouTube videos designed to promote the law and to encourage millennials in particular to sign up for health insurance (Leonhardt 2015). When enrollment numbers were running below projections, the administration stepped up its efforts on Twitter with hashtags like #getcovered (Leonhardt 2015).

As the struggle to win the public relations war continued, the Obama team asked the president's supporters to reclaim the word "Obamacare," encouraging the president's Twitter followers to tweet what they liked about the new law (Hopper 2017). As he embraced the term, the president argued that the eventual success of the health care reform plan would be a net plus for his public opinion ratings and for other Democrats (Ceaser et al. 2015). But there are limits to efforts to reframe a term that already was being widely used negatively by the president's critics. Despite the Obama team's best efforts to generate more positive sentiments around the word "Obamacare," media reports that used that term still tended to be more negative than positive (Hopper 2017).

Opposition to the ACA following its enactment also moved forward on more communication-oriented tracks. As the new health care regulations and plans began to roll out, Republicans frequently repeated Obama's ill-fated promise "If you like your insurance, you can keep it," a comment named the "Lie of the Year" by Politifact in 2013 (Busch 2016). (Of course, Sarah Palin's claim that the health care bill contained "death panels" was the organization's 2009 "Lie of the Year" [Hopper 2017].) Republicans kept up the pressure against the law in the courts and on conservative media, convinced that the legislation would continue to drag down Democrats, including the president himself, in 2012 (Ceaser et al. 2015).

Even so, arguably the biggest problem that the ACA faced during its early implementation was not the litigation, not the angry Tea Party movement, and not Republican legislative opposition in Washington and in many state capitals. Rather it was the misfire of the health care registration website itself. People trying to enroll in the insurance program via healthcare.gov faced frozen computer screens, painfully long waits, and other obstacles that made it difficult for people who wanted to buy a policy to actually do so (Busch 2016).

In the face of these problems, Obama sought to increase enrollment in the health exchanges via an appearance on *Between Two Ferns*, an online comedy program hosted by Zach Galifianakis, and that effort did drive more people—particularly young people—to the government's health insurance website shortly before an enrollment deadline (Azari 2014; Blake 2014). To promote the video's release, FunnyorDie.com tweeted a link to the video. This tweet received about 2,500 retweets and 1,400 "favorites" in just a few hours and generated considerable attention in the mainstream media (Leonhardt 2015).

Other celebrities joined the call to sell the plan. The Obama administration used basketball legends Magic Johnson and Alonzo Mourning to help build up interest in signing up for ACA via light-hearted YouTube videos (Leonhardt 2015). At best, though, these efforts limited the damage caused by the mis-firing government website. As the saying goes, one does not get a second chance to make a first impression—not even Magic could turn negative impressions around.

Republicans sought to portray the ACA website crash as "Obama's Katrina," but social media did not adopt the analogy. A sample of Twitter users using the term during the crisis rejected the comparison by a more than two-to-one margin (Hopper 2017). These GOP efforts fared better in traditional media. The Katrina-Obamacare comparison appeared in many media reports at the time, with a plurality of reports saying that linking those two matters was legitimate (Hopper 2017).

Ironically, the best promoters for Obamacare turned out to be President Trump and U.S. House Speaker Paul Ryan. In early 2017, as Republicans began their efforts to repeal and replace the Affordable Care Act, public support for the controversial health care plan surged and Republicans in Congress abandoned—at least temporarily—the "repeal and replace" promise (Hohmann 2017a). Even though House Republicans eventually crafted a bill that could pass the chamber during Trump's first months in office, Senate Republicans voted down a number of efforts to repeal and/or replace parts of the Affordable Care Act in July 2017 (Sullivan et al. 2017).

President Obama, the Affordable Care Act, and Public Opinion

Public opinion regarding the health care plan was consistently negative during the health care rollout and through the end of Obama's presidency. As shown in Table 4.7, support for the Affordable Care Act never topped 50 percent during Obama's second term, though it came close a few times, like in November 2012, right after Obama's reelection, and after the administration established more user-friendly enrollment systems towards the end of his term (e.g., the surveys conducted in July 2015 and May 2016). Most of the surveys showed support for the measure in the lower 40s, and sometimes under 40 percent support. The high level of consistency in the public's views regarding the law once again demonstrates how hard it is even for a president, who possesses a greater ability than other politicians do to shape policy discourse, to use public relations to generate significant change in public opinion (Edwards 2003).

The political situation in the fall of 2010, a high point in political discussion of the health care law that passed into law earlier that year, deserves a closer look. As shown in Table 4.8, the public did not view the Obama presidency or the policy actions of Obama and the Democrats all that unfavorably going into the 2010 midterm elections. The president's overall job approval rating stood at 50 percent in October 2010, roughly where presidents usually are at the mid-point of their first terms (cf., Balz

Table 4.7 Public Opinion Regarding ACA

Do you generally approve or disapprove of the 2010 Affordable Care Act, signed into law by President Obama, that restructured the U.S. health care system?

	Approve	Disapprove
2016 Nov 9–13	42%	53%
2016 Aug 30–31	44%	51%
2016 May 6–8	47%	49%
2015 Nov 4–8	44%	52%
2015 Jul 1–5	47%	48%
2015 Apr 1–4	41%	53%
2014 Nov 6–9	37%	56%
2014 Oct 1–2	41%	53%
2014 May 21–25	43%	51%
2014 Apr 7–8	43%	54%
2014 Feb 28-Mar 2	40%	55%
2014 Jan 31-Feb 1	41%	51%
2014 Jan 3–4	38%	54%
2013 Dec 11–12	41%	51%
2013 Nov 23–24	40%	54%
2013 Nov 7–10	40%	55%
2013 Oct 26–28	44%	47%
2013 Oct 18–20	45%	50%
2013 Aug 17–18	41%	49%
2013 Jun 20–24	44%	52%
2012 Nov 15–18	48%	45%

Note: Don't Know responses are not reported here, so percentages do not sum to 100.

Source: Brands and Newport 2016.

and Cohen 2010). In addition, he remained far more popular than Congress, as presidents nearly always are (Farnsworth 2009).

On specific issue areas, the Democrats also did pretty well. More voters favored the Democrats over the Republicans on several issues, including the key issues of the economy and health care and particularly helping the middle class. While Republicans had slight public opinion advantages on policies relating to the federal budget deficit in taxes, the differences were within the margin of error. There was also the issue of the high expectations that accompanied Obama's election, and the natural frustration among his supporters that they did not see as much change as they expected (Aberbach 2012). Where the GOP really had its greatest advantage, though, was in voter intensity, and differing levels of voter enthusiasm are particularly important in midterm elections. While the public remained split nearly 50/50 on the health care bill, the GOP's newly energized congressional leadership said after the 2010 elections that they would try to repeal the new law (Herszenhorn and Pear 2010; Murray and Bacon 2010).

Table 4.8 Partisan Conflict, 2010

Do you approve or disapprove of the way ____ are/is doing their/his job?

	Approve	*Disapprove*
Barack Obama	50%	47%
Congress	24%	73%
Democrats in Congress	36%	61%
Republicans in Congress	30%	67%

Which political party, the (Democrats) or the (Republicans), do you trust to do a better job handling ____? [political parties rotated] *

	D	R	Both (vol.)	Neither (vol.)
The economy	44%	37%	4%	14%
Health care	46%	38%	1%	12%
Immigration issues	37%	37%	3%	17%
The situation in Afghanistan	39%	34%	4%	19%
The federal budget deficit	39%	40%	2%	18%
Taxes	40%	43%	3%	13%
Helping the middle class	50%	34%	2%	11%

Do you think the money the federal government has spent on the economic stimulus has been mostly (well spent) or mostly (wasted)?

Well spent	*Wasted*
29%	68%

Given what you know about them, would you say you support or oppose the changes to the health care system that have been enacted by (Congress) and (the Obama administration)? [Congress/Obama order is rotated]

	Support	*Oppose*
October 2010	47%	48%
March 2010	46%	50%

Notes: Don't Know responses are not reported here, so percentages do not sum to 100.
* A half sample was asked first six questions, and the last question was asked of the full sample.

Source: Balz and Cohen 2010.

Academic critics of Obama's marketing of the health care bill faulted him for not doing more to promote the issues on inequality found in the status quo, an environment where people had vastly different levels of access to health insurance and therefore vastly different levels of access to health care (Lynch and Gollust 2010). Those messages would likely have been most effective on individuals less likely to participate in the public discussion of possible health care reforms and not the key pivotal elements of the electorate (Druckman et al. 2012). In contrast, securing passage of the Affordable Care Act involved focusing on issues of great salience to middle class voters who are more likely to participate in politics and for whom health care inequalities were not likely to be salient (Jacobs and Skocpol 2010). Indeed, critics of the Affordable Care Act tried to turn the health care pressures to their advantage, arguing that middle class access to quality health care might worsen if more people had insurance. This approach effectively targeted those people most likely to be engaged in the debate and to vote in the midterm election (Skocpol and Williamson 2012). In other words, Obama probably did the right thing, politically speaking. Had the president focused more on inequality issues in his appeal, the opposition to his health care bill among the currently insured might have been stronger and Democratic losses might have been even greater (Druckman et al. 2012). In other words, the Tea Party would have used any Obama emphasis on inequality in health care to exacerbate concerns about the president's greater concern for specific sectors of the electorate.

The Obama Communication Legacy

As the Obama presidency reached its end, 35 percent of Americans thought the Affordable Care Act defined his years in office. As shown in Table 4.9, that topic ranked first, ahead of becoming the first African American president (17 percent) or his positive personal qualities, including his compassion, dignity, and intelligence (10 percent). No other topic received more than 10 percent support among those respondents, who were able to give up to three answers to this question of Obama's legacy. While some presidential scholars may point to Obama's economic policies in preventing a second Great Depression as worthy of particular note, only 7 percent listed economic matters of any kind as a key policy matter for the president. Ironically, for all the attention that George W. Bush once gave to his promise to hunt down Osama bin Laden "dead or alive," Obama received little credit for being the president who actually ordered the strike that killed the terrorist leader (only 2 percent listed it as a major achievement).

Overall, the assessments of Obama's tenure divided roughly 50–50, with 49 percent saying that his administration's accomplishments outweigh its failures, and 46 saying the reverse. The numbers were far better than those for George W. Bush when he left office, when public opinion tilted strongly negative, 64 percent to 24 percent. Obama's numbers were worse than Bill Clinton's, who left office with 60 percent saying he was likely to have a positive legacy as compared to 27 percent who thought he would have a negative one.

As Obama gave way to his successor, 46 percent of Americans said he would likely be remembered as an above average or excellent president,

Table 4.9 Obama Legacy, December 2016

Thinking ahead, what do you think Barack Obama will be most remembered for after he has left office? (accept up to three responses)

Domestic Policy (net)	49%
Affordable Care Act/Obamacare/health care	35%
Economy/taxes/budget/trade	7%
Gay marriage/women's rights/civil rights	2%
Immigration	1%
Race/racial issues	1%
Military/veterans	1%
Other domestic policy	5%
First Black President	17%
Positive assessments (net)	13%
Compassionate/intelligent/humble/dignity	10%
Positive views of how he ran the country	3%
Foreign Policy (net)	9%
Killing Osama bin Laden	2%
Cuba	1%
Iran/Iran deal	1%
ISIS/terrorism/national security	1%
Other foreign policy	5%
Negative assessments (net)	6%
Ran country poorly	4%
Polarization/divisiveness	2%
Other negative assessments	1%

In the long run, do you think the accomplishments of the Obama Administration will outweigh its failures, or will the failures outweigh the accomplishments?

	Obama 2016	Obama 2012	Bush 2008	Clinton 2001
Accomplishments will outweigh failures	49%	43%	24%	60%
Failures will outweigh accomplishments	44%	44%	64%	27%

How do you think President Obama will go down in history . . . as an outstanding president, above average, average, below average, or poor?

	2016 Obama	2008 G.W. Bush	2001 Clinton	1993 G.H.W. Bush	1989 Reagan
Outstanding	18%	3%	12%	6%	17%
Above average	28%	8%	32%	30%	42%
Average	26%	28%	32%	51%	25%
Below average	11%	24%	10%	8%	9%
Poor	16%	34%	11%	4%	5%

Source: Pew 2016c.

as compared to 11 percent who said that about Bush eight years earlier and to 44 percent who said that about Bill Clinton as he prepared to leave office in 2001. Among recent presidents, Ronald Reagan scored the highest on this measure, with 59 percent describing him as an above average or outstanding president.

Turning now to some final thoughts on the presidential marketing of the Affordable Care Act, one must note above all the difficulty of trying to move public opinion in such a difficult—and emotionally laden—policy area. Few policy areas generate as much fear for as many Americans as does health care, since one never knows when one will be sick and what treatments their insurance will cover—or not cover—for some future illness. Economic uncertainties like those around the time of Obama's election heighten concerns in other ways: even people who have good health insurance today might lose their jobs and therefore their health insurance for themselves and their families in the days ahead. Further, critics of the plan could also underscore concerns among the well-insured that the quality of their health care would deteriorate if the current system of doctors and hospitals suddenly had to take on large numbers of people who would start consuming larger amounts of medical services because they obtained health insurance (Hopper 2017). For all these reasons, health care is one of many areas where the uncertainty of policy change represents a massive barrier blocking any new legislation.

Obama's more diffident media style has its advantages in an era where character counts in terms of presidential communication. His low-key approach seems particularly well suited to those likely to be checking out *Between Two Ferns*, the late night comics, and other places where the policy content of discourse is not emphasized. Likewise, the invitations to participate in Twitter events promoting Obamacare and other administration priorities offered opportunities for presidents to use new media in ways that advance a president's standing. Policymaking, which generally contains greater uncertainty than the status quo, requires a high level of confidence in the policy maker to secure support for change. Obama's popularity was enough to win legislative support, but only enough (at best) to fight the public opinion battles to a draw.

In other words, this Affordable Care Act case study is a story of how effective social media opportunities exist both for a president and for his opponents. Obama's critics convinced many citizens that Obama was not one of them, and that he might even not be a Christian. Likewise, conservative attacks on alleged incompetence by liberals when it comes to health care policy management helped set the stage for high levels of criticism of Obamacare once the website failed to launch promptly and effectively.

Even so, it is important to appreciate that this case study also demonstrates that presidents do have some resilience in the framing of policy matters (Hopper 2017). After all, Obama did succeed in getting Congress to pass a health care bill—something that President Clinton could not accomplish. Further, Obama remained popular despite a highly problematic rollout of the new health insurance program and continuing Republican efforts to undermine the policy initiative (Farnsworth 2015).

In these highly partisan times (Campbell 2016), some voters seem primed to believe the best about a president they support and the worst about the other party's elected officials. The passage of this law, and the continuing fights over it, demonstrate how difficult it is to change policy in a political environment marked by high levels of partisanship. This case study also demonstrates how hard it is to find policy success in a media environment marked by decentralized news that increasingly moves away from policy substance and towards more personalized matters.

The Obama case study reminds presidents that it is particularly important to make the process of policy implementation a high priority. One of the biggest struggles during the implementation of the new health care law was the fact that the government's own enrollment website did not work. Clearly far greater investment in preparation would have helped increase the number of people signing up for the new law right away, as well as helping convince some skeptical citizens about the effectiveness of the health care plan. In these times of wide-ranging social media, many issues generate competing narratives, even if the dominant frame comes from the White House. As a result, it is important for policy makers to avoid crucial mistakes in those areas where one has maximum opportunity to prevent them.

Obama's decision to employ a targeted mass media strategy to maximize policy success was one of the key positive examples for other strategic communication campaigns. The president's decision to appear on certain media outlets like *Between Two Ferns* represented a very effective way to aim a communication message directly at a portion of the uninsured population likely to be using a particular slice of social media: young adults who have jobs that do not come with health insurance. Other Obama media efforts also helped create a positive image of Obama's character, allowing the president to reach people who might not be following traditional news closely. Obama's "March Madness" college basketball post-season picks on ESPN, hyped by the White House on social media, is an effective example of how one can help build support—or at least reduce opposition—to a president by reaching citizens where they are in today's very decentralized media environment. As public opinion data show, Obama's approval ratings remained quite stable throughout much of his presidency, a sharp contrast from the disapproval spiral across the years of many other recent presidents (Farnsworth 2009, 2015).

Finally, the Obamacare marketing case study reminds strategic communicators of the wisdom of trying to help sell the policy by selling the salesperson. For many people, the intricate details of a policy debate are not scintillating reading or viewing. People are often more interested in something other than a bill's subchapters, as Obama realized when he decided to go on ESPN and *Funny or Die*. Likewise, showing up on late night television to "slow jam" the news is another example of how to try to connect with people who are not necessarily political junkies. To some, these efforts may not seem dignified, but being dignified might not move the political merchandise these days. Character may count for more than it used to, but the shape of that character can vary greatly from president to president. That observation seems particularly apt as we turn to the next chapter, where we examine political communication efforts during the 2016 election and during the first year of the Trump presidency.

5   The Twitter Presidency of Donald Trump

Donald Trump's rapid political ascent to the presidency from a career as a real estate tycoon and reality television celebrity speaks to the extreme level of citizen frustration with conventional politics in 2016. Trump's Electoral College victory was truly unprecedented. Never before had a president been elected without having previously won election to a lower office, usually as a governor or senator, or having served in a top rank in the military. In fact, every previous major party *nominee* for decades had served in the military or held civilian public office before becoming president (Ceaser et al. 2017: 3). Of course Trump didn't win the 2016 election by much—a mere 78,000 votes *combined* in the crucial states of Michigan, Wisconsin, and Pennsylvania gave Trump his Electoral College win, even as Hillary Clinton won the national popular vote by roughly 3 million votes out of more than 130 million ballots cast (Sabato 2017: 5).

Anger sometimes directs the trajectory of American politics, and 2016 qualifies as a prime example. The level of citizen frustration with the government in Washington has varied over the years as economic anxiety and political conditions change (Farnsworth 2003a, 2003b). The anti–Wall Street fervor of William Jennings Bryan energized crowds more than a century ago. More recently, anger—primarily conservative anger—intensified during the years of the Jim Crow South, the anti-communism "red scare" led by Senator Joseph McCarthy (R-WI), the John Birch movement, and "massive resistance" to desegregated schools. White working class resentments fueled protests led by Alabama Gov. George Wallace in the 1960s, by independent Ross Perot in the 1992 presidential campaign, and by the Tea Party movement more recently (Adorno et al. 1950; Farnsworth 2001, 2003a; Hibbing and Theiss-Morse 1995; Skocpol and Williamson 2012).

While these earlier movements had some political success, Trump succeeded where many other populist efforts had not. His effective use of Twitter to attack the status quo resonated with many voters, and Trump wrested the Republican nomination away from an experienced field of GOP governors and senators, and then defeated Democratic nominee Hillary Clinton, also a highly experienced politician (Ceaser et al. 2017).

Trump was the culmination of more than two centuries of outsi-derism: a silver-spoon populist (widely seen as a demagogue) who warned of rigged political processes, dangerous foreigners, slick lob-byists, greedy rich people, and snooty intellectual elites. He trafficked in insults and unfounded conspiracy theories, and some of his fol-lowers responded with a nasty zeal that crossed the line into bullying and violence.

(Ceaser et al. 2017: 10–11)

Political science scholars offer three possible explanations for this pat-tern of conservative voting by low-income white Americans. One school of thought argues that white working class voters care more about social issues than a liberal economic agenda, and vote for conservative politi-cians who reflect their intense concerns over abortion and traditional marriage (Frank 2004). A second perspective argues that such voters do care about economic issues but they do not always act in their self-interest, for example by supporting tax cuts that primarily benefit the rich (cf., Bartels 2008).

A third approach argues that one's social identity explains the appar-ent departure from what some would consider self-interested voting on economic matters (Walsh 2012). Research in Wisconsin, a key state in the 2016 election, revealed that rural voters have a collective group consciousness that explains support for small government conservatism among residents of relatively low-income communities. While higher lev-els of government support for the less affluent may be in the economic self-interest of struggling Americans, rural residents in an interview pro-ject expressed objected to such efforts (Walsh 2012). They said that they expected these expanded federal programs would be controlled by urban political elites who disrespected them and also might funnel the money to assist minority groups they do not wish to assist (Walsh 2012). This perceived contempt (or actual contempt, if one prefers) is a key factor in explaining the rise of conservative voting by white low-income voters who would be likely to be subsidized by expanded government programs (Walsh 2012).

These three theories are not mutually exclusive, and further research into the opinions of Trump supporters during his presidency should shed greater light on the relative utility of these explanatory perspectives. One also might note that Republicans would be unlikely to deride guns and religion the way Obama did in 2008 (Owen 2009).

The News Media Environment of the Trump Era

Throughout the 2016 presidential campaign Trump's use of Twitter set the political agenda for the media and the other candidates. His angry cam-paign messages belittled political opponents with personal put-downs, and he attacked the policy status quo on trade, immigration, and other hot-button issues online (Owen 2017).

For news consumers generally, though, media use patterns remained relatively similar to those of recent presidential elections. Overall, campaign 2016 took place within a hybrid media environment, where traditional television media remained highly influential and online media also occupied an important role in providing news (Pew 2016a, 2017a).

As shown in Table 5.1, 57 percent of those surveyed counted television as one of their major news sources on the 2016 election, a significant drop from the 74 percent who identified television as a key news source four years earlier. Even so, television remained in first place among the leading media channels. About as many people in 2016 said that they considered online news outlets a major source of their campaign information as in 2012: 38 percent versus 36 percent in the earlier period. Radio and newspapers lagged behind those two media formats, consistent with recent election cycles. While the percentage of the public identifying online news as a major source of information about the campaign has not moved much in recent election cycles, many people are getting at least *some* news online. Digital sources were used by 65 percent of the electorate for at least some campaign news and nearly half used online resources like Facebook and Twitter for some campaign information (Owen 2017: 172).

Despite all that media consumption, a high level of public skepticism also marked the news environment of 2016. Donald Trump routinely attacked critical reports as "fake news" during the election season and beyond (Owen 2017). Trump banned the authors of critical news reports from his campaign events, and he refused their requests for interviews and documents, especially copies of his tax returns (Owen 2017).

Trump routinely returned fire on his critics, using campaign-style rallies and Twitter to attack mainstream media outlets as failing business entities and as purveyors of "fake news." Those attacks resonated with supporters who also had their doubts about the even-handedness of mainstream news reports, as shown in Table 5.1.

As Trump said of the *New York Times* during the final days of the campaign:

> They are so dishonest, folks. You can't even read articles in certain papers anymore. *New York Times* is a total lie. You can't, I mean you can't—it is so false. Nothing to do with me. I'm just telling you, such lies. Such lies, such fabrications, such made-up stories. Now the *Times* is going out of business pretty soon. That's the good news.
>
> (quoted in Owen 2017: 171)

As shown in Table 5.1, many citizens also had their doubts about reporters. About three-quarters of those surveyed believed the media

Table 5.1 News Sources and Trust in News, 2016

How did you get most of your news about the presidential election campaign? From television, from newspapers, from radio, or from the internet? [randomize options, accept up to two answers]

	2016	2012	2008
Television	57%	74%	68%
Newspapers	20%	23%	33%
Radio	25%	17%	16%
Internet	38%	36%	36%

In presenting the news dealing with political and social issues, do you think that news organizations (deal fairly with all sides) or (do they tend to favor one side)? [randomize options]

Percentage Saying Media Favor One Side

All	74%
Conservative Republicans	87%
Moderate/Liberal Republicans	77%
Conservative/Moderate Democrats	57%
Liberal Democrats	73%

Thinking about the news that your friends, family and acquaintances post or send you online about political and social issues, overall, do you think the mix of news you get from them represents (one side) or (represents more than one side)? [randomize options]*

Percentage Saying They Get News from One Side

All	35%
Conservative Republicans	39%
Moderate/Liberal Republicans	33%
Conservative/Moderate Democrats	29%
Liberal Democrats	44%

Would you prefer that the news your friends, family and acquaintances post or send you online about political and social issues has a greater mix of views from all sides, or do you think it's okay that overall it represents just one side?* §

Percentage Saying It is Okay to Get News from One Side

All	30%
Conservative Republicans	51%
Moderate/Liberal Republicans	27%
Conservative/Moderate Democrats	23%
Liberal Democrats	34%

Notes: Don't Know responses are not reported here, so percentages do not sum to 100.
* Questions asked only of web-using adults.
§ Asked if respondent said they get news from one side in previous question.

Source: Pew 2016a.

were more inclined to favor one side rather than report fairly. Conservative Republicans were most likely to doubt the media, followed by moderate and liberal Republicans.

When asked to assess the news they received from via email and social media posts by friends, family, and acquaintances, 35 percent said they thought those reports were only from one side, a sharp contrast from public evaluations of the news reports themselves. Conservative Republicans and liberal Democrats were most likely to believe they received news from only one side from their key personal contacts, but even in those groups the percentage saying they received one-sided news reports were less than half.

The final question of Table 5.1 demonstrates that many people like being in media cocoons that emphasize news consistent with their views. Among conservative Republicans who said they received one-sided news, 51 percent of those said that it was okay to get the news from just one side, as compared to 34 percent of liberal Democrats and under 30 percent of the two moderate partisan groups.

Traditional Media Focus on Trump, and Not Always in a Good Way

During the presidential primaries, research by news content analysis firm Media Tenor Inc. revealed that candidate Trump received a bumper crop of legacy media attention. More news coverage during the primary campaign focused on Trump than on key rivals Sen. Marco Rubio (R-FL), Sen. Ted Cruz (R-TX), and Gov. John Kasich (R-OH) every single week between Jan. 1 and June 7, 2016 (Patterson 2016a). Taking out the cases with roughly even positive and negative content, the tone of Trump's coverage during the nomination period was 49 percent positive and 51 percent negative, as good as or better than key Republican rivals (Patterson 2016a). During the period they were active candidates, Cruz's coverage was also 49 percent positive in tone. Reports on Rubio were 44 percent positive and on Kasich were 41 percent positive, according to the Media Tenor content analysis of news reports on CBS, CNN, NBC, Fox News, the *Los Angeles Times*, the *New York Times*, *USA Today*, the *Wall Street Journal*, and the *Washington Post* (Patterson 2016a).

These same media outlets were far more critical of Trump during the general election campaign, however. The Media Tenor analysis revealed that coverage of Trump was 23 percent positive during the fall campaign, as compared to 36 percent positive for Hillary Clinton, his Democratic rival (Patterson 2016b). These are exceptionally negative assessments for these nominees, far more critical than candidates in previous general election cycles (cf., Farnsworth and Lichter 2011a; 2016a). Media reports on Trump and Clinton were particularly harsh on character matters: both candidates received news reports that were 87 percent negative regarding their fitness for office, which includes content on candidates' policy positions, personal qualities, leadership abilities and ethical standards (Patterson 2016b).

Once he became president, Trump continued to face highly critical television news coverage. A Media Tenor research report of news stories on the new president's first month in office found that, excluding mixed evaluations, 6 percent of the reports about Trump that aired on the evening newscasts of NBC and CBS were positive, while 94 percent were negative (Farnsworth, Lichter and Schatz 2017). During his first 100 days in office, Trump's news coverage on the evening news reports were 20 percent positive in tone, far below the 59 percent positive tone Obama received during that same period eight years earlier. Trump's critical coverage was also worse than the 43 percent positive tone George W. Bush had received in early 2001 and the 40 percent positive tone Bill Clinton received in early 1993 (Patterson 2017; Farnsworth and Lichter 2006, 2011b). No doubt the highly controversial nature of some of Trump's initiatives pushed his numbers downward.

Fox News and Conservative Visions of News

As discussed above, Trump's campaign benefitted from mass media consumption patterns that enabled conservatives to use Fox News and online news outlets to receive largely congenial news reports of Republican causes and candidates. During Obama's presidency, Fox News expanded beyond its previous role as a right wing information source that connected and mobilized conservatives and became a national advocacy organization for channeling protest against Democrats (Jamieson and Cappella 2008; Williamson et al. 2011). In other words, Fox News viewers were primed to see a Republican candidate who echoed the fullthroated attacks on Democrats frequently seen on Fox programming, something Trump demonstrated repeatedly during his own very combative 2016 campaign (cf., Ceaser et al. 2017).

Even as technological change has widened the range of media options, many conservatives continued to find Fox News cable programming worth watching. A CBS/*New York Times* poll in April 2010 found that 63 percent of Tea Party supporters watched Fox News, as compared to 11 percent of all respondents. The big three networks received little attention from this group: only 11 percent of Tea Party supporters watch ABC, CBS, or NBC for news, as compared to more than a quarter of Americans overall (Williamson et al. 2011).

> It is not only in the quantity of Fox News coverage that we can see the media organization's role as an organizer of the community, because the *quality* of coverage the Tea Party has received on Fox is fundamentally different from the coverage on other major networks.

Fox News has explicitly mobilized its viewers by connecting the Tea Party to their own brand identity. In early 2009, Fox News dubbed the upcoming Tea Party events as "FNC [Fox News Channel] Tea Parties." Fox hosts Glenn Beck, Sean Hannity, Greta Van Susteren, and Neil Cavuto have broadcast their shows from Tea Party events.

(Williamson et al. 2011: 29–30, italics in original)

The impact of Fox News extends beyond its audience size as news reports there can affect the news agenda of other, more mainstream, media outlets that do not want to be accused of ignoring topics that get considerable attention on conservative media (Dreier and Martin 2010). Other conservative media outlets are often willing to follow the lead of Fox News, whose viewers may overlap with a significant part of their own audiences (Dreier and Martin 2010).

Even so, Trump's treatment on Fox News's *Special Report* during the 2016 presidential campaign was not particularly upbeat, though Fox was less critical than other comparable news programs. A Media Tenor analysis of Fox News coverage on that evening newscast between mid-August and Election Eve 2016 found that coverage of Trump was 27 percent positive, compared to 11 percent positive on CBS News and 17 percent positive on NBC News (Patterson 2016b). Trump's Fox News coverage was less critical than Fox's treatment of Clinton, who received only 19 percent positive coverage (Patterson 2016b). Indeed, the harsh treatment of Hillary Clinton on Fox News helped crystallize the very negative feelings many of that channel's viewers had for her, making them resistant to reports by other media and independent fact-checking organizations that revealed that Trump had major problems with accuracy and competence throughout the campaign (cf., Farnsworth and Lichter 2016b).

Fox News also was not all that kind to Trump during his first month in office, though it was less critical than the mainstream media outlets discussed above. A Media Tenor research report revealed that on *Special Report*, the Fox News program that most closely resembles the evening network news, 32 percent of the reports on Trump were positive and 68 percent were negative. In other words, even the conservative-leaning Fox News featured twice as much bad press as good press for the new president (Farnsworth, Lichter and Schatz 2017). During the first 100 days, the Fox News coverage became less critical, with 48 percent positive coverage of the new president on *Special Report* (Patterson 2016b). These studies of Fox News content excluded the commentary programs like those of Sean Hannity and Bill O'Reilly or *Fox & Friends*, which offered more opinion and likely more positive treatment of Trump than the network's evening news program (cf., Chang 2017).

Other conservative media outlets also looked out for Trump. In a February 2017 staff meeting, Gerry Baker, editor in chief of the *Wall Street*

Journal, owned by a company controlled by media mogul Rupert Murdoch, rejected concerns by some of the paper's reporters that the paper was not being tough enough on the new president (Lichter et al. 2017). The disagreement between some of the paper's reporters and its top editor came in the wake of a memo objecting to use of the term "majority Muslim nations" in the *Journal* when referring to the majority Muslim nations covered in the original Trump administration travel ban (Pompeo and Gold 2017).

> Concerns about the *Journal*'s Trump reporting have been simmering since at least the fall, when the paper garnered a reputation for access-driven campaign coverage that stood in contrast to aggressive investigations being pursued by competitors like the *New York Times* and the *Washington Post*.
>
> (Pompeo and Gold 2017)

Trump routinely found that conservative media had his back, sometimes in ways that undermined professional journalism. Consider another matter involving the *Wall Street Journal*, which scored a highly valuable interview with President Trump during July 2017. In an unusual move, the paper's editor in chief participated in the presidential interview, and in an even more unusual move the paper's top editors warned staffers not to let the transcript become public, perhaps concerned about the coziness apparent in the friendly banter between Baker and the president (Dawsey and Gold 2017). By keeping the transcript to itself, the paper kept other media outlets from citing the *Journal* in their own reporting on that highly newsworthy interview. The paper's effort to keep it private was futile, and *Politico* quickly acquired a leaked copy of the interview (Dawsey and Gold 2017).

Working with friendly media is a key Trump media strategy to minimize critical press commentary. During his first 48 briefings (which corresponded roughly to the first four months of the Trump administration), Press Secretary Sean Spicer's "top five go-to questioners were all from right-leaning outlets: Fox News, Fox News Radio, Newsmax, Fox News Business, and the One America News Network" (Savillo 2017). Spicer also allowed fewer follow-up questions, the part of the briefing when reporters try to pin down unclear or unresponsive responses, and reduced the length of the briefings when compared to those held during the Obama administration (Savillo 2017).

As he has in other areas of online discourse, Trump has gone further than his predecessors have when it came to his version of the White House website. As seen in Figure 5.1, this page contains a larger picture of the president than the other pages examined here, with any reference to policy issues placed lower on the page in order to have a photo splayed across the entire top of the web page. What's more, the Trump photo is

"Believe in yourselves. Believe in your future.
And believe, once more, in America."

- President Donald J. Trump

Sign Up to Receive Updates

Email Address*   Zip Code*   JOIN US

1600 Daily: Everything White House 10/30/2017

READ MORE

West Wing Reads for 10/27/17

Each day we round up the best stories the West Wing is reading and share them with you.

READ MORE

Figure 5.1 White House Website, Trump Presidency, 2017

one of presidential adoration: the image is of Trump addressing a joint session of Congress, with Vice President Pence and House Speaker Paul Ryan standing and applauding the new president. The Trump webpage places the president in an even larger and more central position than did the webpages of previous administrations, drawing as much attention as possible to the president as a person.

Below the opportunity to sign up for a presidential mailing list, the White House web page offers a chance for page visitors to read from *1600 Daily*, a collection of news items curated to show the president in as positive a light as possible (Gorman 2017). Those who dig still deeper into the White House website can find information about the president's policies.

The Rising Influence of Twitter

Twitter had been around for several election cycles but before the 2016 campaign its impact had been modest. Its potential, though, was clear, as the brevity of 140-character messages allows for wide and easy peer-to-peer dissemination of messages via hashtags, retweets, and the like (Gross and Johnson 2016). Twitter's users say that hearing directly from candidates allows citizens to get news faster and feel more personally connected to their favored candidates (Owen 2017).

Many people were ready to hear directly from Donald Trump. As of the election he had 16 million followers on Twitter, as compared to 11 million for Hillary Clinton (Owen 2017). Of course, Twitter's utility for a presidential campaign was much more than just the opportunity to connect with other users. This free, unlimited resource of information snippets was particularly useful for candidates hoping to spread their messages via journalists, as "tweets themselves have become news and thus essentially free advertising for the candidates" (Gross and Johnson 2016: 748). Indeed, the many high-quality investigative reports during the campaign provided by the *New York Times*, the *Washington Post,* and other news outlets received less attention than the breathless news reports about the latest Trump tweet or scandal (Owen 2017).

The campaign tweets among the candidates for the 2016 Republican nomination were notable for their harshness, with the eventual nominee dominating the field as the author of—and target of—the largest number of negative tweets (Gross and Johnson 2016). One general exception to the pattern of negativity is the hesitation of the Republican candidates to "punch down," that is, to attack via tweets rivals doing worse in the polls than the tweeter—but here, once again, Trump was an exception, directing brutal remarks at all rivals regardless of poll standings (Gross and Johnson 2016).

Trump also was effective in his topic selection for his tweets. He empha-sized morally charged content in three different issue areas highly salient to conservatives: gay marriage, gun control, and climate change (Van Bavel and Brady 2017). Trump's effective use of moral and emotional orientations in his tweets on these subjects led to extensive re-tweeting, far more than Clinton's tweets on these topics (Van Bavel and Brady 2017).

The Rise of Disinformation on Social Media

When Barack Obama ran for president in 2008, and during his years in office, ever more influential social media networks spread the false rumor that Obama was not born in this country and therefore not eligible to be president (Chadwick 2013). With the expansion of social media's reach and visibility over the years of the Obama presidency, America's voters faced a growing challenge when it came to obtaining accurate information in a media environment populated by entrepreneurs promoting fake news for profit and Russian-backed hackers releasing misleading or false information on Hillary Clinton (Fisher et al. 2016).

A study of online news content published in the *Columbia Journalism Review* found that the conservative website Breitbart was at the center of a network of false information making its way across the web, a conservative disinformation campaign that had no comparable effort on the Democratic side (Benkler et al. 2017).

> Our own study of over 1.25 million stories published online between April 1, 2015 and Election Day shows that a right-wing media network anchored around Breitbart developed as a distinct and insulated media system, using social media as a backbone to transmit a hyper-partisan perspective to the world. This pro-Trump media sphere appears to have not only successfully set the agenda for the conservative media sphere, but also strongly influenced the broader media agenda, in particular coverage of Hillary Clinton.
>
> While concerns about political and media polarization online are longstanding, our study suggests that polarization was asymmetric. Pro-Clinton audiences were highly attentive to traditional media outlets, which continued to be the most prominent outlets across the public sphere, alongside more left-oriented online sites. But pro-Trump audiences paid the majority of their attention to polarized outlets that have developed recently, many of them only since the 2008 election season.
>
> (Benkler et al. 2017)

During the 2016 election Facebook, which has more than a billion daily users, became a powerful vehicle for spreading disinformation.

> During the U.S. election, propagandists—some working for money, others for potentially state-sponsored lulz—used the service to turn

fake stories into viral sensations, like the one about Pope Francis endorsing Trump (he hadn't). And fake news was only part of a larger conundrum. With its huge reach, Facebook has begun to act as the great disseminator of the larger cloud of misinformation and half-truths swirling about the rest of media. It sucks up lies from cable news and Twitter, then precisely targets each lie to the partisan bubble most receptive to it.

(Manjoo 2017)

For an extreme example of how false news permeates the online world, consider the case of Pizzagate, which started with a false report that the basement of a pizza parlor in a leafy upper-income neighborhood of Washington, D.C., housed a pedophilia ring involving Hillary Clinton (Fisher et al. 2016). The absurd claim was retweeted thousands of times day after day and recirculated, often anonymously, on online platforms Reddit, 4chan and Instagram, as well as through InfoWars. Employees of the pizza restaurant and those working at other businesses on the same block of Connecticut Avenue NW began receiving threatening calls and disturbing emails. Eventually a gun-toting man from North Carolina waged a one-man assault on the restaurant, only to discover that there was no pedophilia ring, and not even a basement (Fisher et al. 2016).

In response to criticisms that it had not done enough to stem the tide of false news making its way across social media, after the 2016 election Facebook instituted new programs to link fact-checking and other sources of information to posted material, and to engage more effectively with third-party fact-checkers to challenge misleading or false claims (Su 2017). By late 2017, Facebook said it would flag as many questionable claims as possible with a warning. This improved accountability mechanism, of course, came too late to affect the 2016 election. Fake news companies that rely upon large numbers of clicks to generate revenue may be looking at a minor reduction in income in the wake of this effort. They will likely continue to thrive on social media because many people continue to click on information that they would like to believe is true (Sandler 2017; Silverman et al. 2017). Twitter is likewise trying to cut down on the trolling and false information found in its service, in part by banning problematic users from the site (Streitfeld 2017).

Nastiness is another problem exacerbated by social media. An analysis of political information posted on Reddit, another popular online site, offers another example of social media's further coarsening of political discourse. The study of 39 million political comments on Reddit from January 2015 to January 2017 found that an increasing number of offensive posts that focused on political content appeared leading up to the 2016 election, a trend not seen in nonpolitical posts from the same period (Nithyanand et al. 2017). Those offensive posts, defined as those that used profanity, engaged in name calling, or compared someone to Hitler or a pedophile, were also more popular on the site (as measured by up-votes minus down-votes by those reacting to the posts) than comments that were not deemed offensive (Nithyanand et al. 2017). As the parent of any toddler soon learns, rewarded behavior is repeated behavior, and so the forwarding of nasty comments online should lead to even more such commentary on social media.

Getting to Know Donald Trump

Trump was a celebrity long before he became a presidential candidate. Before the 2016 campaign, Trump had been known for his branded casi-nos and hotels, for his best-selling book *The Art of the Deal*, and as the host of the reality television shows *The Apprentice* and *The Celeb-rity Apprentice*, where he would utter his famous tagline "you're fired" (Ceaser et al. 2017). Trump had been married three times and lived a lavish lifestyle that for decades drew the attention of the New York tabloids. His background made him an odd choice to be the voice of religious conservatives and angry working-class populists (Ceaser et al 2017). "Trump was the people's billionaire, offering unashamedly what the average American wanted, a Trump steak or a night at a casino, or showing the kind of luxury people could only yearn for" (Ceaser et al. 2017: ix).

Long before he became a candidate, Trump was prone to exaggera-tion, as he admitted in *The Art of the Deal*: "I play to people's fantasies. I call it truthful hyperbole. It's an innocent form of exaggeration—and a very effective form of promotion" (quoted in Swanson 2016). Trump took risks, and he endured several bankruptcies of his businesses over the years, making him less of a financial success story than he appeared to be on TV (Swanson 2016).

In terms of politics, Trump in the years before 2016 had given money to Democrats and to Republicans, and changed his party registration back and forth (Ceaser et al. 2017). Trump considered running for office off and on over the years, and renewed his interest in politics during the Obama presidency, when he became a spokesperson for the "Birther" movement, which alleged that Obama was not born in this country and therefore ineligible to be president (Williamson et al. 2011).

From the start, voters had their doubts about Trump. As shown in Table 5.2, Clinton bested Trump in many public evaluations. In a Sep-tember 2016 survey, Trump had a 40-point deficit on the question of whether he had the experience to be president and double-digit deficits on the question of whether he would display good judgment in a cri-sis, could manage the government effectively and was likeable. Survey respondents split roughly evenly on which candidate would be better at getting things done, which one was stronger, and which one was more honest and trustworthy. The only double-digit advantage Trump had

Table 5.2 Comparing the Character of the Presidential Candidates, September 2016

Thinking about the following characteristics and qualities, please say whether you think each applies or doesn't apply to Hillary Clinton/Donald Trump. How about ___?

	Applies to Clinton	Applies to Trump	Difference (Clinton—Trump)
Has the experience it takes to be president	69%	29%	+40
Would display good judgment in a crisis	54%	39%	+15
Can manage the government effectively	54%	41%	+13
Is likable	50%	38%	+12
Cares about the needs of people like you	48%	40%	+8
Can get things done	60%	56%	+4
Can bring about the changes country needs	41%	41%	—
Is a strong and decisive leader	56%	57%	−1
Is honest and trustworthy	33%	35%	−2
Stands up to special interest groups	46%	52%	−6
Is healthy enough to be president	60%	77%	−17

Source: Newport 2016.

here was on being healthy enough to be president. These numbers speak to the uphill nature of the Trump campaign during the fall of 2016.

The Pitch

Trump's main argument was that the nation needed to reverse course and he was the only person who could "Make America Great Again," in the words of a key Trump campaign slogan. He vowed that his business experience would lead to a presidency that would "drain the swamp" of corruption in Washington and make government work more effectively on behalf of American workers who Trump said had lost out in international trade agreements (Ceaser et al. 2017).

Simply put, Trump presented himself to voters as a highly combative populist tribune. In the presidential nomination debates, Trump very effectively demonstrated he was willing to go where many Republican candidates were not: divisive attacks on immigrants for allegedly taking jobs away from American workers (Cohen et al. 2016). Since Trump had little support among party elites or regular donors, some of whom might rely on immigrant labor or offshore production in their businesses,

Trump could say what he wanted with little loss of GOP establishment support. In fact, Trump's distance from party elites allowed him to decry the blue-chip connections of his GOP rivals and wear his outsider temperament as a badge of honor (Cohen et al. 2016). The anger was not his alone: Trump's campaign benefitted from increasing citizen fears of violence, bolstered by terrorist incidents in Paris and San Bernardino, California (MacWilliams 2016).

Trump's aggressive character generated extreme loyalty from some. From the start, Trump's combative campaign was tailor-made to appeal to angry voters, people who felt left behind in a rapidly changing economy and in a rapidly diversifying nation. Political science scholars said Trump particularly appealed to voters with authoritarian tendencies, generally defined as people who perceive the world in black and white terms, who seek a leader to restore order, who fear diversity and who sometimes act aggressively to those they consider outsiders (Adorno et al. 1950; Fromm 1941; Hetherington and Weiler 2009; MacWilliams 2016). Multivariate analysis of likely 2016 Republican primary voters revealed that an individual's authoritarian orientations and fear of a personal threat from terrorism were two statistically significant variables that predicted whether one supported Trump rather than another Republican candidate (MacWilliams 2016).

> Throughout his campaign, Trump constantly used us-versus-them language to define the others who allegedly pose a threat to us and order. From Mexicans to Muslims, the others, as described by Trump, do not hold our values and are not like us. To Trump and the crowds who follow his lead, he alone recognizes the threat the others pose and he alones possesses the will to neutralize them. . . . Trump's messaging and strongman manner was a practical application of authoritarian theory to real politics—a clear, clarion call to American authoritarians that drove them to support his candidacy.
>
> (MacWilliams 2016: 717)

As he reflected on the large, emotional crowds standing before him at campaign rallies, Trump came to think his popularity was bulletproof. As Trump said in January 2016: "I could stand in the middle of Fifth Avenue and shoot somebody. And I wouldn't lose any voters. OK. It's like incredible" (quoted in MacWilliams 2016: 720). Trump believed his supporters were very loyal and they were. Trump got into political troubles repeatedly and yet survived those many scandals (Sabato 2017).

The Problem

From the start, candidate Donald Trump presented himself as a highly combative person. That was a double-edged sword, as was the intense loyalty of his supporters. Some Republicans, for example, were troubled by his harsh rebuke of immigrants, as many in the party leadership had hoped to win over a greater percentage Latino voters in 2016 (Barbour et al. 2013). Trump was not going to be much help, as he demonstrated in his campaign announcement:

> When Mexico sends its people, they are not sending their best. . . . They're sending people that have lots of problems, and they're bringing those problems with them. They're bringing drugs. They're bringing crime. They're rapists. And some, I assume, are good people.
>
> (quoted in Ceaser et al. 2017: 72)

Trump did not spare other Republicans from his wrath. Early in the campaign, Trump savaged Sen. John McCain (R-AZ), the party's 2008 nominee for president, and a prisoner of war during the Vietnam years. Trump said: "I like people who weren't captured" (quoted in Ceaser et al. 2017: 72). Trump's attacks on McCain seemed particularly risky politically, given McCain's heroic status as a former POW, and Trump's very different status, having received several military deferments and never serving in the Armed Forces because of a high draft number (Barbaro 2015). As the nomination campaign progressed, Trump's anger fanned out in all directions: he developed twitter-length insults of his rivals, including "Lyin' Ted" Cruz, "Low Energy Jeb" Bush, "Little Marco" Rubio, and eventually, "Crooked Hillary" Clinton (Ceaser et al. 2017: 102). These personal attacks highlighted his anger and sent a simple message to his followers: ignore policy differences and focus on Trump's personal toughness (cf., Ceaser et al. 2017).

Trump insults targeted more than just other political candidates and elected officials. He attacked Megyn Kelly, then of Fox News, "blaming her menstrual period for tough questions" during one debate (Ceaser et al. 2017: 72). On camera, Trump mocked a disabled *New York Times* reporter by imitating his spastic movements (Ceaser et al. 2017). Trump also attacked a Muslim-American family who had lost a son fighting for the U.S. military (Ceaser et al. 2017).

Taken together, Trump's harsh insults were un-presidential, at least as one would define the term before 2016, and his rhetoric gave many citizens pause (Pew 2016b). They were a sharp contrast with previous presidential elections, where candidates spent much of their time making a positive, upbeat case for why they should be president (cf., Ceaser and Busch 1993, 2001; Ceaser et al. 2009, 2015). Sometimes, Trump even advocated violence at his campaign rallies, encouraging supporters to attack and manhandle hecklers (Parker 2016). As president, he sometimes continued to offer endorsements of violence, at one point encouraging police officers not to be concerned about using excessive force against criminal suspects (Berman 2017a). In response to that unprecedented presidential encouragement of law enforcement lawlessness, many prominent police chiefs objected; several days later Trump's spokeswoman rather implausibly claimed the president had been joking (Berman 2017b).

Six months into Trump's term, senators were already talking among themselves about whether Trump was mentally ill. "I think he is crazy," Sen. Jack Reed (D-RI) told Sen. Susan Collins (R-ME) on July 25, 2017, who replied "I am worried" in an exchange inadvertently captured on a live microphone (Osnos 2017). When an audio recording of the exchange became public, Collins said that her statement referred to upcoming budgetary deadlines, not to Trump's alleged mental illness. For his part, Reed offered no apologies: "The Trump Administration is behaving erratically and irresponsibly" (quoted in Osnos 2017).

Many mental health professionals have hesitated to offer professional assessments of the president, raising concerns that one should not diagnose a person one has not treated—or even met. That concern stems from the so-called Goldwater Rule, where the 1964 presidential candidate successfully sued for libel after psychologists questioned his mental fitness for office (Mayer 2017). But Trump's extremely unusual actions—his belittling of some of his most loyal subordinates, such as Attorney General Sessions; his frequent expressions of obviously false claims, like the claim that he won the popular vote—have renewed concerns from some mental health professionals that they should be speaking out about a president whose character troubles them deeply (Mayer 2017).

Debate over the president's mental fitness intensified in January 2018, as Trump attacked a book critical of him: *Fire and Fury: Inside the Trump White House*, which reported that White House staff regularly doubted the president's competency and fitness for office. Trump elevated the book to best-seller status as he vigorously defended his mental fitness for office, calling himself a "very stable genius" (Baker and Haberman 2018). Trump's legal team tried through threats of legal action to block publication of the book, and the publisher rushed the text into bookstores ahead of schedule in response. The book, by Michael Wolff, emerged days after Trump boasted on Twitter that his "nuclear button was bigger" than that of North Korea leader Kim Jong-un (Baker and Haberman 2018).

Debates over Trump's unconventional personal demeanor as a candidate and a president made him a valuable subject of personal ridicule to the late night comedians. The New York developer turned presidential candidate was the subject of 1,817 jokes between Jan. 1, 2016 and Nov. 11, 2016—more than triple the 506 jokes directed at Hillary Clinton during that same period (Farnsworth, Lichter and Canieso 2017). Many of those jokes focused on his alleged character flaws and his general unfitness for office (Farnsworth, Lichter and Canieso 2017). Going back to the 1992 contest, the Center for Media and Public Affairs at George

Mason University found that the late night comedians never focused on a presidential candidate the way they focused on Trump (Farnsworth, Lichter and Canieso 2017).

Applying Character Models to Donald Trump

Throughout his career in business and his new career in politics, Trump has invested a great deal in getting even with those who he believed had offended him, even when it might hurt his own interests in the end (Isenstadt 2017). Trump's pattern of concentrating on short-term, emotional responses and not considering long-term costs resembles the short-sightedness of Richard Nixon, the quintessential active-negative president (Barber 1992). It also demonstrates an unusually high level of conflict, a key component of the George and George (1998) model of for analyzing presidential behavior.

> Trump's obsession with loyalty and his penchant for keeping close track of personal slights—both well-documented by his biographers and in coverage of his presidency—color his approach not only toward his political foes but toward his own party's candidates, even at the risk of jeopardizing GOP incumbents.
>
> (Isenstadt 2017)

Trump's desire to keep re-litigating the 2016 presidential election throughout 2017 also suggests an active-negative temperament. The intense focus on domination, even when it concerns defeated rivals, speaks to a dimension of relatedness, his combative way of dealing with others, a key component of the Renshon (1998) model of presidential behavior. These qualities suggest a somewhat insecure president who will place a premium on loyalty and surround himself with people who are clearly subordinate and therefore unlikely to challenge him (George and George 1998).

In his *Wall Street Journal* interview in July 2017 Trump repeatedly turned back to issues relating to the election, focusing on Hillary Clinton's email scandal, his advantage in the Electoral College, and how the Russia investigation was a fraud created to explain Clinton's defeat (Dawsey and Gold 2017). In addition, the public rage of Trump on Twitter is not unlike the private rage of Lyndon Johnson, another active-negative president, who felt surrounded by enemies in the media and in the nation (cf., Barber 1992; Goodwin 1991).

Another issue that points in the direction of Trump's counterproductive personality traits as identified by the model offered by George and George (1998) is his narcissism, which was on display in a leaked January 2017 conversation with the Mexican president where Trump discussed his campaign vow that Mexico would pay for a border wall (Miller 2017). While we discuss it further below, what is interesting about the conversation from the perspective of both the Barber and Renshon models is the extent to which difficulties in U.S.-Mexico relations were viewed by Trump primarily as PR problems for himself.

As Jennifer Rubin, a conservative, albeit anti-Trump, columnist for the *Washington Post*, observed:

> Trump is frighteningly obsessed with himself and his image to such an extent that he cannot fulfill the role of commander in chief. He cannot frame logical arguments based on public policy, and therefore comes across as, well, a fool to foreign leaders. His desire to maintain his own image suggests he'd be more than willing to make the country's interests subordinate to his own need for personal affirmations. Dealing with foreign allies is bad enough, but one can only imagine what he has said to adversaries. This, in turn, raises a third critical issue: Trump's narcissism leaves him open to flattery and threats—to reveal embarrassing material, for example.
>
> (Rubin 2017b)

In a relatively uncommon moment of self-reflection, Trump said of himself: "When I look at myself in the first grade and I look at myself now, I'm basically the same. The temperament is not that different" (quoted in Barbaro 2015). That lack of personal flexibility with respect to circumstances in the external world is a quality of relatedness, which influences how presidents interact (or not) with others in ways that affect their abilities to respond to their external environment, a key component of presidential success or failure (George and George 1964).

News Management and Character Challenges

Trump often chooses a combative approach with mainstream media outlets, including CNN and the *New York Times*, calling reporters "the enemy of the American people" a month after taking office (Grynbaum 2017). Carl Bernstein, one of the reporters who broke the Watergate story that brought down Richard Nixon, said Trump's rhetoric "may be more insidious and dangerous than Richard Nixon's attacks on the press. But there is a similarity in trying to divide the country, and make the conduct of the press the issue, instead of the conduct of the president" (quoted in Grynbaum 2017).

Research into how the public reacts to news relating to immigration, which would later become a key Trump campaign issue, has shown that "polarization decreases the impact of substantive information and, perhaps ironically, stimulates greater confidence in those—less substantively grounded—opinions" of political parties (Druckman et al. 2013: 57). The research found a twofold impact, with more extreme issue positions among partisans and higher salience for immigration (Druckman et al. 2013).

Trump's victory had much to do with the so-called culture war that Republicans used in recent election cycles to pull some voters away from their traditional loyalties to the Democratic Party (Frank 2004). Race-based appeals to white voters have been a key part of that strategy (Anderson 2017). A recent examination of data from four panel studies conducted between 1992 and 2012 reveal that cultural attitudes, particularly views relating to abortion and gay rights, can explain fundamental belief systems in ways comparable to partisanship and religious affiliation (Goren and Chapp 2017). Abortion and gay rights appear to have particular influence in public opinion because of the central role they play in family organization and human sexuality (Jelen 2009). For many individuals, those matters are also key issues in the establishment and maintenance of religious beliefs and behavioral orientations through childhood and beyond (Sears 2001). Further, abortion and gay rights can trigger deeply ingrained gut reflexes and moral judgments, making them durable components of one's political orientation (Hibbing et al. 2014a, 2014b).

Public Opinion

As shown in Table 5.3, the early months of Donald Trump's presidency generated relatively low public opinion numbers (Jones 2017; Swift 2017). Gallup polls reveal a president who took office with roughly half the nation opposed. The 45 percent approval rating he received during his Inauguration weekend looks good when compared to tracking polls conducted for each of the first six months in office. In recent months, Gallup and other surveys have shown Trump's approval near or below 40 percent, a very low number from which to try to secure legislative victories on Capitol Hill, particularly for a controversial measure like repealing and replacing the Affordable Care Act.

Table 5.3 Trump Presidential Approval, 2017

Do you approve or disapprove of the way Donald Trump is handling his job as president?

	Approve	Disapprove
July 21, 2017	38%	57%
June 21, 2017	39%	56%
May 21, 2017	37%	56%
April 21, 2017	42%	52%
March 21, 2017	40%	55%
February 21, 2017	42%	52%
January 22, 2017	45%	45%

Source: Jones 2017.

Six months into his presidency, Donald Trump had the worst net approval rating of any modern president. As shown in Table 5.4, only two of the past thirteen presidents have had a net negative evaluation after six months in office: Gerald Ford, who generated a furor when he pardoned Richard Nixon (cf., Woodward 1999), had a minus 6 rating, and Donald Trump, with a minus 16 rating. Harry Truman had the highest score half a year into his presidency, with a net approval rating of 84 shortly after the end of World War II.

Trump's results are striking: the average for Trump's twelve most recent predecessors was a net approval score of 38. Recent presidents generally have fared worse in this comparison than earlier ones, but even so, their ratings—Obama and Bush each at 19 and Clinton at zero—were far better than Trump's.

Growing citizen partisanship helps explain this downward trend. Over the past several presidencies, fewer citizens are willing to support a president of the opposite party. As shown in Table 5.5, only 8 percent of Democrats supported Trump in an average of polls across his second quarter in office. Trump had the support of 85 percent of Republicans, a 77-point partisan gap. Eight years earlier, Obama had the support of 91 percent of Democrats and 26 percent of Republicans, a 65-point partisan gap. In 2001, Bush's partisan gap was smaller still, a 61-point gap. Eight years earlier, in 1993, Clinton had a 50-point partisan gap.

Trump's character is part of the explanation for his negative standings in these comparisons as well. Trump intensifies the partisanship as he appeals to his base by such things as insisting that Hillary Clinton should be in jail (Ceaser et al. 2017) and that Republicans should ignore

Table 5.4 Presidential Public Approval at Six Months

President	Year	Approve	Disapprove	Net Approval
1. Harry Truman	1945	87%	3%	+84
2. Lyndon Johnson	1964	75%	10%	+65
3. John Kennedy	1961	72%	14%	+58
4. Dwight Eisenhower	1953	69%	15%	+54
5. George H. W. Bush	1989	67%	18%	+49
6. Richard Nixon	1969	63%	16%	+47
7. Jimmy Carter	1977	62%	22%	+40
8. Ronald Reagan	1981	58%	30%	+28
9. George W. Bush	2001	52%	33%	+19
10. Barack Obama	2009	56%	37%	+19
11. Bill Clinton	1993	46%	46%	—
12. Gerald Ford	1975	35%	41%	–6
13. Donald Trump	2017	39%	55%	–16
Average without Trump		62%	24%	+38

Note: Results are poll aggregations.

Source: Enten 2017.

Table 5.5 Trump Presidential Approval, 2017

Average approval rating by political party for elected presidents during second quarter in office

	Approval	Approval	Party gap*
	Democrats	Republicans	
Donald Trump	8%	85%	77
Barack Obama	91%	26%	65
George W. Bush	29%	90%	61
Bill Clinton	71%	21%	50
Ronald Reagan	44%	87%	43
George H. W. Bush	48%	84%	36
Richard Nixon	50%	82%	32
John Kennedy	87%	57%	30
Dwight Eisenhower	60%	88%	28
Jimmy Carter	73%	48%	25

Note: Party gap is calculated by subtracting the presidential approval rate among those who identify with the opposing party from those who identify with the president's party.

Source: Jones 2017.

Democrats when they work on health care bills (cf., Sullivan et al. 2017). As president, he continued to focus on Clinton's emails. He also angered both liberals and conservatives when he said that all sides were to blame for violence at a neo-Nazi, white nationalist rally in Charlottesville, Virginia, in August 2017 (Clement and Nakamura 2017).

The highly critical revelations regarding Trump contained in *Fire and Fury* reflected public impressions of the forty-fifth president as his first year in office drew to a close. A national survey conducted by Quinnipiac University in the days after Trump's January 2018 declaration that he was a "very stable genius" found that only 27 percent of Americans considered Trump both "smart" and "level-headed" (Bump 2018). Just under half of those surveyed (43 percent), said neither of those terms applied to Trump (Bump 2018). In addition, 57 percent of those surveyed considered him not fit to serve as president (Bump 2018).

Is Trump Reckless?

Many conservatives have had their doubts about Trump as a candidate and as president, wondering whether he was a true conservative or simply an opportunist using the movement for his own advancement. Could Trump, who was once a Democrat, be a reliable Republican partner?

Sara Fagen, a White House political director under President George W. Bush, said in July 2017 that the chaos of the president's administration relates to Trump's character, not to actions by White House staff.

Everybody knows what needs to be done to fix it, and I think everybody is coming to accept that they're not going to happen. And the reason they're not going to happen is the person at the top of the food chain is not going to change. This is the new normal. This goes down as one of the worst weeks he's had politically and P.R.-wise, but I don't think anything will change.

(quoted in Baker 2017)

Trump frequently belittled his first chief of staff before colleagues, repeatedly drawing attention to Reince Priebus's request in October 2016 that Trump drop out of the presidential campaign after a lewd audiotape emerged where Trump's bragged to an *Access Hollywood* host that he could grab a woman's crotch with impunity because of his celebrity status. Priebus, who left his job as head of the RNC to become White House chief of staff, endured the frequent presidential hazing in silence (Baker and Haberman 2017).

In July 2017, Gallup conducted a survey that asked in more detail than most why one supported or opposed the president. In this survey, 38 percent of those surveyed said they approved of Trump's presidency, while 56 disapproved. As shown in Table 5.6, 65 percent of those who disapproved of Trump's presidency said it was mainly because of his personal characteristics. Only 16 percent of those disapproving of Trump mentioned issues or policy.

When one compares these responses to the results in similar surveys conducted during the first year of the Obama and Bush presidencies it becomes clear how much Trump's character shapes his public evaluations. For Obama and for George W. Bush, fewer people expressed disapproval at comparable points in their presidencies—36 percent and 34 percent respectively. While nearly two-thirds of those objecting to Trump listed character matters, only 14 percent surveyed in 2009 mentioned Obama's character and only 17 percent surveyed in 2001 mentioned character issues involving Bush.

Of the Trump objectors who focused on matters of character, nearly half of them described the new president as not presidential, of having a bad temperament or being arrogant or obnoxious. A somewhat smaller group said that Trump did not know what he was doing, and a still smaller group said Trump was looking out mainly for himself or they objected to Trump's heavy use of Twitter.

Those who objected to Trump for policy reasons focused on a range of issues, including foreign affairs, health care and policies that favor the rich. For those who expressed negative broad performance evaluations, most said Trump was doing a poor job.

Table 5.7 considers why people who approve of Trump's performance do so. A plurality (38 percent) mentioned general performance matters, saying that the new president was doing the best he could under difficult

Table 5.6 Character Concerns and Trump Presidential Disapproval, July 2017

Responses are based on those surveyed who said they disapproved of the way the president is handling his job. For Trump, 56 percent disapproved. . .

Why do you disapprove of the way [Trump/Obama/Bush] is handling his job as president? (Broad categories)

	Trump 2017	Obama 2009	Bush 2001
Broad performance evaluations	12%	15%	43%
Issues/Specific policies	16%	65%	31%
Personality/Personal characteristics	65%	14%	17%

Why do you disapprove of the way Trump is handling his job as president? (Detailed Categories, Percentage mentioning)

Character/Personality-related (net)	65%
Not presidential/Bad temperament/Arrogant/Obnoxious	29%
Inexperienced/Doesn't know what he is doing	10%
Looking out for himself/Doesn't consider people's needs	6%
Use of social media/Twitter	6%
Untrustworthy	6%
Racist/Sexist	3%
Not knowledgeable	3%
Wishy-washy	2%
Issue/Policy-related (net)	16%
Disagree with his policies (nonspecific)	4%
Disapprove of his handling of foreign affairs	4%
Disapprove of his healthcare policies	3%
Favors the rich	2%
Needs to unify the country	1%
Disapprove of his environmental policies	1%
Disapprove of his handling of the economy	1%
Broad performance evaluations (net)	12%
Disagree with what he is doing/Doing a poor job	7%
Not fulfilling his campaign promises/All talk and no action	3%
Trying to do too much	1%
Doesn't have qualified advisers/staff	1%

Note: Not all response options are listed here.

Source: Newport 2017.

circumstances, that he was keeping his promises or and that he was looking out for America's best interests. One third of those who approved of Trump mentioned specific issue and policy concerns, particularly that he was bringing jobs back to the nation and that he was working on doing a better job with the economy, immigration, or terrorism.

In sharp contrast from those who disapproved of Trump, supporters of the president rarely mentioned character to explain why they approved of his job performance. Only 24 percent of those who thought Trump

Table 5.7 Performance Evaluations Enhance Trump Presidential Approval, July 2017

Responses are from those who said they approved of the way the president is handling his job. For Trump 38 percent approved.

Why do you approve of the way [Trump/Obama/Bush] is handling his job as president? (Broad Categories)

	Trump 2017	Obama 2009	Bush 2001
Broad performance evaluations	38%	41%	50%
Issues/Specific policies	33%	40%	9%
Personality/Personal characteristics	24%	15%	24%

Why do you approve of the way Trump is handling his job as president? (Detailed Categories)

Broad performance evaluations (net)	38%
Doing a good job/best he can under difficult circumstances	12%
Keeping his promises	11%
Does what is best for America	10%
Better than Obama	4%
Willing to give him a chance	1%
Issue/Policy-related (net)	33%
Creating job opportunities/Bringing jobs back to America	6%
Agree with his policies/actions (nonspecific)	5%
Active/Taking on many issues	5%
Economy is getting better/Fixing the economy	5%
Handling of immigration/terrorism	4%
Trying new, different things/Changing things	4%
Foreign policy	2%
Conservative	2%
Character/Personality-related (net)	24%
Doesn't back down/Shows strong leadership	9%
Not part of the Washington establishment/Not a politician	7%
Transparent/Straightforward with the people	3%
Honest/Has integrity	3%
Intelligent/Smart	1%
Like his handling of the media	1%

Note: Not all response options are listed here.

Source: Newport 2017.

was doing a good job mentioned character issues, and the top two issues for those supporters was his strong, uncompromising leadership and the fact that he was not part of the Washington establishment.

Is the Trump Administration Dishonest?

Questions of the Trump administration's honesty emerged anew during the hours after the Inauguration, when Trump bragged that the crowd for his Inauguration was bigger than Obama's ceremony eight years earlier. Both the president and Sean Spicer, Trump's press secretary, falsely claimed that Obama's crowds were smaller. Photographic evidence demonstrated that Obama's crowds were much larger and the crowd for the Women's March in Washington the next day to protest Trump's inauguration was about three times larger than Trump's crowd (Wallace and Parlapiano 2017).

Of course controversies over crowd sizes are one thing, while questions over possible Russian collusion with the Trump team during the election and during the final weeks of the Obama presidency are quite another. Early on, the Trump administration struggled with whether National Security Advisor–designate Michael Flynn had discussed sanctions policy with Russian government representatives. Shortly before Inauguration Day, Vice President-elect Pence said those meetings did not discuss sanctions (Blake 2017a). Flynn left office a few weeks later, when it became clear that the former general had indeed discussed sanctions with the Russians despite Flynn's own reports to Pence and to others in the administration (Blake 2017a). In December 2017, Flynn plead guilty to lying to the FBI about his contacts with the Russians. He promised to cooperate with the Justice Department investigation into possible Russian collaboration with the Trump campaign and the Trump White House (Leonnig et al. 2017).

Other key officials also faced credibility problems. In May, H.R. McMaster, a subsequent National Security Adviser, denied media reports that Trump had discussed classified information with the Russian Foreign Minister during an Oval Office meeting. A day later McMaster said Trump acted appropriately when he released classified information to the Russians, because the president has the final say on whether to declassify national security information (Blake 2017a).

These comments by Spicer, Flynn, McMaster and others are not merely misstatements made by people at the highest levels of the Trump administration. The president himself consistently fails to remember—or chooses not to repeat—the truth. He had received an exceptionally large number of red flags over his fact-challenged comments from independent fact-checkers. During his first six months in office, the *Washington Post* "fact checker" found Trump made 836 false or misleading comments, an unprecedented level of roughly 4.6 a day (Kessler et al. 2017).

The Trump White House pattern of telling the truth after the deceits become unsustainable has touched a variety of issues. When President Trump fired FBI Director James Comey in May 2017, administration officials insisted the dismissal had nothing to do with Comey's investigation of possible contacts between Russian officials and the Trump campaign. Trump's Justice Department originally claimed that the president dismissed Comey because of the way he communicated with the press over the Hillary Clinton email investigation a year earlier. But that incredible story fell apart when Trump said on NBC News shortly afterwards: "And in fact, when I decided to just do it, I said to myself—I said, you know, this Russia thing with Trump and Russia is a made-up story" (quoted in Blake 2017a).

During that same interview, Trump also demolished his own administration's previous claim that the president was just following a Justice Department recommendation to fire Comey, as Press Secretary Sean Spicer originally stated (Blake 2017a). After Spicer's statement, Trump said that the recommendation was not decisive: "I was going to fire Comey . . . Oh, I was going to fire regardless of recommendation" (quoted in Blake 2017a).

When Donald Trump Jr. put out a misleading statement relating to a meeting with Russian intermediaries before his father's election, Jay Sekulow, one of the president's top lawyers, said that the president had nothing to do with drafting the statement. That claim subsequently was contradicted by President Trump's own tweets and by a statement by Sarah Huckabee Sanders, who replaced Spicer as Trump's press secretary, who said that Trump was involved "as any father would" be (Blake 2017a).

Trump repeatedly promised during the presidential campaign that if he became president he would build a wall along the U.S.-Mexico border— and that Mexico would pay for it (Blake 2017b). In fact he abandoned that vow, privately at least, within days of becoming president (Miller 2017). A leaked White House transcript of a January 27, 2017 call between Trump and President Enrique Peña Nieto of Mexico revealed that Trump had already abandoned his frequently stated claim that Mexico would pay for the wall. In that call, he was instead focusing on the public relations aspect of Mexico's public refusal to pay for the barrier (Miller 2017). In the call, Trump described the wall as "the least important thing we are talking about, but politically this might be the most important" (quoted in Miller 2017).

These remarks with the Mexican leader were very different from what Trump was telling Americans even several months later about who would pay for the wall.

> The [January 27] exchange suggests that even at the outset of his presidency, Trump regarded the prospect of extracting money from Mexico as problematic but sought to avoid acknowledging that reality publicly. Trump reiterated that vow as recently as [July], when he said during a summit of foreign leaders in Germany that he "absolutely" remained committed to forcing Mexico to pay for the wall.
>
> (Miller 2017)

In addition to the factual errors, Trump demonstrated a high level of hypocrisy, even when compared to other politicians. Trump's early political activities included serving as one of the leading voices of the "Birther" movement, arguing that Obama was not born in the United States

(Abramowitz 2017). In addition, Trump repeatedly called during the 2016 presidential election for greater public disclosure from Hillary Clinton, insisting she release more emails from her personal email accounts (Owen 2017). Trump did not believe in transparency for himself, however: as a presidential candidate and as president, Trump repeatedly refused to release his tax returns, a departure from previous presidents and presidential candidates of both parties (Owen 2017). The *New York Times* published a story related to a few pages of Trump's return from the 1990s that revealed that he paid no taxes for several years; Trump said he was being "smart" for not paying taxes and blamed Clinton for not closing the loopholes he employed when she was a senator (Owen 2017).

Hypocrisy appears in smaller matters as well. During Obama's years as president, Trump routinely needled the president on Twitter, arguing that he was spending too much time on the golf course. Trump vowed, if he became president "I'm not going to have time to go play golf" (quoted in Bump 2017b). In fact, by the end of August 2017 Trump spent more than 50 days as president on the golf course, as compared to 15 days for Obama during the same seven-month period eight years earlier (Bump 2017b).

An April 2017 poll by Pew (2017b) revealed that many Americans considered the new president reckless. As reported in Table 5.8, 63 percent he was too impulsive, 2 percent said he was too cautious, and 32 percent said he was about right. In January 2010, when Americans answered the same question about Obama, only 26 percent said he was too impulsive, versus 20 percent who said he was too cautious and 46 percent who said he was about right. Trump also had a credibility problem. As shown in Table 5.8, 51 percent said they trusted Trump less than his predecessors, as compared to 30 percent who trusted him more and 16 percent who trusted him about the same as other presidents.

Table 5.8 also reveals the profound policy divisions found in America as the new president made his way through his first months in office. In the survey, Democrats had a clear advantage on health care, by a margin of 54 percent versus the 34 percent who thought that the Republicans could do a better job. Citizens favored Democrats by wide margins on foreign policy, immigration, abortion, the environment and educational policy, a surprisingly long list for a party that could not win the White House or majority control of either chamber of Congress a few months earlier. Republicans had a large advantage when it came to dealing with the threat of terrorism, but negligible advantages on managing the economy, taxes and international trade.

International Perspectives

In many ways, the Trump administration represented a major departure from the bipartisan foreign policy consensus that has governed U.S.

Table 5.8 Trump's Temperament and Partisan Policy Differences, 2017

In making important decisions, do you think Donald Trump is ___?

	Trump	Obama
		(January 2010)
Too impulsive	63%	26%
Too cautious	2%	20%
About Right	32%	46%

Would you say you trust what Donald Trump says more, about the same, or less than you trust what previous presidents said while in office?

	Trump	Bush
		(June 2003, Gallup/ CNN/USA Today)
More	30%	41%
About the same	16%	25%
Less	51%	32%

Which political party could do a better job of ___?

	Democrats	Republicans	Both (vol.)	Neither (vol.)
Handling the economy	43%	46%	5%	5%
Dealing with health care	54%	34%	2%	6%
Dealing with the terrorist threat at home	36%	48%	8%	6%
Dealing with taxes	43%	44%	4%	5%
Making wise decisions about foreign policy	49%	36%	5%	6%
Dealing with immigration	50%	39%	2%	6%
Dealing with policies abortion/ contraception	53%	33%	3%	6%
Dealing with the environment	59%	28%	3%	5%
Dealing with education policy	53%	27%	5%	4%
Representing your views on govt. spending	48%	40%	2%	7%
Reflecting your views on gun policy	41%	46%	2%	5%
Dealing with trade agreements	42%	45%	4%	4%

Note: Don't know responses are not reported here, so percentages do not sum to 100.

Source: Pew 2017b.

international relations since the end of the Cold War (Quealy 2017). While there were differing views over how to handle Iraq, the Reagan, Clinton, Obama, and both Bush presidencies all were deeply committed to increased international trade and strong international organizations, as well as (generally) casting a wary eye on potential adversaries like China and Russia. All five presidents likewise focused on promoting democracy around the world as a vital American interest (Rogin 2017). Six months into his presidency, though, the Trump administration was debating whether to drop democracy promotion as a national goal (Rogin 2017).

The Trump administration also largely silenced the State Department in its early months. Under Presidents Obama, George W. Bush, Clinton, and George H. W. Bush the State Department routinely conducted at least four briefings a week. For the first six months of the Trump adminis- tration, the average was 1.1 briefings per week (Quealy 2017). By failing to do more to promote its views of the world to foreign leaders and their publics, the Trump team reduced its own opportunities to try to shape the global conversation.

President Trump inspired little confidence among citizens of other nations. As shown in Table 5.9, nearly every country listed in these Pew surveys witnessed major declines in the belief that the American president would do the right thing in world affairs when Trump replaced Obama. In a variety of America's key allies—including G-20 nations such as Germany, South Korea, France, Spain, Canada, the U.K., Australia and Japan—the drop exceeded 50 percentage points. Many of those Trump numbers were about as low, and sometimes lower, than those of George W. Bush in 2008 (Pew 2017c). Low international approval of a president limits the abilities of foreign leaders to collaborate with this country. If less than one in four residents of the U.K. believe Trump would do the right thing internationally, for example, a British prime minister would be taking a huge risk to stand shoulder to shoulder with Trump.

Public confidence in Trump to do the right thing in world affairs fell in the U.S. as well, but the 12-point drop in the U.S. post-Obama was much smaller than in nearly all of the regionally influential nations listed in Table 5.9. Of the 22 international publics sampled in the nations listed here, only two nations were more positive about Trump than Obama: Russia, where Trump marked a 42-point gain, and Israel, where Trump registered a 7-point gain over Obama.

International evaluations of Trump's character are also quite critical in most of America's key allies. As shown in Table 5.10, in a number of key NATO allies, including Germany, France, Spain, Canada, and the U.K., more than two-thirds of people surveyed said that Trump was dangerous. Less than one person in five surveyed in Germany, Spain, Canada, the U.K., Japan, and Mexico considered Trump well qualified to be president.

Once again, Trump scored well in Russia, where 62 percent of those surveyed considered him well qualified to be president and only 31 per- cent considered him dangerous. More than half of those surveyed in Israel (54 percent) considered Trump well qualified to be president, and only 42 percent considered him dangerous. Trump also scored relatively well in India, a nation where he has courted Prime Minister Modi, with

Table 5.9 International Evaluations of Recent Presidents

For each, tell me how much confidence you have in each leader to do the right thing regarding world affairs: a lot of confidence, some confidence, not too much confidence, or no confidence at all [George W. Bush/Barack Obama/ Donald Trump].

	Bush 2008	Obama 2016	Trump 2017	Change (Obama/Trump)
U.S.	37%	58%**	46%	−12
Germany	14%	86%	11%	−75
South Korea	30%	88%**	17%	−71
France	13%	84%	14%	−70
Spain	8%	75%	7%	−68
Canada	28%*	83%	22%	−61
UK	16%	79%	22%	−57
Australia	23%	84%	29%	−55
Japan	25%	78%	24%	−54
Brazil	17%	63%	14%	−49
Mexico	16%	49%**	5%	−44
Italy	43%*	68%	25%	−43
Indonesia	24%	64%**	23%	−41
Poland	41%	58%	23%	−35
South Africa	32%	73%	39%	−34
Turkey	2%	45%**	11%	−34
Argentina	7%	40%	13%	−27
Lebanon	33%	36%**	15%	−21
India	55%	58%	40%	−18
Jordan	7%	14%**	9%	−5
Nigeria	—	63%	58%	−5
Israel	57%*	49%**	56%	7
Russia	22%	11%**	53%	42

Notes: The percentages combine the first two categories.
Dashes signify that the question was not asked by Pew in that country in that year.
*   Results from 2007 survey.
** Results from 2015 survey.

Source: Pew 2017c.

41 percent of those surveyed saying Trump was well-qualified to be president and only 28 percent considering him dangerous.

Case Study: Selling the Obamacare "Repeal and Replace" Plan

Efforts to eliminate the Affordable Care Act make a compelling case study for Donald Trump's first year in office for several reasons. First, ending Obamacare was a key promise of the presidential candidate (Ceaser et al. 2017). In addition, it is more specific—and therefore more subject to analysis—than a general desire to "make America great again." (That is

Table 5.10 International Evaluations of Presidential Character, 2017

Please tell me whether you think the following describes U.S. President Donald Trump. Do you think of Donald Trump as ___?

	Well-qualified to be president	Strong Leader	Dangerous	Arrogant
Germany	6%	54%	76%	91%
South Korea	18%	47%	76%	85%
France	21%	44%	78%	93%
Spain	13%	58%	76%	94%
Canada	16%	38%	72%	93%
UK	16%	39%	69%	89%
Australia	22%	45%	71%	89%
Japan	15%	51%	56%	80%
Brazil	24%	64%	63%	75%
Mexico	11%	77%	83%	91%
Italy	25%	62%	58%	77%
Indonesia	22%	49%	68%	70%
Poland	24%	62%	45%	71%
South Africa	41%	47%	41%	53%
Turkey	27%	40%	72%	64%
Argentina	26%	73%	70%	82%
Lebanon	28%	43%	66%	77%
India	41%	42%	28%	26%
Jordan	18%	30%	62%	91%
Nigeria	66%	69%	33%	33%
Israel	54%	69%	42%	65%
Russia	62%	67%	31%	44%

Source: Pew 2017c.

why "hope and change" was not the case study analysis of the Obama presidency). Second, there has been specific legislative action on this key matter: the U.S. House voted to approve a "repeal and replace" plan and the Senate voted to reject several alternative plans. Those governmental actions allow for a more precise evaluation of Trump's efforts to market a key policy agenda than a bill that was still working its way through Capitol Hill.

While another issue may emerge as a better choice for a case study of the Trump years, the timing of this book required an important decision action to take place during the first year of the new president's term. Even health care reform may rise again as the Trump presidency unfolds. Indeed, perhaps a future "repeal and replace" plan may gain legislative approval in the months ahead. For now, Trump has emphasized the "repeal and replace" effort more than any other matter during his time in office so far. By any measure, Congress has not provided Trump with legislative success on his diesire to repeal the ACA.

President Trump, Repealing the Affordable Care Act, and Public Opinion

In the same way that Trump wanted to chart a different course than Obama did on health care, Trump also charted a different course in trying to make his favored policy change. Trump did not engage in town hall meetings where citizens could ask questions about his health care proposals, as President Obama had done (Hopper 2017). Rather Trump focused on tweeting frequently his displeasure with the Affordable Care Act (Ingraham 2017). Trump's few events that addressed the "repeal and replace" concept did not involve audience questions; those events were more like campaign rallies rather than reasoned efforts to hear public concerns and to persuade people of the merits of the legislation (Baker 2017; Hohmann 2017a).

Trump also did not emphasize working with individual Republican senators to develop a deal that would win majority support. At a White House meeting with Republican senators, Trump insisted he was waiting for them to act. "I am sitting in the Oval Office with a pen in hand," Trump told them (quoted in Marcus 2017), not exactly a measure of presidential negotiating commitment.

The experiences of many presidents demonstrate that senators do not respond well to rough treatment from the White House. Even so, Trump threatened the Obamacare repeal holdouts. Trump endorsed the attack advertisements launched by an outside conservative group on Sen. Dean Heller (R-NV), who faces a tough re-election contest in 2018. Heller drew Trump's ire because he did not want to reverse Medicaid expansion, which was part of the "repeal and replace" bill the Senate rejected in July 2017 (Isenstadt 2017).

The six-year terms that senators enjoy make them unlikely to succumb to threats from Trump or any other president. They are not members of a municipal zoning board looking at a plan for a new apartment building, nor do they work for the White House. In fact, Trump's threats to Capitol Hill rang hollow. Most Republican senators elected in 2016 won by a wide margin and did not come into office riding on the new president's electoral coattails. So they owed him little (Bump 2017a).

> Trump treats loyalty the way that he treats bipartisan unity: He invokes it regularly but repeatedly demonstrates that he simply means that people should rally around and unconditionally back him, not that he'd do his part in the bargain. After the election, he kept insisting on unity, but did little or nothing to actually reach out to or consider the viewpoints of his Democratic opponents. He asks for loyalty, cajoling Republican members of the House for their votes on that chamber's version of the health-care bill, only to later throw them under the bus by describing the legislation as "mean."
>
> (Bump 2017a)

In his July 25, 2017 interview with the *Wall Street Journal*, Trump was not articulate concerning the health care plan he was supporting, and offered only vague generalities about the bill. In response to a question about the specifics of health care policy, Trump said:

> So I'd rather see—I'd rather see replace. I'd rather add the replace. And we have a very good plan. That's the one thing, we really have a good plan. We've covered a lot of territory. It's a very, very difficult situation because you move a little bit to the left and you lose four guys, you move a little bit to the right all of a sudden you have a bloc of people that are gone. You have about a one-inch road and it wheels through the middle of the valley, and if it's even slightly off. It's a very difficult—it's a very difficult thing, always has been.
>
> (quoted in Dawsey and Gold 2017)

In addition to the absence of policy specifics, one can note that Trump's political assessments contrast with what he originally said about health care. He previously promised it would be easy to repeal and replace Obamacare and that he would exchange it for a better health insurance plan, one that would insure more people and cost less than the Affordable Care Act. In the end, he supported a variety of different Congressional plans, all of which independent analysts said would have eliminated affordable coverage for tens of millions of Americans, exactly the opposite of what Trump promised as a candidate (Baker 2017; Hohmann 2017a).

In that same *Journal* interview, Trump got even the small things wrong. He said that Hillary Clinton worked on the health care bill for eight years as First Lady (Dawsey and Gold 2017), while in fact the Clinton plan was abandoned in less than two years, once the 1994 midterm elections installed Republican majorities in Congress (Skocpol 1997).

Trump's most frequently repeated false claim during his first six months as president, according to the *Washington Post* Fact Checker, is that Obamacare was dying, which the president said 44 times during his first six months in office (Kessler et al. 2017). Not only was it not true, the repeated comment did not persuade the public to endorse the "repeal and replace" alternative that the Senate debated and rejected in July 2017 (Hohmann 2017a).

Finally, Trump also ignored that old adage about not counting one's chickens before the eggs have hatched. When the House passed a "repeal and replace" health care bill, Trump held a "victory" celebration at the White House, even though the bill was pending before the Senate, where it eventually died.

Mindful of the possibility that it might not be able to kill Obamacare legislatively, at least not on the first try, the Trump administration has sought to undermine the law through a series of administrative actions. These actions included shortening the 2017 ACA enrollment period, reducing the availability of trained staffers at call-in centers to help would-be enrollees, discouraging insurance company participation by increasing the uncertainty over the future availability of government subsidies, and even using Obamacare budget funds dedicated to expanding health care to launch a public relations campaign against the law (Edsall 2017). That administrative undermining approach may end up being more successful in weakening the ACA than the legislative route.

Trump's first year did include one major legislative victory, passage of a measure that included the largest revisions to the federal tax code in three decades (Wagner 2017). The $1.5 trillion measure, which secured no Democratic support, included permanent tax cuts for business and temporary ones for many individual taxpayers (Wagner 2017). Polls conducted before Trump signed the bill showed that it was unpopular, but he predicted that more Americans would support the tax plan once its impacts became clear during 2018 (Wagner 2017).

Lessons (So Far) From Trump's Communication Efforts

Six months into his presidency, Republicans in Congress began to turn on the controversial chief executive. Just in July 2017, Senate Republicans refused to pass a replacement health care bill, one of Trump's major campaign themes, and Congress with near-unanimity passed legislation to limit Trump's ability to reduce the sanctions in place against Russia. In addition, a congressional committee forced Trump's son-in-law, Jared Kushner, a top White House official, to testify about meetings with Russians during the 2016 campaign, and many in Congress objected to Trump's decision to ban transgender people from serving in the U.S. military. Also during that month, a number of conservative Republicans, including Senate Judiciary Chairman Charles Grassley (R-Iowa), spoke up in defense of Attorney General Sessions, after Trump insulted Sessions over what the president considered insufficient loyalty to the White House (Baker 2017).

As his troubles mounted in late July, Trump pushed out his first chief of staff, replacing him with a general whom Trump said will bring more discipline to the administration.

> The shake-up followed a week that saw the bombastic, with-me-or-against-me president defied as never before by Washington and its institutions, including Republicans in Congress, his own attorney general, the uniformed military leadership, police officers, and even the Boy Scouts. No longer daunted by a president with a Twitter account that he uses like a Gatling gun, members of his own party made clear that they were increasingly willing to stand against him on issues like health care and Russia.
>
> (Baker 2017)

The departure of Chief of Staff Reince Priebus followed a profanity-laced tirade by White House Communications Director Anthony Scaramucci, who attacked Preibus and Stephen K. Bannon, the president's chief strategist, in extremely vulgar terms (Baker and Haberman 2017). While such unprofessional behavior by any staffer would likely have led to an immediate resignation in a previous White House, Scaramucci's departure came the following week, on the day a new chief of staff took office.

Around the time Priebus left, Trump also attacked his own Attorney General, saying on Twitter that William Sessions was "VERY weak [Trump's capitalization]" and criticized him for not doing enough to investigate Hillary Clinton and recusing himself from the FBI's Russia investigation the previous spring (Baker 2017). The message of the Trump presidency on many days is chaos.

> So many figures inside Mr. Trump's orbit have been declared on their way out that it takes a scorecard to keep track. Aside from Mr. Priebus and Mr. Sessions, many wonder about the future of Lt. Gen. H. R. McMaster, the national security adviser whose Afghanistan war plan was rejected by the president last week. Secretary of State Rex W. Tillerson disappeared for a few days off, stoking speculation that he may leave. ("Rexit," it was called on Twitter.) And the president, who has already fired one F.B.I. director, this week called for the acting head of the bureau to be dismissed too. The clash between Mr. Scaramucci and Mr. Priebus offers a case study in how the Trump White House operates, a conflict divorced from facts, untethered from the basics of how government works, enabled by the lack of any organizational structure and driven by ambition, fear, animosity and envy.
>
> (Baker and Haberman 2017)

That is not to say Trump is getting nothing accomplished. The most effective presidential efforts, in the longer term, may be those activities that do not generate much public or media attention. Amid the chaos of the opening act of the Trump presidency, for example, the new president engaged in an extensive rewriting and blocking of a number of administrative rules put forward by President Obama. Those adjustments include curtailing Obama administration efforts to limit greenhouse gas emissions from power plants, to protect streams from coal mining activities, and to increase protections for transgender students (Bump 2017c).

Those efforts may allow Trump to advance the interests and values of white working class Americans at the expense of others in ways that may not draw a lot of attention. "The guiding principle in Mr. Trump's government is to turn the politics of white resentment into the policies of white rage—that calculated mechanism of executive orders, laws and agency directives that undermines and punishes minority achievement and aspiration" (Anderson 2017). In time, administration actions to curtail immigration or gay rights and reduce trade may lead to better presidential public opinion standings and thereby revive respect in the legislative branch. Perhaps a crisis will generate support for the president that has been absent from policy debates early in his presidency. Alternatively, Trump's relationship with his fellow Republicans could deteriorate further in response to ongoing events. We will see.

6 Successes and Failures in Presidential Communication

Presidential candidates campaign for the nation's highest office by convincing the nation that they have the best—or at least the better—character for taking on the immense challenges that await the victor. Persuasion is also central to governing, where presidents try to shape the American future they wish to see. The character of any person, formed throughout a lifetime of experiences, is not likely to change dramatically from the personal qualities revealed during his or her decades of adulthood. Chief executives are no different in this regard. Indeed, as Americans have seen from president after president, what you see in a presidential candidate's character is largely what you get in a president's character.

Not everything will remain as consistent as the qualities of one's character, though, if a presidency is to be successful. Campaign marketing approaches must give way to governing marketing approaches, and that requires a new set of staffers who are expert in dealing with Congress, the federal bureaucracy, and foreign leaders. Such Washington professionals must supplement campaign workers with their demonstrated capacity in public relations and election mechanics or a presidency will probably not accomplish much. To put it another way, the soaring rhetoric of an election sprint to November must give way to four years of long marches of persuasion relating to legislation, administrative rule making, and international relations. Character continues to matter, of course. By force of personality, presidents have to persuade both governing officials as well as voters to follow his or her lead, usually a more difficult task than running for office.

In this final chapter, we consider how modern presentations of presidential character have helped presidents succeed in the job, and how they have not. We consider how character conversations have changed as the presidents—and their media environments—have varied. As we have done throughout this book, this analysis focuses on the public communication strategies of recent presidents. We review how Americans have viewed presidents elected during the internet age across their years in office, paying particular attention to presentations and evaluations of character. We also consider presidential legislative successes and failures.

As the president is the most visible representation of the United States on the world stage, we also consider how well presidents have connected with people in other nations. Taken together, these matters offer a range of ways to consider the effectiveness of media strategies employed by various presidents to sell their policies and themselves. We consider as well as how future presidents might learn from the communication experiences of the Clinton, Bush, Obama and Trump years to shape their own presentations of themselves and their policies to citizens, to Congress, and to the world.

The Value of Emphasizing Presidential Character

Conversations that focus on character may humanize presidents, and that sometimes leads citizens to feel more positively about the president as a person. A friendly, open personal demeanor in most election years is a prerequisite for obtaining the office and for governing successfully. Even when the public generally likes a political figure as a person, that fact does not ensure political success. Sometimes, Americans want a pit bull in charge. Sometimes the political environment demands one.

Even if a modern political figure did not wish to emphasize his or her own character as a candidate or as a president, he or she has little choice but to do so. For nearly a century, Americans have become increasingly used to hearing (and then seeing) candidates in their living rooms and sometimes even their bedrooms via radio, television and now online. The intimacy conferred by these direct, albeit one-way, media connections can make many people feel like they can judge presidential candidates the way they judge the other people one meets in person over the course of a day. We routinely evaluate the people we encounter by considering questions like these: is this person honest, is this person sufficiently competent to handle the job he or she has, is this person likeable? When it comes to evaluating individuals, public policies, and even presidents, people often trust their gut instincts (Popkin 1991). Such an evaluation strategy may not be wise; nevertheless, citizens often employ that technique.

While the stage-managed nature of modern presidential communication leads to an "intimacy" that can reasonably be described as a faux connection, the public expects presidents to make the effort to connect on a personal level. Indeed, the polls cited throughout this project demonstrate that people often feel quite comfortable in evaluating presidents observed almost entirely through the sometimes distorting lenses of mass media on dimensions of their character, including honesty, decisiveness, and even whether a given president shares one's own values. People feel quite confident they have enough information to make those personal assessments for president after president—only a tiny number of people hesitate to offer these evaluations when pollsters ask them to do so.

As many have noted, every modern White House is engaged in permanent marketing campaigns to build and retain public affection for the president and win over some of the less-committed moderates who, with persuasion, may come to view the president in a positive light. Today's hyper-partisan political debates mean that every president has a group of die-hard supporters who will support nearly every policy and a core of die-hard opponents who will reject nearly every policy (each group is roughly one-third of the electorate). Beyond those two groups, there are significant numbers of persuadable voters who might support nearly any president's initiatives at least some of the time once the election is over.

Presidents and presidential candidates spend so much time discussing their character because they believe that winning and retaining high public approval ratings is an essential prerequisite for a president's political success, even though evidence suggests it is not a good use of their time (cf., Edwards 2003). Though presidents and their public relations staffers carefully tend these reputations, public assessments may shift in an instant in response to external events over which presidents have little control.

As we have seen in a previous chapter, the horrific attacks of 9/11 created a huge and durable increase in George W. Bush's approval numbers. Souring conditions eventually pushed Bush's ratings into far more negative territory, as the administration reeled from the aftershocks of Hurricane Katrina, the unexpectedly long-running occupation of Iraq, and as an economic crisis hit during Bush's final year in office. No other president examined here has had higher highs or lower lows (at least so far).

How Congress reacts to a president, and to White House policy preferences, also affects presidential public approval numbers. Executive branch credibility and competence, as seen through interactions with the legislative branch, shape public evaluations of the national executive, in other words. Congress's decision to abandon debate over Clinton's health care bill in 1994 hurt his standing with the public (and it did not help congressional Democrats running for office that year either). Americans restored Clinton's approval numbers a few years later when congressional Republicans tried to drive him from the White House in the wake of the Clinton-Lewinsky scandal. Obama's numbers also sank as he promoted a controversial health care bill in the face of a vigorous opposition from a new Tea Party movement during 2009 and 2010, and his approval numbers did not get much better even after Congress approved the Affordable Care Act. Public approval of Obama increased as economic conditions improved somewhat during 2012 and the years that followed. For Trump, public opinion of the new president started out unusually negative and remained there, even falling lower as the first year of his chaos-filled presidency unfolded.

Although over-promising, or at least rhetorical inconsistency, may work to secure some short-term policy goals at first, a persistent credibility gap can really hurt a president's standing over time. Presidents who sell themselves and their policies through less-than-honest marketing often face an eventual day of reckoning. Public perceptions of George W. Bush's credibility declined sharply after the Iraq operation turned out to be far more difficult than predicted. Obama's credibility suffered because the administration underestimated the severity of the economic crisis it inherited, overestimated the economic gains the administration could generate quickly, and did not realize how hard it would be for some people to keep their own doctors under the Affordable Care Act. Voters then punished the Democrats in 2010 because things did not get better as quickly as administration officials had promised. Trump's wild and unsupported claims that Obamacare was collapsing likewise created a White House credibility gap, though that gap emerged more rapidly than it had for his predecessors (Kessler et al. 2017).

Both overall public evaluations and public assessments of character, including whether a president is honest or shares the public's values, routinely trend downward over the course of a presidency. Donald Trump, who started with far more negative character evaluations and general public approval numbers than did previous presidents, saw his numbers tumble during his first year in office. His approval ratings fell at the same time he struggled to keep promises that he said would be easy to accomplish. The list includes the promise to build a U.S.-Mexico border wall that Mexico would pay for, the vow to offer a better and cheaper health care system to replace Obamacare, and the largely abandoned commitment to "drain the swamp" of corruption in Washington. The *Art of the Deal* author found it difficult to reach agreement with Republican majorities in both the House and the Senate on a variety of issues. As shown in Chapter 5, strong doubts about Trump's character animate many of his critics.

Each president has a base of support that remains loyal almost regardless of how bad things get for a particular administration. What is particularly interesting about Trump is the extent to which he retained his base despite the very rocky start to his presidency and his many departures from the populist campaign promises made during the campaign, as discussed in Chapter 5. Trump's persuasiveness as a candidate might seem to fly in the face of the best interests, for example, of relatively low-income voters who might reject politicians and political parties promising to cut government aid to the poor, an apparent choice against their self-interest. Even if one imagined that Donald Trump would provide an economic boom to once-thriving industrial communities, the Trump presidency's first year offered little encouragement that the new administration would focus on economic concerns of the Rust Belt. Yet still much of his support remained among his partisan backers.

Media Changes and the Communication
of Presidential Character

Although Clinton, Bush, and Obama won their elections at least in part because they possessed effective media management teams, their strategies sometimes diverged in response to different policy challenges they faced. Trump's support, in contrast, sprang from the character of Trump himself: he promoted himself as a no-nonsense business executive who could "drain the swamp" of Washington. He won office despite powerful divisions within the Republican Party and without a traditional campaign organization along the lines of the ones that helped propel Clinton, Bush and Obama to victory (cf., Ceaser et al. 2017).

Even though voters selected Barack Obama on a wave of enthusiasm for his optimistic and confident character in 2008, Obama never had the public opinion highs Bush did after 9/11. (Of course, taking over in the midst of a devastating global financial crisis did not help). Obama had two years of Democratic legislative control as president, and once Republicans took over the House of Representatives, Obama faced far greater partisan opposition than Bush found in his years with Democratic congressional majorities. Little bipartisanship also marked the Clinton years. Like Obama, Clinton's first-term media management efforts were not sufficient to prevent a mid-term electoral backlash: both Democratic presidents lost Democratic House majorities two years into their presidencies. Bush lost his Senate majority even sooner, at the hands of a renegade Republican senator who broke from the party during Bush's first year. Bush regained a GOP Senate majority in the midterm election of 2002, held just a year after the terrorist attacks on the World Trade Center and the Pentagon.

Indeed, the 2001 terrorist attacks pushed foreign affairs to the forefront. This is the issue area where the presidential communication advantage in shaping public opinion is strongest. Crises are also good times for presidents to emphasize character. Presidents also get to act tough in a crisis, and that often improves a president's standing with the public, particularly in the early going. In addition to being something approaching the role of a national father in times of heightened public anxiety, wartime presidents can also make far greater use of an administration's inherent advantages in releasing—and not releasing—information to reporters relating to national security matters.

Domestic programs such as the economic recovery efforts and the Affordable Care Act were far more prominent policy concerns during Obama's presidency. Many sources of information can address domestic policy, making it easier for others to challenge presidential framing in domestic issue areas. In contrast with Bush, Obama rarely focused on foreign policy, and even when he did, he found military matters were not as subject to bipartisanship or as salient to citizens as they had been a decade earlier. Trump likewise started his presidency by focusing on domestic concerns, particularly those relating to job loss and illegal immigration, thereby reducing the chances his supporters would concentrate on international matters.

The media changes since the 1980s have expanded greatly the communication channels with which presidents and presidential candidates can reach out and connect with citizens. They also give the president's critics new venues to reach the public. The now wide-open media landscape also gives citizens greater opportunity to join in the political debate, be it via e-mails, blogging, or posting political videos online. This greater democratization of the modern media system, as Obama, Bush, and Trump have learned, does not always assist in disseminating the president's favored narrative to the nation. Presidents and their opponents employ character construction and reconstruction to shape personality debates through an ever-growing list of media channels.

Recent presidents nevertheless have developed media strategies that seemed very effective in the context of the media environments they encountered as they sought to influence the public. All employed extensive use of character-based arguments as candidates and as presidents, and did so in different ways that took account of the different media environments as well as the different temperaments of these individual presidents.

Perhaps Americans want what they do not have, at least when it comes to presidential character. In presidential elections during the past several decades, voters have turned to candidates who are strong in the personal qualities their predecessor lacked. Earnest Jimmy Carter seemed like an antidote in 1976 to the deceit and corruption of Richard Nixon and Watergate. Four years later, the tough Ronald Reagan seemed like an effective response to a challenging international environment, with U.S. diplomats turned hostages languishing in Iran and rising Soviet influence, particularly in Latin America. In 1988, Reagan's appeal had diminished in the wake of the Iran-Contra scandal, and voters backed the competent and professional George H. W. Bush as a replacement. Four years later, Americans turned to Bill Clinton because he seemed more in touch with economic hard times than the more patrician incumbent he faced in 1992. Eight years after that, George W. Bush seemed likely to operate on a far higher moral plane than Clinton ever could. Obama's promise of a better economic future, greater domestic cooperation and less contentious international relations seemed like an effective counter to the harsh economic times and stubborn global conflicts of the Bush years. Trump's backward-looking anger was the polar opposite of Obama, who offered a forward-looking, multicultural optimistic orientation that generated conservative hostility that Trump exploited effectively, first as a Birther and then as a combative presidential candidate.

The first president in our sequence of four, Bill Clinton, possessed an informality that seemed ideally suited to the talk shows of the 1990s. He appeared on these conversational programs and won over crowds despite widespread public concerns over his personal morality. In an era where traditional media outlets like television news continued to dominate information consumption patterns, his plainspoken politics provided soundbite-ready materials for the news. Clinton, like many presidents of the television age, used the "bully pulpit" of the White House to dominate the political discourse, a task that was far easier when a handful of editors who worked in influential newsrooms in Washington and New York largely set the national news agenda. Clinton's personal misconduct raised questions about his character, but he remained in the public's good graces by relying upon biblical invocations of forgiveness, as well as effective attacks on his rivals for allegedly attempting to overthrow an election. Having a healthy economy also undermined efforts by Republicans to turn public opinion against a president many considered an unprincipled rogue, albeit a likeable one.

For all their differences in personality, both Clinton and Bush seemed very committed to the Sun King vision of presidential media management, placing their character conversations front and center, weighing in on just about every topic, and trying to shape the discourse on public policy issues to the maximum extent possible. The traditional presidential venues for mass communication, the network television evening newscasts and the *New York Times* and the *Washington Post*, continued to shape White House efforts to connect with the American public. Like Clinton, Bush had a direct approach to public commentary that generated many effective White House soundbites. Bush provided a very clear presentation of his views and often offered Manichean assessments, particularly when discussing foreign or military policy. These black-and-white statements about the world did not always go over well with independent voters or global audiences, but they offered citizens a clear policy vision.

Bush also presented the nation and the world with a presidential toughness that helped him win greater public support. For a nation traumatized by 9/11, these us-versus-them story lines worked very well at Fox News, a conservative news outlet that often provided friendlier treatment of Bush than was the case at mainstream media outlets. Other conservative news outlets on talk radio and online followed Fox News in offering pro-Bush reporting, providing a place for conservatives seeking an interpretation of current events favorable to Bush to find such media content.

While Bush and Clinton sought to dominate the discourse, Obama's presidential news efforts were more defensive and less focused on dominating the stories reported on larger news outlets like broadcast and cable television. He was more inclined to pick his battles, choosing to engage in certain corners of cable news or on social media now and then, with the expectation that many of those efforts would filter back into the programming of traditional news outlets. Obama achieved extraordinary legislative success in his first two years. He secured passage of a major health care reform, a major economic stimulus package and a wide-ranging financial industry regulatory package designed to prevent future fiscal meltdowns—and he did so with a far more modest, diffident public communications strategy than the constant efforts employed by his two immediate predecessors to dominate the news cycle. (Obama did have larger partisan legislative majorities in the Senate than did his predecessors, which helped a good deal at first). Obama's understated public communications style, even in the face of unrelenting conservative criticism and doubts over whether he was even legally eligible to be president, made him a modern-day version of Cool Hand Luke, an iconic long-suffering character played by Paul Newman in the landmark 1967 film of the same name.

Obama's modest approach made sense, though, for the far more decentralized media environment during his years as president. Winning the framing battles on the network evening news programs mattered less during Obama's presidency than it had for his predecessors. The understated style worked well in the key social media outlets of the Obama years, as on YouTube, where audiences younger than those tuning in to television news would likely not be moved by old-style media rhetoric, complete with critical soundbites and attack ads. Humor, such as Obama's appearance on the parody talk show *Between Two Ferns*, was a particularly effective way of engaging with social media and a more youthful audience that increasingly focused on political humor. This lighter touch to presidential communication, "slow-jamming the news" and so on, seemed more consistent with Obama's personality. Pronouncements like those offered by George W. Bush (like his argument that foreign leaders were either with America or with the terrorists) would have seemed very discordant had they come out of Obama's mouth, given the less-aggressive character he had presented to the nation and the world.

Arguably, Obama had little choice but to present himself as even-tempered and maybe even resistant to conflict. As the first African-American president, Obama had to be cautious in his public appearances and on social media lest he trigger even more hostility to his presidency than had already been generated by the Birther movement. During more than a decade in public life, Barack Obama never revealed whether he had an "inner Al Sharpton" dying to shout aloud his frustrations, but had Obama sounded like an angry activist in public that would probably not have gone over well. The idea that Obama had a private rage that he did not or could not express was in fact the source of a long-running "Obama anger translator" comedy routine by African American humorists Keegan-Michael Key and Jordan Peele (Merry 2017).

For Donald Trump, there was no question about whether he was angry on the inside, since he so frequently expressed his anger on the outside. Even before he became a political candidate, his "You're fired!" catchphrase on television and his "Birther" commentary online demonstrated his combativeness. As discussed earlier, his campaign announcement speech called Mexican immigrants rapists and criminals, still more evidence of his anger and his desire to present it as a centerpiece of his campaign. That campaign featured an extraordinarily wide range of personal insults directed at his fellow candidates, as well as at federal judges who issued rulings that upset him and at individual citizens who made comments that he did not like. Trump sought to dominate the discourse as Clinton and Bush had done, but he sought to do so largely through nasty put-downs of rivals and through bullying on Twitter. His approach generated a very large amount of news attention during his early months as president, and much of it revolved around the anger expressed online.

Trump's presidency borrowed almost nothing from Obama's examples of character presentation. Indeed Trump often seemed to be the precise opposite of his predecessor. Where one sought to portray himself as multicultural cool, the other offered white-hot anger. Where one sought to include many people and build coalitions with them, the other sought to divide, and divide with intense passion. Where one sought to work with Congress by cooperation and with respect for another branch of government, the other sought to bully, degrade, and intimidate those at the other end of Pennsylvania Avenue.

So far, the results have not been particularly encouraging for Trump's media management style as president: his low approval ratings have fallen further as more Americans found themselves frustrated with the chaos in Washington and angry over the continuing efforts to divide (cf., Newport 2017; Pew 2017b). With the exception of an unpopular tax bill, Congress has largely rejected his legislative initiatives, including plans to repeal and replace Obamacare, or delayed acting on them. In addition, the extremely high level of staff turnover in the upper ranks of the administration and the administration's many legal challenges made it difficult to recruit the best possible replacements.

Presidents Can't Escape Character Conversations

As the examples of recent presidents have shown, the modern media environment has at least encouraged, if not made it essential for, presidential candidates and presidents to give their fellow citizens an extensive view into their own psyche. Reporters push for personal details regarding the childhood of presidential candidates, as well as details about their families, and how they functioned in the workplace and in previous government positions. These matters make for interesting reading and viewing to be sure, but at the core of these investigations is an effort aimed at using character to predict how a candidate would actually behave as president and what a president will do next.

These character conversations are ideal for a modern media environment that gives rise to short-attention-span politics. They also serve the politicians' interests, as constantly distracted news consumers may not remember, much less punish, politicians if they said one thing yesterday and the opposite thing today. Over-promising, the staple of presidential spinning, seems like a particularly high-risk strategy when virtually every presidential utterance is recorded for posterity. The late-night comedians on the *Daily Show*, for example, excel in pointing out the hypocrisy of politicians, and air the news clips to prove their inconsistencies if not hypocrisy (Lichter et al. 2015).

In such an environment, an angry approach on social media can energize followers and attract media attention, as Trump demonstrated throughout his campaign and during his presidency. While it may be effective as a campaign strategy, Allen Frances, a professor emeritus at Duke University Medical College, found what Trump's anger generated among his supporters, many of whom voted for him despite their doubts about his character.

> We need to be looking in the mirror to see what's wrong with us that would allow someone who is so unsuitable for the Presidency to rise to the highest and most dangerous office in the world. Trump's psychology is far too obvious to be interesting. You don't have to be a psychoanalyst to understand Trump. He's the most transparent human being who ever lived.
>
> (quoted in Osnos 2017)

In addition to anger, Trump comments demonstrate a lack of honesty, if not a desire to deceive the public (cf., Kessler et al. 2017). Dishonesty may matter less than used to be the case, though. Not every news consumer sees the range of presidential deceits these days, particularly if one watches Fox News during a Republican presidential administration. In other words, lying to the public in an environment of polarized media may mean never having to admit to your followers (or to anyone, for that matter) that you did not tell the truth. One can simply dismiss any unappealing media reports as "fake news," as Trump often responds on Twitter in the wake of critical news reports. The White House press secretary can simply deny the obvious contradictions and reversals as figments of biased reporter imaginations.

With the various modern media cocoons that exist today a person may never hear a president called to account for a comment that turned out to be false. On Fox News, for example, a conservative can hear news that largely agrees with his or her beliefs, and therefore the price a conservative politician pays for lying drops considerably (Stolberg 2017). While left-looking news consumers could also find like-minded news reports, the tables in this book demonstrates that the Fox audience is far larger than that of liberal media.

Over the past two decades, institutional changes in American politics have made it easier for politicians to lie. The proliferation of television political talk shows and the rise of the internet have created a fragmented media environment. With no widely acknowledged media gatekeeper, politicians have an easier time distorting the truth. And in an era of hyper-partisanship, where politicians often are trying to court voters at the extreme ends of the political spectrum, politicians often lie with impunity.

(Stolberg 2017)

There are exceptions, of course, to the pro-Trump narratives on Fox News. During mid-2017, when most Fox News programming argued that the investigation of possible pre-election misconduct by the Trump campaign and officials connected with the Putin government was nothing more a phony issue raised by the sore losers of 2016, Shepard Smith objected, describing the Trump administration's changing stories as lies, a word reporters often hesitate to use.

If there's nothing there—and that's what they tell us, they tell us there's nothing to this and nothing came of it, there's a nothing-burger, it wasn't even memorable, didn't write it down, didn't tell you about it, because it wasn't anything so I didn't even remember it—with a Russian interpreter in the room at Trump Tower? If all of that, why all these lies? Why is it lie after lie after lie? If you clean, come on clean, you know? My grandmother used to say when first we practice to—Oh what a tangled web we weave when first we practice to deceive. The deception, Chris [Wallace], is mind-boggling.

(quoted in Blake 2017c)

Presidents and the Search for America's Moral Core

Presidents have often summoned Americans to a higher moral purpose, to live up to the exemplary vision of the "city upon a hill" referenced in the Bible and used by John Winthrop as an inspiration for the early Massachusetts Bay settlers more than 350 years ago. Lincoln's second inaugural address in 1865 urged an America bloodied and bitter over an ongoing Civil War to come together "with malice toward none, with charity for all." Theodore Roosevelt thought that the government should protect the vulnerable from the predations of big business. In his 1989 farewell address Reagan returned to that seventeenth-century vision by saying that America "is still a beacon, still a magnet for all who must have freedom, for all the pilgrims from all the lost places who are hurtling through the darkness, toward home" (quoted in Landler 2017).

Trump, in contrast to these noble and uplifting sentiments from his Republican and conservative predecessors, repeatedly refused to pass judgment on the violence at an August 2017 white supremacist rally in Charlottesville, Virginia that killed one peaceful protestor and led to the deaths of two state police officers in a helicopter crash after monitoring

the incident from the air. In remarks that gave succor to white national-
ists, the president said: "I'm not putting anybody on a moral plane. What
I'm saying is this. You had a group on one side and you had a group on
the other, and they came at each other with clubs and it was vicious and
it was horrible" (quoted in Landler 2017). Other Republicans quickly
condemned his remarks, saying that Trump should condemn bigotry,
particularly in the wake of the violent Virginia rally.

Trump also refused to condemn the autocratic rule of Putin and President Rodrigo Duterte of the Philippines. In a Fox News interview where
then-host Bill O'Reilly asked about Putin, Trump undermined the image
of America as a place that holds democratic values dear. Trump said:
"There are a lot of killers. You think our country's so innocent?" (quoted
in Landler 2017). His remarks about Putin represented a stark departure
from what American presidents have said about the Soviet Union and
Russia over the past 70 years. Democratic and Republican presidents
before Trump have consistently argued that there are fundamental moral
differences between the U.S. and the USSR or Russia. Until Trump, a
bipartisan American foreign policy stretching back decades sought to
build support for human rights and democracy around the world to further American interests of a peaceful world that recognizes human rights
as a core principle of modernity—and one of our nation's key advantages
over authoritarian regimes.

The Uphill Struggle: Presidential Challenges on Capitol Hill

The modern 24/7 media management system, one peppered with some
friendly reporters as well as harsh critics in the cable and online environments, tempts White House staffers to try to win the news cycle min-
ute-by-minute. Failing to take more of a long-term perspective, though,
can be self-defeating over time. The Bush administration, for example,
offered short-term goodies like tax cuts to boost public approval, but
at devastating long-term costs to the national debt (Farnsworth 2009).
The short-term gains of Bush's "mission accomplished" moment come at
the long-term budgetary, human, and political costs of an occupation of
Iraq that turned out to be far worse than advertised (Tanter and Kersting 2008). We also can see the costs of short-term actions by examining
Obama's promise that one can keep one's own doctor under the Affordable Care Act. Once again, fleeting efforts to boost public opinion for a
controversial bill came at substantial long-term costs to Democrats running for office as well as for a president's credibility (Hopper 2017).

Bill Clinton suffered from the consequences of short-term-itis of a different sort. The Clinton scandals likewise demonstrate very effectively
how a president's character flaws can hurt one's political standing. Clinton's immediate physical desires and the subsequent televised denials of

his misbehavior cost him dearly during the yearlong impeachment effort, when his sordid behavior was on full display (Berman 2001). Even so, Clinton demonstrated throughout 1998 that he could play defense effectively, particularly when he turned the tables on Republicans pushing for impeachment.

Of course, campaigns win elections in the short term. Bush's intense public focus on the War on Terror clearly helped create a discourse framework that favored the Republicans in 2002 and 2004. That same War on Terror framework probably also undermined the GOP's chances in 2006, as the occupation's duration—one of many departures from the administration's prewar promises—angered many voters (Balz and Cohen 2007). Bush's stumbles also gave rise to Obama's victory in 2008. Obama's presidency, with its heavy focus on passing a very controversial health care bill, cost Democrats dearly in the elections that followed. While Obama's health care law will likely end up improving health care conditions compared to the status quo, Democratic electoral prospects clearly suffered following the law's passage.

In short, partisan legislative control of Congress does not guarantee success, even for presidents with solid personal reputations. Furthermore, such partisan control may turn out to be fleeting. Given such painful realities of governing, and the fact that few Republicans in Congress favored Trump as the party's nominee, President Trump faced immense challenges from the outset of his presidency. Trump's popular vote loss, along with the vibrant anti-Trump movement that emerged during the 2016 campaign and the many positions that Trump took that departed from Republican orthodoxy, meant that the new president would struggle to convince Congress to back his agenda. Despite the challenging environment, Trump could not muster the personal discipline to present himself, to organize his administration, or to create his policy agenda in ways that would maximize the chances of legislative success (Azari 2017).

Lawmakers generally try not to turn on presidents of their own political party, particularly during a president's first year. Even so, Republican members of Congress have launched attacks on Trump's character, something not seen in Washington since the final days of Nixon and Watergate. Sen. Jeff Flake (R-AZ) took the extraordinary step during Trump's first year in office to denounce him as dangerous to conservative causes, including traditional GOP values of free trade, limited government, and standing up in defense of human rights in the face of global authoritarians. Flake objected to the president's pattern of repeating falsehoods and otherwise not living up to presidential standards of credibility and respect for facts.

> We're only as good as our information, and if we lose our sense of objective truth, we lose everything. Whatever the source, a steady

diet of bad information, conveyed in bad faith, can over time become a serious threat to a democracy. Over time, a determined effort to undermine the very idea of truth softens the ground for anti-demo-cratic impulses. . . . Enduring democracies depend on the acceptance of shared facts, facts such as: certified elections are valid, millions of votes were not illegally cast in the 2016 election, vaccinations don't cause autism, and two Hawaiian newspapers announcing the birth of Barack Obama more than 50 years ago probably means that Obama was born in Hawaii—just to highlight a few of the more colorful examples of nonsense that has made the rounds in recent years.

(quoted in Hohmann 2017b)

To be sure, there has been a lengthy disagreement between the two men. Flake said Trump should end his campaign after the *Access Hollywood* tape surfaced, and relations have been sour ever since. Trump often seeks to avenge slights, and he had threatened to spend $10 million to defeat Flake in an upcoming Republican primary (Isenstadt 2017). Flake subsequently chose not to seek re-election in 2018.

The *National Review*, a key voice of American conservativism for more than half a century, said the failure of the health care bill repeal in mid-2017 demonstrated that Trump is more talk than action and that his "cartoon tough guy act" works better on television than in the Oval Office (Williamson 2017).

We did not elect Donald Trump; we elected the character he plays on television. He has had a middling career in real estate and a poor one as a hotelier and casino operator but convinced people he is a titan of industry. He has never managed a large, complex corporate enterprise, but he did play an executive on a reality show. . . . He isn't much of a negotiator, manager, or leader. He cannot negoti-ate a health-care deal among members of a party desperate for one, can't manage his own factionalized and leak-ridden White House, and cannot lead a political movement that aspires to anything greater than the service of his own pathetic vanity.

(Williamson 2017)

Presidential Character and the White House Staff

Congress is not the only Washington constituency that watches a presi-dent closely for signals on how to behave, as Neustadt (1990) observed. As in any workplace, people who work around the president often get to know him well. That familiarity sometimes breeds contempt, as the many White House tell-all books that emerge following changes of power in Washington demonstrate. Many people work for bosses they do not respect, and even in the White House there are those who work for a president they consider dangerous. Such people sometimes justify working for a problematic president if for no other reason than to prevent something even worse from happening. The Nixon White House offers a clear example of this pattern of self-justification.

> It is difficult to understand how anyone could work for someone as volatile and irrational as Nixon sometimes was. Most likely (Secretary of State Henry) Kissinger and others rationalized their collaboration as helping to save Nixon from himself. After all, he was a democratically elected president and they saw themselves as serving the national well-being by reining him in. Yet what seems so striking in the record is how often the people around Nixon catered to his outbursts and flights of fancy rather than challenging some of his most unsavory and unenforceable demands. It was a way to remain at Nixon's side but it was a disservice to sensible policy-making.
>
> (Dallek 2007: 316)

Trump's anger became particularly apparent during the days after violence erupted in Virginia at a rally of white supremacists that killed a young woman. He then resisted admitting he made a mistake in his original response in blaming both sides (Hohmann 2017c). This led to days of chaos in the West Wing (Cook and Dawsey 2017).

> Trump's temper has been a constant force in this eight-month-old White House. He's made policy decisions after becoming irritated with staffers and has escalated fights in the past few weeks with everyone from the Senate majority leader to the volatile dictator of North Korea. The controversy over his response to the Charlottesville violence was no different. Agitated about being pressured by aides to clarify his first public statement, Trump unexpectedly unwound the damage control of the prior two days by assigning blame to the "alt-left" and calling some of the white supremacist protesters "very fine people."
>
> (quoted in Cook and Dawsey 2017)

As Timothy Naftali, a presidential historian at New York University, observed: "It's not unusual to have presidents motivated by anger. The difference with Trump is the lack of filter, so we're seeing much more of his thinking than we ever saw with past presidents" (quoted in Cook and Dawsey 2017).

As an ex-president, Obama continued to show his ability to work with social media. He also provided a powerful contrast to his successor. When Trump struggled to express himself in a series of inconsistent statements about the neo-Nazi violence in Charlottesville in August 2017, Obama issued an optimistic tweet that captured the feelings of many. His tweet, quoting Nelson Mandela, expressed more optimism than Trump: "No one is born hating another person because of the color of his skin or his background or his religion" (quoted in Bromwich 2017). That tweet, and an accompanying photo of Obama talking with a group of multicultural children through an open window, received the most likes of any tweet in the history of Twitter (Bromwich 2017).

The virulent hostility to Trump found among many Democrats can offer a comforting cocoon to the like-minded in 2017. Of course, a year earlier Democrats enjoyed a similar comfort among themselves with their profound conviction that Donald Trump's unpresidential temperament made him unelectable in 2016. Liberal optimism that Trump's presidency will self-destruct may be an appealing dream for some, but Trump's ability to survive the difficulties of his business, entertainment, and political careers demonstrates the danger of underestimating the chances that Trump prevails in the end.

Presidential Character and Global Politics

There is always a certain level of international public and elite frustration with American presidents, regardless of who is serving in that office. America's highly influential role in the world, even in places where America may not focus its foreign policy efforts, can generate disagreement over policy ends as well as frustration that one's own nation lacks such global standing. International public opinion of the last two Democratic presidents (Clinton and Obama) was generally higher than that of the two Republican presidents examined here (George W. Bush and Trump). Both Republican presidents sought more aggressively to shape the international environment to their view of American interests with little international consultation, a move certain to create greater doubts in most world capitals than the more multilateral foreign policy orientations of Clinton and Obama.

A president's international popularity does not generate policy success, to be sure. For all of its multilateralism, the Obama administration struggled to deal with the wars it inherited in Iraq and Afghanistan, as well as the instability it faced in Libya and especially Syria. Trump's threats of nuclear war with North Korea and an expanded military engagement in the Middle East, and deference to authoritarian leaders in several nations, including Russia, the Philippines, and Turkey, mark an international presidency that is just getting started. It is far too soon to tell whether Trump will succeed where other presidents have struggled, or whether he will be less successful in the international arena than his predecessors were.

Trump's presidency offers an interesting test of his self-proclaimed negotiating shrewdness. Some White House officials have suggested that Trump's erratic approach to international matters is a rebirth of the "madman" international relations approach pioneered by Richard Nixon more than four decades ago. If a negotiator acts in irrational ways, the theory goes, the unpredictable negotiator has an advantage. If one cannot predict an adversary's next move based on a rational calculation, it could increase caution on the part of that adversary, according to this theory. Of course, it might also increase recklessness on both sides of a negotiation. It is too soon to tell whether Trump's threats to North Korea, for example, will lead to a moderation of the behavior of that rogue nation's leader. What is clear about the Trump presidency is that the forty-fifth president greatly desires to place issues of character at the center of conversations of international relations as well as domestic politics.

Presidential Character and the Future

People who expect the mass media to provide better political discourse that would assist in the rise of more qualified presidential candidates seem destined to be disappointed. Parts of the mass media certainly could have done far better in 2016 (Owen 2017), as well in previous elections marked by excessive horse-race coverage and a shortage of policy discussions (Farnsworth and Lichter 2011a). For much of the campaign reporters covered Trump as a novelty act, a newsworthy sideshow that would attract eyeballs and clicks for a while but would soon grow out of favor with a fickle audience. The cutbacks in the financially strapped newsrooms around the nation limited the amount of investigative journalism that takes place these days, but even so there were first-rate investigative pieces by places like the *New York Times* and the *Washington Post* that found problematic if not disqualifying matters from Trump's personal and financial history.

What's more, Trump himself often spoke in ways that would have been disqualifying for any previous presidential candidate, including the bragging of groping women's genitals on the *Access Hollywood* tape, attacking former prisoner of war Sen. John McCain (R-AZ) because he was captured in North Vietnam, and the idea that he was smart because he avoided paying taxes. A person who consumed news from a range of media outlets during 2016 would have found ample evidence to suggest that Trump's temperament made him an unsuitable if not a dangerous choice for the Oval Office.

Of course, many people do obtain news from a diverse range of media outlets. Fox News and other conservative news outlets, while not consistently all that enthusiastic about Trump, regularly made the case that this recent convert to conservatism was less dangerous as a president than Hillary Clinton would be. A never-ending diet of Benghazi reports and continuing allegations of email misconduct as well as a last-minute restart of an FBI investigation added up to a powerful case against her for those who were looking for one. The world of social media, where millions of humans and anti-Clinton bots posted and reposted false stories with impunity, provided a twenty-first century version of the age-old political art of candidate character assassination. Some people, at least, seem more inclined to recognize and focus on negative news (Soroka 2006, 2014), and Donald Trump responded to that human trait with a steady stream of anger, invective, and hostility directed at many perceived enemies foreign and domestic: be they Mexicans, immigrants, reporters, global traders, Democrats, elite Republicans, and especially Hillary Clinton. The more a politician can direct public attention to the faults of one's opponent the less one observes the faults found in the attacker. That approach seems to work better for a candidate than a president; after all, attacks on Hillary Clinton in 2017 seem stale, and even more so as the attacks continue in 2018. What's more, continuing White House criticism of fellow Republicans does not help move a president's legislative agenda.

While reporters at some media outlets may admit they need to change, it is not clear that those efforts will add up to much. The trajectory of media change has not always been in the direction of improved public discourse, to say the least. Social media providers promised after the 2016 election to improve the content on their sites. Those vows seem unlikely to alter things all that much for future elections. Platforms like Facebook and Twitter and YouTube profit from the volume of discourse and the public attention they receive, not from the quality of content. A business does not kill the goose (or the bot) that lays a golden egg with every click, after all.

Even if these social media providers succeeded in their promised efforts to flag false content with their own fact-checking algorithms, that vow also does not seem likely to elevate the discourse. If these outlets do change in the way that some think would lead to more elevated public discourse, what is to keep the people who want to receive stories about the next "Pizzagate" from migrating to another media platform that has no such "good government" compunctions? Indeed, irresponsibility on the web may be a profitable way to distinguish one's web operations.

Perhaps the fault, to paraphrase Shakespeare, is more in ourselves than it is in our URLs.

Donald Trump and the Future of Candidates and Presidential Character

Trump has emphasized discussion of Trump the person. He has not encouraged discussion of the administration's policy specifics, even less any legislative success. While many presidents have sought to emphasize the personal to maximize their popularity and their chances of success, Trump is a departure from the previous norm that presidents should try to maximize how likeable they seem to the public as part of that process. Trump offers the aggressiveness of Bush, without the "good old boy" demeanor that might smooth off his rougher edges for public consumption. Trump argues that he understands the troubles that ordinary Americans face in tough economic times as Clinton did a quarter-century ago, but he does so without the charm offensive that marked the personality presentation of the forty-second president. Trump cultivates his base with his hot rhetoric, and makes little effort to reach beyond the roughly one-third of the country that is always in the president's corner to block what the opposing party has to offer. The combativeness and aggressiveness of candidate Trump and his tweets, if anything, have intensified since he took office. Like other presidents before him, Trump is a man of the media moment, with his presidential communication efforts effectively tailored to the news environment of his time.

Whether Trump is the start of a new era in presidential communication will depend largely on the success of his presidency. Nothing succeeds like success, as the saying goes. A number of business and Hollywood celebrities are debating whether to launch their own political careers in the wake of Trump's presidential election victory. If his presidency succeeds in passing more legislation or in improving Trump's evaluation numbers there may be a number of political newbies thinking that they can be the next Trump. If Trump is re-elected in 2020, expect even more celebrity-turned-politicians running for office.

That scenario seems less likely than the alternative, for three reasons. There is, above all, the most powerful tradition in presidential elections: the idea that we want what we do not have in a leader. As we have discussed earlier, successful presidential candidates offer things their predecessors lacked, and Trump's negative, divisive approach may not wear well with most Americans year after year. Indeed, the polls show an unusually negative public reaction to the first year of the Trump presidency. A more unifying, upbeat message that speaks to America's aspirations rather than its fears may be appealing to more Americans in 2020 than a replay of Trump's downbeat message of economic anxiety, external threats, and personal attacks.

A second problem Trump faces is his slow start as president. Presidents tend to have their most political and legislative success during their first two years in office, but Trump has taken longer than many of his predecessors to staff his administration and put together a detailed legislative agenda (Azari 2017). Midterm elections often hurt a president's prospects in Congress: both Clinton and Obama had Democratic majorities in both the House and Senate for only the first two years of their term, as examples. By the end of any president's first year, many of the president's co-partisans are paying close attention to presidential popularity, and Trump's extremely low approval numbers will not convince

Republicans in Congress to gamble that Trump can save them in the traditionally harsh midterm reaction against nearly every president that hurts a president's fellow partisans on Capitol Hill. In 2018, these elected officials will be looking out for themselves, not for him, and that does not increase Trump's chances of legislative success in the years that follow.

A third reason why Trump may not be the pattern of future politicians trying to follow his lead concerns Trump himself. He may be one of a kind. Trump demonstrated an extraordinary ability to connect with millions of evangelical Christians and economically struggling small-town voters who one might have thought would be ill disposed to support a blustery New York City billionaire on his third marriage who bragged of his ability to get away with grabbing women, stiffing contractors, and evading tax bills. Trump's regular attempts to denigrate his fellow Republicans did not create nearly the opposition within the party that one might have expected—note how the GOP's "Never Trump" movement fizzled before the election despite some big-name supporters. Trump's many scandals and deceits, exhaustively covered by the media, did not sink his candidacy, though these problems would have been the end of many a campaign with a candidate who lacked Trump's extraordinary, instinctive ability to connect with the public's distrust of government.

In other words, the way to be the next LeBron James is to play basketball like LeBron James. Well, almost no one can play the game as well as LeBron James can, which is why he has won all those NBA MVP trophies. It may be equally difficult for would-be future Trump-style candidates to capture his magical bluster, the celebrity candidate secret sauce that allowed Trump to survive and then succeed when so many rivals with years of public service could not.

Regardless of whether or not the Trump presidency becomes more successful after a very rough first year, we can see that his aggressive use of modern media technology to shape public opinion surrounding his presidency and his character will lead to greater emphasis on personality matters in the selection of future presidential candidates and the evaluation of future presidents. Reporters and voters will continue to look at who the presidents present themselves to be as people and consider how well the character of would-be presidents matches public preferences and public policy needs at the time of that election. Twitter, YouTube, and other social media outlets now allow presidential candidates and presidents to present themselves far more extensively, and in a far more unmediated manner, than was possible even a decade ago. They will, as have the presidents before them, take advantage of the dominant technologies in ways that maximize their chances of winning an election and securing the positive public approval that helps increase presidential leverage in policy-making in domestic and international venues.

At the same time, new media will continue to magnify and amplify the character traits of candidates and presidents in ways that can make or break campaigns and administrations. The dynamic interactions among personalities, media venues, and messages are bound to grow in importance as every candidate struggles to prove that he or she is worthy of being president and as every president seeks to demonstrate that he or she is succeeding at the world's most challenging—and most visible—job.

References

Aaker, Jennifer, and Andy Smith. 2010. *The Dragonfly Effect: Quick, Effective and Powerful Ways to Use Social Media to Drive Social Change*. New York: Jossey-Bass.

Aberbach, Joel D. 2012. "'Change We Can Believe In' Meets Reality." In *The Obama Presidency: Appraisals and Prospects*, eds. Bert A. Rockman, Andrew Rudalevige, and Colin Campbell. Washington: Sage/CQ Press.

Abramowitz, Alan I. 2017. "It Wasn't the Economy, Stupid: Racial Polarization, White Racial Resentment and the Rise of Trump." In *Trumped: The 2016 Election That Broke All the Rules*, eds. Larry J. Sabato, Kyle Kondik, and Geoffrey Skelly. Lanham, MD: Rowman & Littlefield.

Abramson, Paul R., John H. Aldrich, and David W. Rohde. 2012. *Change and Continuity in the 2008 and 2010 Elections*. Washington: CQ Press.

Adatto, Kiku. 1990. "Sound Bite Democracy." Research paper, Kennedy School Press Politics Center, Harvard University, June.

Adorno, Theodor, Else Frankel-Brunswick, Daniel J. Levinson, and Nevitt R. Sanford. 1950. *The Authoritarian Personality*. New York: Harper and Row.

Aitken, Jonathan. 1993. *Nixon: A Life*. Washington: Regnery.

Alter, Jonathan. 2010. *The Promise*. New York: Simon & Schuster.

_____. 2013. *The Center Holds*. New York: Simon & Schuster.

Altman, Lawrence K., and Todd S. Purdum. 2002. "In Kennedy File, a Portrait of Illness and Pain." *New York Times*, November 17.

Anderson, Carol. 2017. "The Policies of White Resentment." *New York Times*, August 6. URL: www.nytimes.com/2017/08/05/opinion/sunday/white-resentment-affirmative-action.html?smid=tw-share

Azari, Julie. 2014. "How Obama's 'Between Two Ferns' Appearance Compares to FDR's Fireside Chats." *Washington Post*, March 12. URL: www.washingtonpost.com/news/monkey-cage/wp/2014/03/12/how-obamas-between-two-ferns-appearance-compares-to-fdrs-fireside-chats/?utm_term=.c2b494db7791

_____. 2017. "Trump Came in as A Weak President, and He's Made Himself Weaker." *FiveThirtyEight.com*, August 1. URL: https://fivethirtyeight.com/features/trump-weak-president/

Baker, Peter. 2017. "Trump Tries to Regroup as the West Wing Battles Itself." *New York Times*, July 29. URL: www.nytimes.com/2017/07/29/us/politics/trump-presidency-setbacks.html?smid=tw-share&_r=0

Baker, Peter, and Maggie Haberman. 2017. "Anthony Scaramucci's Uncensored Rant: Foul Words and Threats to Have Priebus Fired." *New York Times*,

July 27. URL: www.nytimes.com/2017/07/27/us/politics/scaramucci-priebus-leaks.html

Baker, Peter, and Maggie Haberman. 2018. "Trump, Defending His Mental Fitness, Says He's a 'Very Stable Genius.'" *New York Times*, January 6. URL: www.nytimes.com/2018/01/06/us/politics/trump-genius-mental-health.html

Balz, Dan, and Jon Cohen. 2007. "Confidence in Bush Leadership at All-Time Low, Poll Finds." *Washington Post*, January 22.

Balz, Dan, and Jon Cohen. 2010. "Democrats Gain in Poll, But GOP Still Leads as Midterm Elections Near." *Washington Post*, October 5. URL: www.washingtonpost.com/wp-dyn/content/article/2010/10/05/AR2010100500005.html

Barbaro, Michael. 2015. "Donald Trump Likens His Schooling to Military Service in Book." *New York Times*, September 8. URL: www.nytimes.com/2015/09/09/us/politics/donald-trump-likens-his-schooling-to-military-service-in-book.html

Barber, James David. 1992. *Presidential Character: Predicting Performance in the White House*. Englewood Cliffs, NJ: Prentice-Hall.

Barbour, Henry, Sally Bradshaw, Ari Fleischer, Zori Fonalledas, and Glenn McCall. 2013. "Growth and Opportunity Project." Republican National Committee. URL: www.gop.com/growth-and-opportunity-project/

Bartels, Larry. 2008. *Unequal Democracy: The Political Economy of the New Gilded Age*. Princeton, NJ: Princeton University Press.

Baum, Matthew A., and Samuel Kernell. 1999. "Has Cable Ended the Golden Age of Presidential Television?" *American Political Science Review* 93(1): 99–114.

Benda, Peter M., and Charles H. Levine. 1988. "Reagan and the Bureaucracy: The Bequest, The Promise and the Legacy." In *The Reagan Legacy: Promise and Performance*, ed. Charles O. Jones. Chatham, NJ: Chatham House.

Benkler, Yochai, Robert Faris, Hal Roberts, and Ethan Zuckerman. 2017. "Study: Breitbart-Led Right-Wing Media Ecosystem Altered Broader Media Agenda." *Columbia Journalism Review*, March 3. URL: www.cjr.org/analysis/breitbart-media-trump-harvard-study.php

Bennett, W. Lance. 1995. "The Clueless Public: Bill Clinton Meets the New American Voter in Campaign '92." In *The Clinton Presidency: Campaigning, Governing and the Psychology of Leadership*, ed. Stanley A. Renshon. Boulder, CO: Westview.

_____. 2012. *News: The Politics of Illusion*. Boston, MA: Longman. Ninth Edition.

Bennett, W. Lance, Regina G. Lawrence, and Steven Livingston. 2007. *When the Press Fails: Political Power and the News Media from Iraq to Katrina*. Chicago: University of Chicago Press.

Berman, Mark. 2017a. "Trump Tells Police Not to Worry About Injuring Suspects During Arrests." *Washington Post*, July 28. URL: www.washingtonpost.com/news/post-nation/wp/2017/07/28/trump-tells-police-not-to-worry-about-injuring-suspects-during-arrests/?utm_term=.9c4e5ed88ea0

_____. 2017b. "White House Says Trump Was Kidding About Police Mistreating Suspects, But Cops Say 'it Doesn't Matter If He Was Joking.'" *Washington Post*, July 31. URL: www.washingtonpost.com/news/post-nation/wp/2017/07/31/why-police-departments-lashed-out-at-trump-for-his-comments-on-how-they-treat-suspects/?utm_term=.df1591ef0b28

Berman, William C. 2001. *From the Center to the Edge: The Politics and Policies of the Clinton Presidency*. Lanham, MD: Rowman & Littlefield.

Beschloss, Michael. 2002. *The Conquerers: Roosevelt, Truman and the Destruction of Hitler's Germany*, 1941–1945. New York: Simon & Schuster.

Blake, Aaron. 2014. "White House: Obama's 'Between Two Ferns' Cameo Driving Traffic to HealthCare.gov." *Washington Post*, March 11. URL: www.washingtonpost.com/news/post-politics/wp/2014/03/11/white-house-obamas-between-two-ferns-cameo-driving-traffic-to-healthcare-gov/?utm_term=.c3cfd70ea2dc

_____. 2017a. "8 Things the Trump Team Denied, and Then Later Confirmed." *Washington Post*, August 2. URL: www.washingtonpost.com/news/the-fix/wp/2017/08/02/7-things-the-trump-team-denied-and-then-later-confirmed/?hpid=hp_hp-more-top-stories_fix-trump-1020pm%3Ahomepage%2Fstory&utm_term=.e3bea52058be

_____. 2017b. "Trump Admits He Punked His Supporters on Mexico Paying For the Wall." *Washington Post*, August 3. URL: www.washingtonpost.com/news/the-fix/wp/2017/08/03/trump-admits-he-punked-his-supporters-on-mexico-paying-for-the-wall/?utm_term=.3fa9f7c02341

_____. 2017c. " 'Lie After Lie After Lie': Fox News's Shepard Smith Has a Cronkite Moment on Russia." *Washington Post*, July 17. URL: www.washingtonpost.com/news/the-fix/wp/2017/07/14/lie-after-lie-after-lie-fox-news-shepard-smith-has-a-cronkite-moment-on-russia/?utm_term=.936fdfd64bd4

Blaney, Joseph R., and William L. Beniot. 2001. *The Clinton Scandals and the Politics of Image Restoration*. Westport, CT: Praeger.

Bonner, Raymond, and Jane Perlez. 2007. "British Report Criticizes US Treatment of Terror Suspects." *New York Times*, July 28.

Bonner, Raymond, and Sara Rimer. 2000. "Executing the Mentally Retarded Even as Laws Began to Shift." *New York Times*, August 7.

Boorstin, Daniel. 1961. *The Image: A Guide to Pseudo-Events in America*. New York: Atheneum.

Brader, Ted, Nicholas A. Valentino, and Elizabeth Suhay. 2008. "What Triggers Public Opposition to Immigration? Anxiety, Group Cues and Immigration Threat." *American Journal of Political Science* 52(4): 959–978.

Brands, Riley, and Frank Newport. 2016. "Most Americans Want Changes to Affordable Care Act." *Gallup.com*. URL: www.gallup.com/poll/198158/americans-changes-affordable-care-act.aspx?g_source=Affordable+care+act&g_medium=search&g_campaign=tiles

Broder, John M. 2006. "Democrats Take Senate: Concession in Virginia Completes Midterm Sweep." *New York Times*, November 10.

Bromwich, Jonah Engel. 2017. "Obama's Charlottesville Response, Boosted by Nostalgia, Becomes Most-Liked Tweet Ever." *New York Times*, August 17. URL: www.nytimes.com/2017/08/16/us/politics/obama-charlottesville-tweet.html?_r=0

Brooks, Stephen. 2006. *As Others See Us: The Causes and Consequences of Foreign Perceptions of America*. Peterborough, ON: Broadview.

Brown, Robin. 2003. "Clausewitz in the Age of CNN: Rethinking the Military-Media Relationship." In *Framing Terrorism: The News Media, the Government and the Public*, eds. Pippa Norris, Montague Kern and Marion Just. New York: Routledge.

Bumiller, Elisabeth. 2003. "Keepers of Bush Image Lift Stagecraft to New Heights." *New York Times*, May 16.

_____. 2004. "Lawyer for Bush Quits over Links to Kerry's Foes." *New York Times*, August 26: A1.

Bump, Philip. 2017a. "Trump Insists That Senators (who won without him) Owe Him Loyalty (that isn't returned)." *Washington Post*, July 24. URL: www.washingtonpost.com/news/politics/wp/2017/07/24/trump-insists-that-senators-who-won-without-him-owe-him-loyalty-that-isnt-returned/?utm_term=.6e77dde8cfe2

_____. 2017b. "By End of August, Trump Will Have Spent Three Times as Many Days at Leisure as Obama." *Washington Post*, August 3. URL: www.washingtonpost.com/news/politics/wp/2017/08/03/by-end-of-august-trump-will-have-spent-three-times-as-many-days-at-leisure-as-obama/?tid=sm_tw&utm_term=.3c549df9b2d2

_____. 2017c. "What Trump Has Undone." *Washington Post*, December 15. URL: www.washingtonpost.com/news/politics/wp/2017/08/24/what-trump-has-undone/?utm_term=.c934e55fa750

_____. 2018. "Trump Says He's a Stable Genius. Only a Quarter of Americans Agree." *Washington Post*, January 10. URL: www.washingtonpost.com/news/politics/wp/2018/01/10/trump-says-hes-a-stable-genius-only-a-quarter-of-americans-agree/?tid=sm_tw&utm_term=.63bea346746a

Burden, Barry C. 2005. "The Nominations: Technology, Money and Transferrable Momentum." In *The Elections of 2004*, ed. Michael Nelson. Washington: CQ Press.

Burns, John F., Sabrina Tavernise, and Marc Santora. 2007. "U.S. and Iraqis Are Wrangling Over War Plans." *New York Times*, January 15.

Burns, James MacGregor, and Susan Dunn. 2001. *The Three Roosevelts: Patrician Leaders Who Transformed America*. New York: Atlantic Monthly Press.

Busch, Andrew. 2016. "The Limits of Governmental Accomplishment." In *Debating the Obama Presidency*, ed. Steven E. Schier. Lanham, MD: Rowman & Littlefield.

Campbell, Colin. 2000. "Demotion: Has Clinton Turned the Bully Pulpit Into a Lectern?" In *The Clinton Legacy*, eds. Colin Campbell and Bert A. Rockman. New York: Chatham House.

_____. 2004a. "Managing the Presidency or the President?" In *The George W. Bush Presidency: Appraisals and Prospects*, eds. Colin Campbell and Bert A. Rockman. Washington, DC: CQ Press.

_____ 2004b. "Unrestrained Ideological Entrepreneurship in the Bush II Advisory System: An Examination of the Response to 9/11 and the Decision to Seek Regime Change in Iraq." In *The George W. Bush Presidency: Appraisals and Prospects*, eds. Colin Campbell and Bert A. Rockman. Washington, DC: CQ Press.

Campbell, David E. 2009. "Public Opinion and the 2008 Presidential Election." In *The American Elections of 2008*, eds. Janet M. Box-Steffensmeier and Steven E.Schier. Lanham, MD: Rowman & Littlefield.

Campbell, James E. 2012. "Political Forces on the Obama Presidency: From Elections to Governing." In *The Obama Presidency: Appraisals and Prospects*, eds. Bert A. Rockman, Andrew Rudalevige, and Colin Campbell. Washington: Sage/CQ Press.

_____. 2016. *Polarized: Making Sense of a Divided America*. Princeton: Princeton University Press.

Cannon, Lou. 1991. *Ronald Reagan: Role of a Lifetime*. New York: Simon & Schuster.

Carey, George, and James McClellan, eds. 1990. *The Federalist*. Dubuque, Iowa: Kendall/Hunt.

Caro, Robert A. 2002. *The Years of Lyndon Johnson: Master of the Senate*. New York: Knopf.

Carr, David. 2011. "How Drudge Has Stayed on Top." *New York Times*, May 16. URL: www.nytimes.com/2011/05/16/business/media/16carr.html

Ceaser, James. 1988. "The Reagan Presidency and American Public Opinion." *The Reagan Legacy: Promise and Performance*, ed. Charles O. Jones. Chatham, NJ: Chatham House.

Ceaser, James, and Andrew Busch. 1993. *Upside Down and Inside Out: The 1992 Elections and American Politics*. Lanham, MD: Rowman & Littlefield.

_____. 1997. *Losing to Win: The 1996 Elections and American Politics*. Lanham, MD: Rowman & Littlefield.

_____. 2001. *The Perfect Tie: The True Story of the 2000 Presidential Election*. Lanham, MD: Rowman & Littlefield.

_____. 2005. *Red Over Blue*. Lanham, MD: Rowman & Littlefield.

Ceaser, James, Andrew Busch, and John J. Pitney, Jr. 2009. *Epic Journey: The 2008 Elections and American Politics*. Lanham, MD: Rowman & Littlefield.

_____. 2015. *After Hope and Change: The 2012 Elections and American Politics* (Post 2014 Election Update). Lanham, MD: Rowman & Littlefield.

_____. 2017. *Defying the Odds: The 2016 Elections and American Politics*. Lanham, MD: Rowman & Littlefield.

Chadwick, Andrew. 2013. *The Hybrid Media System*. Oxford: Oxford University Press.

Chandrasekaran, Rajiv. 2006. *Imperial Life in the Emerald City: Inside Iraq's Green Zone*. New York: Knopf.

Chang, Alvin. 2017. "We Analyzed 17 Months of Fox & Friends Transcripts. It's Far Weirder Than State-Run Media." *Vox.com*, August 7. URL: www.vox.com/2017/8/7/16083122/breakfast-club-fox-and-friends

Christenson, D. P., and Kriner, D. L. 2017. "Mobilizing the Public Against the President: Congress and the Political Costs of Unilateral Action." *American Journal of Political Science*. doi:10.1111/ajps.12298

Clarke, Richard A. 2004. *Against All Enemies: Inside America's War on Terror*. New York: Free Press.

Clement, Scott, and David Nakamura. 2017. "Poll Shows Clear Disapproval of How Trump Responded to Charlottesville Violence." *Washington Post*, August 21. URL: www.washingtonpost.com/politics/poll-shows-strong-disapproval-of-how-trump-responded-to-charlottesville-violence/2017/08/21/4e5c585c-868b-11e7-a94f-3139abce39f5_story.html?utm_term=.4e11bc6e9f19

Cohen, Jeffrey E. 2002a. "The Polls: Policy-Specific Presidential Approval, Part I." *Presidential Studies Quarterly* 32(3): 600–609.

_____. 2002b. "The Polls: Policy-Specific Presidential Approval, Part II." *Presidential Studies Quarterly* 32(4): 779–788.

_____. 2008. *The Presidency in the Era of 24-Hour News*. Princeton, NJ: Princeton University Press.

Cohen, Marty, David Karol, Hans Noel, and John Zaller. 2016. "Party Versus Faction in the Reformed Presidential Nominating System." *PS: Political Science & Politics* 49(4): 701–708.

Conley, Patricia. 2009. "A Mandate for Change? Decisive Victory in a Time of Crisis." In *Winning the Presidency, 2008*, ed. William J. Crotty. Boulder, CO: Paradigm.

Conway, Bethany A., Kate Kenski, and Di Wang. 2013. "Twitter Use by Presidential Candidates during the 2012 Presidential Campaign." *American Behavioral Scientist* 57(11): 1596–1610.

Cook, Nancy, and Josh Dawsey. 2017. " 'He is Stubborn and Doesn't Realize How Bad This is Getting,' The Charlottesville Furor is the Latest Example of the Chaos That Can Result From Trump's Temper and Refusal to Back Down." *Politico*, August 17. URL: www.politico.com/story/2017/08/16/trump-charlottesville-temper-chaos-241721

Cook, Timothy E. 1989. *Making Laws and Making News*. Washington, DC: Brookings Institution.

_____. 2005. *Governing With the News: The News Media as a Political Institution* 2nd ed. Chicago: University of Chicago Press.

Cooper, John M., Jr. 1983. *The Warrior and the Priest: Woodrow Wilson and Theodore Roosevelt*. Cambridge, MA: Harvard University Press.

Copeland, Lauren, and Bruce Bimber. 2015. "Variation in the Relationship between Digital Media Use and Political Participation in U.S. Elections over Time, 1996–2012: Does Obama's Reelection Change the Picture?" *Journal of Information Technology & Politics* 12(1):74–87.

Cronin, Thomas E., and Michael A. Genovese. 2013. *The Paradoxes of the American Presidency* 4th ed. New York: Oxford University Press.

Dallek, Robert. 2003. *An Unfinished Life: John F. Kennedy*. Boston, MA: Little, Brown & Co.

_____. 2007. *Nixon and Kissinger: Partners in Power*. Boston, MA: Little, Brown & Co.

Davis, Richard. 1999. *The Web of Politics: The Internet's Impact on the American Political System*. New York: Oxford University Press.

Davis, Richard, and Diana Owen. 1998. *New Media and American Politics*. New York: Oxford University Press.

Dawsey, Josh, and Hadas Gold. 2017. "Full Transcript: Trump's Wall Street Journal Interview." *Politico*, August 1. URL: www.politico.com/story/2017/08/01/trump-wall-street-journal-interview-full-transcript-241214

Denton, Robert E. 2009. "Identity Politics and the 2008 Presidential Campaign." In *The 2008 Presidential Campaign: A Communication Perspective*, ed. Robert E. Denton. Lanham, MD: Rowman & Littlefield.

Destler, I. M. 1988. "Reagan and the World: An 'Awesome Stubbornness.' " In *The Reagan Legacy: Promise and Performance*, ed. Charles O. Jones. Chatham, NJ: Chatham House.

Dimock, Michael A. 2004. "Bush and Public Opinion." In *Considering the Bush Presidency*, eds. Gary L. Gregg II and Mark Rozell. New York: Oxford University Press.

Dowd, Maureen. 1999. "Name That General!" *New York Times*, November 7.

_____. 2005. "The United States of Shame." *New York Times*, September 3.

Dreier, Peter, and Christopher R. Martin. 2010. "How ACORN Was Framed: Political Controversy and Media Agenda Setting." *Perspectives on Politics* 8(3): 761–792.

Druckman, James N., Jordan Fein, and Thomas J. Leeper. 2012. "A Source of Bias in Public Opinion Stability." *American Political Science Review* 106(2): 430–454.

Druckman, James N., Erik Peterson, and Rune Slothuus. 2013. "How Elite Partisan Polarization Affects Public Opinion Formation." *American Political Science Review* 107(1): 57–79.

Drudge, Matt. 2000. *Drudge Manifesto*. New York: New American Library.

Easton, Nina, Michael Kranish, Patrick Healy, Glen Johnson, Anne E. Kornblut, and Brian Mooney. 2004. "On the Trail of Kerry's Failed Dream." *Boston Globe*, November 14.

Edge, Thomas. 2010. "Southern Strategy 2.0: Conservatives, White Voters and the Election of Barack Obama." *Journal of Black Studies* 40(3): 426–444.

Edsall, Thomas B. 2017. "Killing Obamacare Softly. *New York Times*, July 27. URL: www.nytimes.com/2017/07/27/opinion/health-care-obamacare.html

Edwards, George C. III. 2000. "Campaigning Is Not Governing: Bill Clinton's Rhetorical Presidency." In *The Clinton Legacy*, eds. Colin Campbell and Bert A. Rockman. New York: Chatham House.

_____. 2003. *On Deaf Ears: The Limits of the Bully Pulpit*. New Haven, CT: Yale University Press.

_____. 2004. "Riding High in the Polls: George W. Bush and Public Opinion." In *The George W. Bush Presidency: Appraisals and Prospects*, eds. Colin Campbell and Bert A. Rockman. Washington, DC: CQ Press.

Elahi, Babak, and Grant Cos. 2012. "An Immigrant's Dream and the Audacity of Hope: The 2004 Convention Addresses of Barack Obama and Arnold Schwarzenegger." In *Barack Obama: Political Frontiers and Racial Agency*, eds. Ama Mazama and Molefi Kete Asante. Los Angeles, CA: Sage/CQ Press.

Enten, Harry. 2017. "Six Months In, Trump Is Historically Unpopular." *FiveThirtyEight*, July 17. URL: https://fivethirtyeight.com/features/six-months-in-trump-is-historically-unpopular/

Entman, Robert M. 2000. "Declarations of Independence." In *Decision-Making in a Glass House: Mass Media, Public Opinion and American and European Foreign Policy in the 21st Century*, eds. B. L. Nacos, R. Y. Shapiro, and P. Isernia. Lanham, MD: Rowman & Littlefield.

_____. 2004. *Projections of Power: Framing News, Public Opinion, and U.S. Foreign Policy*. Chicago: University of Chicago Press.

Farnsworth, Stephen J. 2001. "Patterns of Political Support: Examining Congress and the Presidency." *Congress & the Presidency* 28(1): 45–60.

_____. 2003a. *Political Support in a Frustrated America*. Westport, CT: Praeger.

_____. 2003b. "Congress and Citizen Discontent: Public Evaluations of the Membership and One's Own Representative. *American Politics Research* 31(1): 66–80.

_____. 2009. *Spinner in Chief: How Presidents Sell Their Policies and Themselves*. Boulder, CO: Paradigm/Routledge.

_____. 2015. "Studying the Presidency After 9/11: Re-considering Presidential Character in Domestic and International Contexts." 9/11 and the Academy Conference. Emory & Henry College. Emory, Va.

Farnsworth, Stephen J., and S. Robert Lichter. 1999. "No Small-Town Poll: Public Attention to Network Coverage of the 1992 New Hampshire Primary." *Harvard International Journal of Press/Politics* 4(3): 51–61.

_____. 2003. *The Nightly News Nightmare: Network Television's Coverage of U.S. Presidential Elections, 1988–2000.* Lanham, MD: Rowman and Littlefield.

_____. 2004. "New Presidents and Network News: Covering the First Year in Office of Ronald Reagan, Bill Clinton and George W. Bush." *Presidential Studies Quarterly* 34(3): 674–690.

_____. 2005. "The Mediated Congress: Coverage of Capitol Hill in the *New York Times* and the *Washington Post.*" *Harvard International Journal of Press/Politics* 10(2): 94–107.

_____. 2006. *The Mediated Presidency: Television News and Presidential Governance.* Lanham, MD: Rowman and Littlefield.

_____. 2011a. *The Nightly News Nightmare: Media Coverage of U.S. Presidential Elections, 1988–2008.* Lanham, MD: Rowman and Littlefield. Third edition.

_____. 2011b. "The Return of the Honeymoon: Television News Coverage of New Presidents, 1981–2009." *Presidential Studies Quarterly* 41(3): 590–603.

_____. 2016a. "News Coverage of US Presidential Campaigns: Reporting on Primaries and General Elections, 1988–2012." In *The Praeger Handbook of Political Campaigning in the United States*, ed. William Benoit. Santa Barbara, CA: Praeger, 233–253 (Volume 1).

_____. 2016b. "A Comparative Analysis of the Partisan Targets of Media Fact-checking." Paper presented at the American Political Science Association Annual Meeting. Philadelphia, PA. September 2016.

Farnsworth, Stephen J., S. Robert Lichter, and Deanne Canieso. 2017. "Donald Trump Will Probably Be the Most Ridiculed President Ever." *Washington Post*, January 21. URL: www.washingtonpost.com/news/monkey-cage/wp/2017/01/21/donald-trump-will-probably-be-the-most-ridiculed-president-ever/?utm_term=.3564387e0612

Farnsworth, Stephen J., S. Robert Lichter, and Roland Schatz. 2013. *The Global President: International Media and the US Government.* Lanham, MD: Rowman & Littlefield.

_____. 2017. "News Coverage of Trump is Really, Really Negative: Even on Fox News." *Washington Post*, February 28. URL: www.washingtonpost.com/news/monkey-cage/wp/2017/02/28/news-coverage-of-trump-is-really-really-negative-even-on-fox-news/?utm_term=.c4b2c79b1085

Fiorina, Morris P. 2008. "A Divider, Not a Uniter—But Did it Have to Be?" In *The Bush Legacy*, eds. Colin Campbell, Bert A. Rockman, and Andrew Rudalevige. Washington, DC: CQ Press.

Fisher, Louis. 2004. "The Way We Go to War: The Iraq Resolution." In *Considering the Bush Presidency*, eds. Gary Gregg II and Mark J. Rozell. New York: Oxford University Press.

Fisher, Marc, John Woodrow Cox, and Peter Hermann. 2016. "Pizzagate: From Rumor, to Hashtag, to Gunfire in D.C." *Washington Post*, December 6. URL: www.washingtonpost.com/local/pizzagate-from-rumor-to-hashtag-to-gunfire-in-dc/2016/12/06/4c7def50-bbd4-11e6-94ac-3d324840106c_story.html?utm_term=.f26c611c40e1

Foreman, Jr. Christopher H. 2008. "The Braking of a President: Shifting Context and the Bush Domestic Agenda." In *The Bush Legacy*, ed. Colin Campbell, Bert A. Rockman, and Andrew Rudalevige. Washington, DC: CQ Press.

Frank, Thomas. 2004. *What's the Matter with Kansas? How Conservatives Won the Heart of America.* New York: Metropolitan Books.

Friedman, Thomas L. 2001. "Foreign Affairs: Soul Brother." *New York Times*, June 29. URL: www.nytimes.com/2001/06/29/opinion/foreign-affairs-soul-brother.html

Freud, Sigmund, and William C. Bullitt. 1967. *Thomas Woodrow Wilson: A Psychological Study*. Boston, MA: Houghton Mifflin.

Fritz, Ben, Bryan Keefer, and Brendan Nyhan. 2004. *All the President's Spin: George W. Bush, the Media and the Truth*. New York: Touchstone.

Fromm, Erich. 1941. *Escape From Freedom*. New York: Henry Holt & Co.

Frum, David. 2003. *The Right Man: The Surprise Presidency of George W. Bush, An Inside Account*. New York: Random House.

Geer, John. G. 2012. "The News Media and the Rise of Negativity in Presidential Campaigns." *PS: Political Science & Politics* 45(3):422–434.

Geidner, Nick, and R. Lance Holbert. 2011. "A Meeting of Broadcast and Post-Broadcast Media in the 2004 American Presidential Election." *Communication Research Reports* 28(1): 43–51.

George, Alexander L., and Juliette L. George. 1964. *Woodrow Wilson and Colonel House: A Personality Study*. New York: Dover.

____. 1998. *Presidential Personality and Performance*. Boulder, CO: Westview.

Germond, Jack, and Jules Witcover. 1993. *Mad as Hell: Revolt at the Ballot Box, 1992*. New York: Warner.

Ginsberg, Benjamin. 1986. *The Captive Public: How Mass Opinion Promotes State Power*. New York: Basic Books.

Glad, Betty. 1995. "How George Bush Lost the Presidential Election of 1992." In *The Clinton Presidency: Campaigning, Governing and the Psychology of Leadership*, ed. Stanley A. Renshon. Boulder, CO: Westview.

Goldberg, Jeffrey. 2016. "The Obama Doctrine." *The Atlantic*, April. URL: www.theatlantic.com/magazine/archive/2016/04/the-obama-doctrine/471525/

Goldberg, Robert, and Gerald J. Goldberg. 1995. *Citizen Turner*. New York: Harcourt Brace.

Goodwin, Doris Kearns. 1991. *Lyndon Johnson and the American Dream*. New York: St. Martin's.

____. 1994. *No Ordinary Time*. New York: Simon & Schuster.

Gordon, Michael R. 2003. "Basra Offers a Lesson on Taking Baghdad." *New York Times*, April 3.

Goren, Paul, and Christopher Chapp. 2017. "Moral Power: How Public Opinion on Culture War Issues Shapes Partisan Predispositions and Religious Orientations." *American Political Science Review* 111(1):110–128.

Gorman, Michele. 2017. "Trump White House Has a Daily Newsletter Featuring Positive Stories about the President." *Newsweek*, June 29. URL: www.newsweek.com/west-wing-reads-best-media-stories-trump-630067

Greenstein, Fred I. 1995. "Political Style and Political Leadership: The Case of Bill Clinton." In *The Clinton Presidency: Campaigning, Governing and the Psychology of Leadership*, ed. Stanley A. Renshon. Boulder, CO: Westview.

Gregg, Gary L. 2004. "Dignified Authenticity: George W. Bush and the Symbolic Presidency." In *Considering the Bush Presidency*, eds. Gary Gregg II and Mark J. Rozell. New York: Oxford University Press.

Gross, Justin H., and Kaylee T. Johnson. 2016. "Twitter Taunts and Tirades: Negative Campaigning in the Age of Trump." *PS: Political Science and Politics* 49(4): 748–754.

Grynbaum, Michael M. 2017. "Trump Calls the News Media the 'Enemy of the American People.'" *New York Times*, February 17. URL: www.nytimes.com/2017/02/17/business/trump-calls-the-news-media-the-enemy-of-the-people.html?_r=0

Gupta-Carlson, Himanee. 2016. "Re-Imagining the Nation: Storytelling and Social Media in the Obama Campaigns." *PS* 49(1): 71–75.

Halberstam, David. 2001. *War in a Time of Peace: Bush, Clinton and the Generals*. New York: Scribner.

Halbfinger, David. 2002. "The 2002 Election: Georgia: Bush's Push, Eager Volunteers and Big Turnout Led to Georgia Sweep." *New York Times*, November 10.

Harris, John. F. 2005. *The Survivor: Bill Clinton in the White House*. New York: Random House.

Harris, John F., and Jonathan Martin. 2009. "The George W. Bush and Bill Clinton Legacies in the 2008 Elections." In *The American Elections of 2008*, eds. Janet M. Box-Steffensmeier and Steven E. Schier. Lanham, MD: Rowman & Littlefield.

Hawkins, Virgil. 2002. "The Other Side of the CNN Factor: The Media and Conflict." *Journalism Studies* 3(2): 225–240.

Heilemann, John, and Mark Halperin 2010. *Game Change: Obama and the Clintons, McCain and Palin and the Race of a Lifetime*. New York: Harper.

Heith, Diane. 2013. *The Presidential Road Show: Public Leadership in an Era of Party Polarization and Media Fragmentation*. Boulder, CO: Paradigm.

Hersh, Seymour M. 1997. *The Dark Side of Camelot*. Boston, MA: Little, Brown.

____. 2006. "The Next Act." *New Yorker*, November 27. URL: www.newyorker.com/magazine/2006/11/27/the-next-act

Hershey, Marjorie Randon. 1989. "The Campaign and the Media." In *The Election of 1988*, ed. Gerald M. Pomper. Chatham, NJ: Chatham House.

____. 2001. "The Campaign and the Media." In *The Election of 2000*, ed. Gerald M. Pomper. New York: Chatham House.

Herszenhorn, David, and Robert Pear. 2010. "Health Vote is Done, But Partisan Debate Rages On." *New York Times*, March 22.

Hetherington, Marc, and Jonathan Weiler. 2009. *Authoritarianism and Polarization in American Politics*. Cambridge: Cambridge University Press.

Hibbing, John R, Kevin B. Smith, and John R. Alford. 2014a. *Predisposed: Liberals, Conservatives and the Biology of Political Difference*. New York: Routledge.

____. 2014b. "Differences in Negativity Bias Underlie Variations in Political Ideology." *Behavioral and Brain Sciences* 37(3): 297–307.

Hibbing, John R., and Elizabeth Theiss-Morse. 1995. *Congress as Public Enemy: Public Attitudes Towards American Political Institutions*. Cambridge, UK: Cambridge University Press.

Hohmann, James. 2017a. "The Daily 202: Threat of Repeal Making it Easier for Democrats to Finally Sell Obamacare." *Washington Post*, February 9. URL: www.washingtonpost.com/news/powerpost/paloma/daily-202/2017/02/09/daily-202-threat-of-repeal-making-it-easier-for-democrats-to-finally-sell-obamacare/589bcddae9b69b1406c75c9f/?utm_term=.f9a5d7a8b180

____. 2017b. "The Daily 202: Jeff Flake Delivers the Most Courageous Conservative Rebuttal of Trumpism Yet." *Washington Post*, August 2. URL: www.washingtonpost.com/news/powerpost/paloma/daily-202/2017/08/02/

daily-202-jeff-flake-delivers-the-most-courageous-conservative-rebuttal-of-trumpism-yet/59812c9b30fb045fdaef10a8/?utm_term=.39b077990187

____. 2017c. "The Daily 202: Trump has Failed to Offer Moral Leadership After Charlottesville. These 10 People Are Filling the Void." *Washington Post*, August 17. URL: https://s2.washingtonpost.com/camp-rw/?e=c2Zhcm5zdz FAZ21haWwuY29t&s=5995788efe1ff63dfea1ceb6

____. 2017d. "The Daily 202: Six Ways Trump's Putin Comments on Asia Trip Erode U.S. Credibility." *Washington Post*, November 13. URL: www.washingtonpost.com/news/powerpost/paloma/daily-202/2017/11/13/daily-202-six-ways-trump-s-putin-comments-on-asia-trip-erode-u-s-credibility/5a09177d30 fb045a2e002fb4/?utm_term=.6e3fdc2b551d&wpisrc=nl_daily202&wpmm=1

Hopper, Jennifer R. 2017. *Presidential Framing in 21st Century News Media: The Politics of the Affordable Care Act*. New York: Routledge.

Hulse, Carl, and Avery Palmer. 2009. "Sweeping Health Care Plan Passes the House." *New York Times*, November 8.

Ingraham, Christopher. 2017. "There's a Trump Tweet For Everything, Failed Obamacare Repeal Edition." *Washington Post*, July 18. URL: www.washingtonpost.com/news/wonk/wp/2017/07/18/theres-a-trump-tweet-for-everything-failed-obamacare-repeal-edition/?utm_term=.df565d7d3292

Isenstadt, Alex. 2017. "President Trump's Enemies List." *Politico*, July 10. URL: www.politico.com/story/2017/07/10/president-trump-enemies-list-240344

Isikoff, Michael. 2000. *Uncovering Clinton: A Reporter's Story*. New York: Three Rivers Press.

Iyengar, Shanto. 1991. *Is Anyone Responsible? How Television Frames Political Issues*. Chicago, IL: University of Chicago Press.

Iyengar, Shanto, and Donald R. Kinder. 1987. *News That Matters*. Chicago, IL: University of Chicago Press.

Jacobs, Lawrence R., and Robert Y. Shapiro. 1995. "Public Opinion in President Clinton's First Year: Leadership and Responsiveness." In *The Clinton Presidency: Campaigning, Governing and the Psychology of Leadership*, ed. Stanley A. Renshon. Boulder, CO: Westview.

Jacobs, Lawrence R., and Theda Skocpol. 2010. *Health Care Reform and American Politics*. New York: Oxford University Press.

Jacobson, Gary C. 2008. "George W. Bush, Polarization and the War in Iraq." In *The Bush Legacy*, eds. Colin Campbell, Bert A. Rockman, and Andrew Rudalevige. Washington, DC: CQ Press.

____. 2011. "Legislative Success and Political Failure: The Public Reaction to Obama's Early Presidency." *Presidential Studies Quarterly* 41: 220–244.

Jamieson, Kathleen Hall, and Joseph N. Cappella. 2008. *Echo Chamber: Rush Limbaugh and the Conservative Media Establishment*. New York: Oxford University Press.

Jamieson, Kathleen Hall, and Paul Waldman. 2003. *The Press Effect: Politicians, Journalists and the Stories that Shape the Political World*. New York: Oxford University Press.

Jeffords, James M. 2003. *An Independent Man: Adventures of a Public Servant*. New York: Simon & Schuster.

Jelen, Ted. 2009. "Religion and American Public Opinion: Social Issues." In *The Oxford Handbook of Religion and American Politics*, eds. Corwin E. Smidt, Lyman A. Kellstedt, and James L. Guth. New York: Oxford University Press, 217–242.

Jensen, Elizabeth, and Lia Miller. 2006. "After Bankruptcy Filing, Recriminations Fly at Air America." *New York Times*, December 18.

Jones, Charles O. 1988. "Ronald Reagan and the US Congress: Visible-Hand Politics." *The Reagan Legacy: Promise and Performance*, ed. Charles O. Jones. Chatham, NJ: Chatham House.

____. 1994. *The Presidency in a Separated System*. Washington: Brookings Institution.

____. 1995. *Separate But Equal Branches: Congress and the Presidency*. Chatham, NJ: Chatham House.

Jones, Jeffrey M. 2014. "Americans' Ratings of President Obama's Image at New Lows." *Gallup.com*, June 12. URL: www.gallup.com/poll/171473/americans-ratings-president-obama-image-new-lows.aspx?g_source=Obama+honest+trustworthy&g_medium=search&g_campaign=tiles

____. 2017. "Trump Sets New Low for Second-Quarter Job Approval." *Gallup.com*, July 21. URL: www.gallup.com/poll/214322/trump-sets-new-low-second-quarter-job-approval.aspx?g_source=PRESIDENTIAL_JOB_APPROVAL&g_medium=topic&g_campaign=tiles

Jones, Jeffrey P. 2010. *Entertaining Politics: Satiric Television and Political Engagement*. Lanham, MD: Rowman & Littlefield.

Katz, James E., Michael Barris, and Anshul Jain. 2013. *The Social Media President: Barack Obama and the Politics of Digital Engagement*. New York: Palgrave Macmillan.

Kellner, Douglas. 1992. *The Persian Gulf TV War*. Boulder, CO: Westview.

____. 2009. "Barack Obama and the Celebrity Spectacle." *International Journal of Communication* 3: 715–741.

____. 2010. "Celebrity Diplomacy, Spectacle, and Barack Obama." *Celebrity Studies* 1(1): 121–123.

Kenski, Kate, Bruce W. Hardy, and Kathleen Hall Jamieson. 2010. *The Obama Victory: How Media, Money and Message Shaped the 2008 Election*. New York: Oxford University Press.

Kernell, Samuel. 2007. *Going Public: New Strategies of Presidential Leadership*. Washington, DC: CQ Press. Fourth Edition.

Kessler, Glenn, Michelle Ye Hee Lee, and Meg Kelly. 2017. "President Trump's First Six Months: The Fact-Check Tally." *Washington Post*, July 20. URL: www.washingtonpost.com/news/fact-checker/wp/2017/07/20/president-trumps-first-six-months-the-fact-check-tally/?utm_term=.53efecfe48bc

Key, V. O. Jr. 1961. *Public Opinion and American Democracy*. New York: Knopf.

Kinsley, Michael. 1992. "Ask a Silly Question." *New Republic*, July 6.

____. 2003. "An Apology Would Help." *Washington Post*, September 12.

Kinzer, Stephen. 2017. *The True Flag: Theodore Roosevelt, Mark Twain and the Birth of the American Empire*. New York: Henry Holt & Co.

Klein, Joe. 2002. *The Natural: The Misunderstood Presidency of Bill Clinton*. New York: Doubleday.

Kristof, Nicholas D. 2004. "Dithering as Others Die." *New York Times*, June 26.

Krugman, Paul. 2006. "The Crony Fairy." *New York Times*, April 28.

Kumar, Martha Joynt. 1995. "President Clinton Meets the Media: Communications Shaped by Predictable Patterns." In *The Clinton Presidency: Campaigning, Governing and the Psychology of Leadership*, ed. Stanley A. Renshon. Boulder, CO: Westview.

Kurtz, Howard. 1994. *Media Circus: The Trouble with America's Newspapers.* New York: Times Books/Random House.

_____. 1998. *Spin Cycle: Inside the Clinton Propaganda Machine.* New York: Free Press.

_____. 2005. "Network Fires Four in Wake of Probe." *Washington Post*, January 11.

_____. 2007a. "Campaign Allegation a Source of Vexation." *Washington Post*, January 22.

_____. 2007b. "Headmaster Disputes Claim That Obama Attended Islamic School." *Washington Post*, January 23.

_____. 2007c. "Journalist Forced to Reveal Her Methods." *Washington Post*, January 31.

Ladd, Jonathan M. 2013. "The Era of Media Distrust and Its Consequences for Perceptions of Political Reality." In *New Directions in Media and Politics*, ed. Travis M. Ridout. New York: Routledge.

Landler, Mark. 2017. "Unlike His Predecessors, Trump Steps Back From a Moral Judgment." *New York Times*, August 17. URL: www.nytimes. com/2017/08/16/us/politics/trump-charlottesville-moral-neo-nazis.html?emc= edit_cn_20170817&nl=first-draft&nlid=42082185&te=1&_r=0

Landy, Marc, and Sidney M. Milkis. 2014. "The Presidency in History." In *The Presidency and the Political System*, ed. Michael Nelson. 10th ed. Los Angeles: Sage/CQ Press.

Laufer, Peter. 1995. *Inside Talk Radio: America's Voice or Just Hot Air?* Secaucus, NJ: Carol Publishing.

Lazarsfeld, P. F., Berelson, B. and Gaudet, H. 1944. *The People's Choice: How the Voter Makes up his Mind in a Presidential Campaign.* New York: Columbia University Press.

Lebow, Richard Ned. 1995. "Psychological Dimensions of Post-Cold War Foreign Policy." In *The Clinton Presidency: Campaigning, Governing and the Psychology of Leadership*, ed. Stanley A. Renshon. Boulder, CO: Westview.

Leonhardt, James M. 2015. "Tweets, Hashtags and Virality: Marketing the Affordable Care Act in Social Media." *Journal of Direct, Data and Digital Marketing Practice* 16(3): 172–180.

Leonnig, Carol D., Adam Entous, Devlin Barrett, and Matt Zapotosky. 2017. "Michael Flynn pleads guilty to lying to FBI on contacts with Russian ambassador." *Washington Post*, December 1. URL: www.washingtonpost.com/ politics/michael-flynn-charged-with-making-false-statement-to-the-fbi/2017/ 12/01/e03a6c48-d6a2-11e7-9461-ba77d604373d_story.html?utm_term=.1b61 766007a0

Lester, Emile. Forthcoming. *Liberalism and Leadership.* Unpublished book manuscript.

Lichtblau, Eric, and David Johnston. 2007. "Court to Oversee U.S. Wiretapping in Terror Cases." *New York Times*, January 18.

Lichter, S. Robert, Jody C. Baumgartner, and Jonathan S. Morris. 2015. *Politics Is a Joke! How TV Comedians are Remaking Political Life.* Boulder, CO: Westview.

Lichter, S. Robert, Stephen Farnsworth, and Roland Schatz. 2017. "How Did the *Wall Street Journal* Get Caught Up in This Mess?" *The American Spectator.* March 29.

Lichter, S. Robert, and Richard E. Noyes. 1995. *Good Intentions Make Bad News: Why Americans Hate Campaign Journalism*. Lanham, MD: Rowman & Littlefield. Second Edition.

Lindsay, James M. 2003. "Deference and Defiance: The Shifting Rhythms of Executive-Legislative Relations in Foreign Policy." *Presidential Studies Quarterly* 33(3): 530–546.

Lipset, Seymour Martin. 1963. *The First New Nation*. New York: Basic Books.

Lowi, Theodore J. 1985. *The Personal President: Power Invested, Promise Unfulfilled*. Ithaca, NY: Cornell University Press.

Lynch, Julia, and Sarah E. Gollust. 2010. "Playing Fair." *Journal of Health Politics, Policy and Law* 35: 849–887.

MacWilliams, Matthew. C. 2016. "Who Decides When the Party Doesn't? Authoritarian Voters and the Rise of Donald Trump." *PS: Political Science & Politics* 49(40): 716–721.

Manjoo, Farhad. 2017. "Can Facebook Fix Its Own Worst Bug?" *New York Times*, April 25. URL: www.nytimes.com/2017/04/25/magazine/can-facebook-fix-its-own-worst-bug.html

Mann, James. 2013. *The Obamians*. New York: Penguin.

Mann, Thomas E., and Norman J. Ornstein. 2006. *The Broken Branch: How Congress Is Failing America and How to Get It Back on Track*. New York: Oxford University Press.

Marcus, Ruth. 2017. "The White House is Imploding." *Washington Post*, July 28. URL: www.washingtonpost.com/opinions/the-white-house-is-imploding/2017/07/28/2143a68a-73cc-11e7-8839-ec48ec4cae25_story.html?utm_term=.2a3d8a41bdc0

Matthews, Chris. 2011. *Jack Kennedy: Elusive Hero*. New York: Simon & Schuster.

Mayer, Jane. 2010. "Covert Operations." *New Yorker*, August 30. URL: www.newyorker.com/magazine/2010/08/30/covert-operations

____. 2017. "Should Psychiatrists Speak Out Against Trump?" *New Yorker*, May 22. URL: www.newyorker.com/magazine/2017/05/22/should-psychiatrists-speak-out-against-trump

McClellan, Scott. 2008. *What Happened: Inside the Bush White House and Washington's Culture of Deception*. New York: PublicAffairs.

McGinniss, Joe. 1969. *The Selling of the President, 1968*. New York: Trident Press.

Media Monitor. 2000. *Campaign News Final*. Washington, DC: Center for Media and Public Affairs.

Mermin, Jonathan. 1997. "Television News and the American Intervention in Somalia: The Myth of a Media-Driven Foreign Policy." *Political Science Quarterly* 112(Fall): 385–402.

Merry, Stephanie. 2017. "Key and Peele Visited the 'Daily Show' For One Last Bit With Obama's Anger Translator." *Washington Post*, January 6. URL: www.washingtonpost.com/news/arts-and-entertainment/wp/2017/01/06/key-and-peele-visited-the-daily-show-for-one-last-bit-with-obamas-anger-translator/?utm_term=.4c76f6e918cf

Milbank, Dana. 2004. "The Administration Versus the Administration." *Washington Post*, June 29.

Milkis, Sidney. 2006. "The Presidency and Political Parties." In *The Presidency and the Political System*, ed. Michael Nelson, 8th ed. Washington, DC: CQ Press.

Miller, Greg. 2017. "Trump Urged Mexican President to End His Public Defiance On Border Wall, Transcript Reveals." *Washington Post*, August 3. URL: www.washingtonpost.com/world/national-security/you-cannot-say-that-to-the-press-trump-urged-mexican-president-to-end-his-public-defiance-on-border-wall-transcript-reveals/2017/08/03/0c2c0a4e-7610-7611e7-8f39-eeb7d3a2d304_story.html?hpid=hp_hp-top-table-main_trumpcalls-915a%3Ahomepage%2Fstory&utm_term=.b49e36060011

Minutaglio, Bill. 1999. *First Son: George W. Bush and the Bush Family Dynasty*. New York: Times Books.

Mitgang, Herbert, ed. 1971. *Abraham Lincoln: A Press Portrait*. Chicago: Quadrangle.

Mooney, Chris. 2004. "Did Our Leading Newspapers Set Too Low a Bar for a Preemptive Attack?" *Columbia Journalism Review*, March—April.

Morris, Edmund. 1979. *The Rise of Theodore Roosevelt*. New York: Ballantine.

_____. 1999. *Dutch: A Memoir of Ronald Reagan*. New York: Random House.

_____. 2001. *Theodore Rex*. New York: Random House.

Morris, Irwin L. 2002. *Votes, Money and the Clinton Impeachment*. Boulder, CO: Westview.

Murray, Shailagh, and Perry Bacon Jr. 2010. "GOP Deciding Which Direction To Go With New Authority After Midterm Victory." *Washington Post*, November 5.

Nagourney, Adam. 2004. "Kerry Might Pay Price for Failing to Strike Back Quickly." *New York Times*, August. 21: A10.

_____. 2006. "Democrats Looking to Use Katrina Like the GOP Used 9/11." *New York Times*, April 22.

Nelson, Michael. 2014. "The Psychological Presidency." In *The Presidency and the Political System*, ed. Michael Nelson, 10th ed., Los Angeles: Sage/CQ Press.

Neustadt, Richard. 1990. *Presidential Power and the Modern Presidents*. New York: Free Press.

Newman, Brian. 2002. "Bill Clinton's Approval Ratings: The More Things Change the More They Stay the same." *Political Research Quarterly* 55(4): 781–804.

Newport, Frank. 2016. "As Debate Looms, Voters Still Distrust Clinton and Trump." *Gallup*, release dated September 23. URL: www.gallup.com/poll/195755/debate-looms-voters-distrust-clinton-trump.aspx?g_source=Obama+honest+and+trustworthy&g_medium=search&g_campaign=tiles

_____. 2017. "Trump Disapproval Rooted in Character Concerns." *Gallup*, release dated July 13. URL: www.gallup.com/poll/214091/trump-disapproval-rooted-character-concerns.aspx

Nithyanand, Rishab, Brian Schaffner, and Phillipa Gill. 2017. "How Offensive Political Rhetoric Affects Online Discourse." *Vox.com*, August 7. URL: www.vox.com/mischiefs-of-faction/2017/8/7/16104902/offensive-political-rhetoric-comments-reddit

Niven, David, S. Robert Lichter, and Daniel Amundson. 2008. "Our First Cartoon President: Bill Clinton and the Politics of Late Night Comedy." In *Laughing Matters: Humor and American Politics in the Media Age*, eds. Jody C. Baumgartner and Jonathan S. Morris. New York: Routledge.

Obama, Barack. 2004. *Dreams From My Father: A Story of Race and Inheritance*. New York: Three Rivers Press.

____. 2006. *The Audacity of Hope: Thoughts on Reclaiming the American Dream*. New York: Three Rivers Press.

O'Brien, David M.1988. "The Reagan Judges: His Most Enduring Legacy?" *The Reagan Legacy: Promise and Performance*, ed. Charles O. Jones. Chatham, NJ: Chatham House.

Okrent, Daniel. 2004. "Weapons of Mass Destruction? Or Mass Distraction?" *New York Times*, May 30.

Oldfield, Duane, and Aaron Wildavsky. 1989. "Reconsidering the Two Presidencies." *Society* 26(July/August): 54–59.

Osnos, Evan. 2017. "Donald Trump's State of Mind, and Ours." *New Yorker*, July 28. URL: www.newyorker.com/news/daily-comment/donald-trumps-state-of-mind-and-ours?mbid=social_twitter

Owen, Diana. 1995. "The Debate Challenge: Candidate Strategies in the New Media Age." In *Presidential Campaign Discourse: Strategic Communication Problems*, ed. Kathleen E. Kendall. Albany: State University of New York Press.

____. 1996. "Who's Talking? Who's Listening? The New Politics of Talk Radio Shows." In *Broken Contract? Changing Relationships Between Americans and Their Government*, ed. Stephen Craig. Boulder, CO: Westview.

____. 2000. "Popular Politics and the Clinton/Lewinsky Affair: The Implications for Leadership." *Political Psychology* 21(1): 161–177.

____. 2002. "Media Mayhem: Performance of the Press in Election 2000." In *Overtime: The Election 2000 Thriller*, ed. Larry Sabato. New York: Longman.

____. 2009. "The Campaign and the Media." In *The American Elections of 2008*, eds. Janet M. Box-Steffensmeier and Steven E. Schier. Lanham, MD: Rowman & Littlefield.

____. 2017. "Twitter Rants, Press Bashing and Fake News: The Shameful Legacy of Media in the 2016 Election." In *Trumped: The 2016 Election That Broke All the Rules*, eds. Larry J. Sabato, Kyle Kondik, and Geoffrey Skelly. Lanham, MD: Rowman & Littlefield.

Pareles, John. 1992. "Dissing the Rappers is Fodder for the Sound Bite." *New York Times*, June 28.

Parker, Ashley. 2016. "Covering Donald Trump, and Witnessing the Danger up Close." *New York Times*, March 12. URL: www.nytimes.com/2016/03/13/us/politics/covering-donald-trump-and-witnessing-the-danger-up-close.html

Parry-Giles, Shawn J., and Trevor Parry-Giles. 2002. *Constructing Clinton: Hyperreality and Presidential Image-Making in Postmodern Politics*. New York: Peter Lang.

Patterson, Thomas E. 1994. *Out of Order*. New York: Vintage.

____. 2016a. "News Coverage of the 2016 Presidential Primaries: Horse Race Reporting Has Consequences." Shorenstein Center on Media, Politics and Public Policy, Kennedy School of Government, Harvard University, Release dated July 11. URL: https://shorensteincenter.org/news-coverage-2016-presidential-primaries/

____. 2016b. "News Coverage of the 2016 General Election: How the Press Failed the Voters." Shorenstein Center on Media, Politics and Public Policy, Kennedy School of Government, Harvard University, Release dated December 7. URL: https://shorensteincenter.org/news-coverage-2016-general-election/

_____. 2017. "News Coverage of Donald Trump's First 100 Days." Shorenstein Center on Media, Politics and Public Policy, Kennedy School of Government, Harvard University, Release dated May 18. URL: https://shorensteincenter.org/news-coverage-donald-trumps-first-100-days/

Pew Research Center. 1996. "Clinton Unites Dems, Gains Working Class Independents." October 25. URL: www.people-press.org/1996/10/25/clinton-unites-dems-gains-working-class-independents/

_____. 2000a. "Voters Unmoved by Media Characterizations of Bush and Gore." July 27. URL: www.people-press.org/2000/07/27/voters-unmoved-by-media-characterizations-of-bush-and-gore/

_____. 2000b. "Media Seen as Fair, But Tilting to Gore." October 15. URL: www.people-press.org/2000/10/15/media-seen-as-fair-but-tilting-to-gore/

_____. 2000c. "Campaign 2000 Highly Rated." November 16. URL: www.people-press.org/2000/11/16/campaign-2000-highly-rated/

_____. 2000d. "Internet Election News Audience Seeks Convenience, Familiar Names." December 3. URL: www.pewinternet.org/2000/12/03/internet-election-news-audience-seeks-convenience-familiar-names/

_____. 2001a. "Clinton Nostalgia Sets in, Bush Reaction Mixed." January 11. URL: www.people-press.org/2001/01/11/clinton-nostalgia-sets-in-bush-reaction-mixed/

_____. 2001b. "Terror Coverage Boosts News Media's Images." November 28. URL: www.people-press.org/2001/11/28/terror-coverage-boost-news-medias-images/

_____. 2003a. "America's Image Further Erodes, Europeans Want Weaker Ties." March 18. URL: www.people-press.org/2003/03/18/americas-image-further-erodes-europeans-want-weaker-ties/

_____. 2003b. "Views of a Changing World 2003." June 3. URL: www.pewglobal.org/2003/06/03/views-of-a-changing-world-2003/

_____. 2004a. "News Audiences Increasingly Politicized." June 8. URL: www.people-press.org/2004/06/08/news-audiences-increasingly-politicized/

_____. 2004b. "Public Support for War Resilient." June 17. URL: www.people-press.org/2004/06/17/public-support-for-war-resilient/

_____. 2005. "The State of the News Media." *Project for Excellence in Journalism.* URL: www.stateofthemedia.org/2005/cable-tv-intro/content-analysis/

_____. 2006. "Online Papers Modestly Boost Newspaper Readership." July 30. URL: www.people-press.org/2006/07/30/online-papers-modestly-boost-newspaper-readership/

_____. 2008a. "High Marks for the Campaign, a High Bar for Obama." November 13. URL: www.people-press.org/2008/11/13/high-marks-for-the-campaign-a-high-bar-for-obama/

_____. 2008b. "Bush and Public Opinion Reviewing the Bush Years and the Public's Final Verdict." December 18. URL: www.people-press.org/2008/12/18/bush-and-public-opinion/

_____. 2010a. "Public's Priorities for 2010: Economy, Jobs, Terrorism." January 25. www.people-press.org/2010/01/25/publics-priorities-for-2010-economy-jobs-terrorism/

_____. 2010b. "Growing Number of Americans Say Obama is a Muslim." August 19, 2010. URL: www.people-press.org/search/?query=growing%20number%20of%20americans%20say%20obama%20is%20a%20muslim

_____. 2015. "Global Publics Back U.S. on Fighting ISIS, but Are Critical of Post-9/11 Torture." June 23. URL: www.pewglobal.org/2015/06/23/global-publics-back-u-s-on-fighting-isis-but-are-critical-of-post-911-torture/

_____. 2016a. "The Modern News Consumer: News Attitudes and Practices in the Digital Era." July 7. URL: www.journalism.org/2016/07/07/the-modern-news-consumer/

_____. 2016b. "Low Approval of Trump's Transition but Outlook for His Presidency Improves." December 8. URL: www.people-press.org/2016/12/08/low-approval-of-trumps-transition-but-outlook-for-his-presidency-improves/

_____. 2016c. "Obama Leaves Office on High Note, But Public Has Mixed Views of Accomplishments." December 14. URL: www.people-press.org/2016/12/14/obama-leaves-office-on-high-note-but-public-has-mixed-views-of-accomplishments/

_____. 2017a. "Trump, Clinton Voters Divided in Their Main Source for Election News." January 17. URL: www.journalism.org/2017/01/18/trump-clinton-voters-divided-in-their-main-source-for-election-news/

_____. 2017b. "Public Dissatisfaction With Washington Weighs On the GOP." April 17. URL: www.people-press.org/2017/04/17/1-views-of-trump/

_____. 2017c. "U.S. Image Suffers as Publics Around World Question Trump's Leadership." June 26. URL: www.pewglobal.org/2017/06/26/u-s-image-suffers-as-publics-around-world-question-trumps-leadership/

Pfiffner, James P. 2004a. *The Character Factor: How We Judge America's Presidents*. College Station: Texas A&M University Press.

_____. 2004b. "Introduction: Assessing the Bush Presidency." In *Considering the Bush Presidency*, eds. Gary L. Gregg II and Mark J. Rozell. New York: Oxford University Press.

Phillips, Kevin. 2004. *American Dynasty: Aristocracy, Fortune and the Politics of Deceit in the House of Bush*. New York: Viking.

Pollack, Kenneth M. 2004. "Spies, Lies and Weapons: What Went Wrong." *The Atlantic* January/February.

Pompeo, Joseph, and Hadas Gold. 2017. "Gerry Baker to Staff: Criticism of Wall Street Journal's Trump Coverage is 'fake news' ." *Politico*, February 13. URL: www.politico.com/media/story/2017/02/gerry-baker-defends-wsj-trump-coverage-004931

Pomper, Gerald M. 1989. "The Presidential Election." In *The Elections of 1988: Reports and Interpretations*, ed. Gerald M. Pomper. Chatham, NJ: Chatham House.

Popkin, Samuel. 1991. *The Reasoning Voter*. Chicago: University of Chicago Press.

Post, Jerrold M. 1995. "The Political Psychology of the Ross Perot Phenomenon." In *The Clinton Presidency: Campaigning, Governing and the Psychology of Leadership*, ed. Stanley A. Renshon. Boulder, CO: Westview.

Power, Samantha. 2002. *"A Problem from Hell:" America and the Age of Genocide*. New York: Basic Books.

Powers, William. 1998. "News at Warp Speed: Coverage of the Scandal Has Turned the Press on Itself—With a Vengeance." *National Journal*, January 31. 30: 220–223.

Quealy, Kevin. 2017. "The Lowest-Profile State Department in 45 Years." *New York Times*, August 3. URL: www.nytimes.com/interactive/2017/08/01/

upshot/lowest-profile-state-department-in-decades.html?_r=2&utm_medium=
social&utm_campaign=hks-twitter&utm_source=twitter

Quirk, Paul J. 2006. "Presidential Competence." In *The Presidency and the Political System*, ed. Michael Nelson, 8th ed., Washington, DC: CQ Press.

Quirk, Paul J., and Sean C. Matheson. 2001. "The Presidency: The Election and Prospects for Leadership." In *The Elections of 2000*, ed. Michael Nelson. Washington, DC: CQ Press.

Rasmussen, Jim. 2004. "Shame on the Swift Boat Veterans for Bush." *Wall Street Journal*, August 10.

Reeves, Richard. 2001. *President Nixon: Alone in the White House.* New York: Simon & Schuster.

Remnick, David. 2010. *The Bridge.* New York: Knopf.

Renshon, Stanley A. 1995a. "The Psychological Context of the Clinton Presidency: A Framework for Analysis." In *The Clinton Presidency: Campaigning, Governing and the Psychology of Leadership*, ed. Stanley A. Renshon. Boulder, CO: Westview.

_____. 1995b. "Character, Judgment and Political Leadership: Promise, Problems, and Prospects of the Clinton Presidency." In *The Clinton Presidency: Campaigning, Governing and the Psychology of Leadership*, ed. Stanley A. Renshon. Boulder, CO: Westview.

_____. 1998. *The Psychological Assessment of Presidential Candidates.* New York: Routledge.

_____. 2012. *Barack Obama and the Politics of Redemption.* New York: Routledge.

Rich, Frank. 2006. *The Greatest Story Ever Sold: The Decline and Fall of the Truth, from Iraq to Katrina.* New York: Penguin.

Rieff, David. 2003. "Blueprint For a Mess." *New York Times Magazine*, November 2.

Rimer, Sara, Ralph Blumenthal, and Raymond Bonner. 2004. "Portrait of George W. Bush in '72: Unanchored in a Turbulent Time." *New York Times*, September 20: A1.

Risen, James, and Eric Lichtblau. 2007. "Concerns Raised on Wider Spying Under New Law." *New York Times*, August 19.

Robinson, Piers. 2002. *The CNN Effect: The Myth of News, Foreign Policy and Intervention.* London: Routledge.

Rockman, Bert A. 1988. "The Style and Organization of the Reagan Presidency." *The Reagan Legacy: Promise and Performance*, ed. Charles O. Jones, Chatham, NJ: Chatham House.

_____. 2004. "Presidential Leadership in an Era of Party Polarization—The George W. Bush Presidency." In *The George W. Bush Presidency: Appraisals and Prospects*, eds. Colin Campbell and Bert A. Rockman, Washington, DC: CQ Press.

Rogin, Josh. 2017. "State Department Considers Scrubbing Democracy Promotion From Its Mission." *Washington Post*, August 1. URL: www.washingtonpost. com/news/josh-rogin/wp/2017/08/01/state-department-considers-scrubbing-democracy-promotion-from-its-mission/?tid=ss_tw-bottom&utm_term=.f5bc 96bc175d

Rosenstiel, Tom. 1994. *Strange Bedfellows: How Television and the Presidential Candidates Changed American Politics, 1992.* New York: Hyperion.

Rubin, Jennifer. 2017a. "The Bully in Chief is Losing His Touch." *Washington Post*, August 3. URL: www.washingtonpost.com/blogs/right-turn/wp/2017/

08/03/the-bully-in-chief-is-losing-his-touch/?tid=hybrid_mostsharedarticles_1_ na&utm_term=.3526f227ac8a

_____. 2017b. "Why the Leaked Presidential Transcripts Are So Frightening." *Washington Post*, August 3. URL: www.washingtonpost.com/blogs/right-turn/wp/2017/08/03/why-the-leaked-presidential-transcripts-are-so-frightening/ ?tid=ss_tw-amp&utm_term=.011fac9ce843

Rutenberg, Jim. 2004a. "CBS News Concludes it was Misled on Guard Memos, Network Officials Say." *New York Times*, September 20.

_____. 2004b. "Broadcast Group to Pre-empt Programs for Anti-Kerry Film." *New York Times*, October 11: A19.

Rutenberg, Jim, and David Cloud. 2006. "Bush, Facing Dissent on Iraq, Jettisons 'Stay the Course.'" *New York Times*, October 24.

Rutenberg, Jim, and Kate Zernike. 2004. "CBS Apologized for Report on Bush Guard Service." *New York Times*, September 21.

Sabato, Larry J. 1993. *Feeding Frenzy: How Attack Journalism Has Transformed American Politics*. New York: Free Press.

_____. 2002. "The Perfect Storm: The Election of the Century." In *Overtime: The Election 2000 Thriller*, ed. Larry Sabato. New York: Longman.

_____. 2017. "The 2016 Election That Broke All, or at Least Most, of the Rules." In *Trumped: The 2016 Election That Broke All the Rules*, eds. Larry J. Sabato, Kyle Kondik, and Geoffrey Skelly. Lanham, MD: Rowman & Littlefield.

Sabato, Larry, Mark Stencel, and S. Robert Lichter. 2000. *Peepshow: Media and Politics in an Age of Scandal*. Lanham, MD: Rowman & Littlefield.

Sandler, Rachel. 2017. "'It's Hurt My Wallet'—How One Fake News Publisher is Faring After Facebook Crackdown." *USA Today*, August 3. URL: www.usatoday.com/story/tech/2017/08/02/its-hurt-my-wallet-how-one-fake-news-publisher-faring-after-facebook-crackdown/486720001/

Sanger, David. E. 2001. "Bush Tells Blair He Doesn't Oppose New Europe Force." *New York Times*, February 24. URL: www.nytimes.com/2001/02/24/world/bush-tells-blair-he-doesn-t-oppose-new-europe-force.html

Savillo, Rob. 2017. "Study: Sean Spicer's First 48 Press Briefings: More Right-Wing Outlets, Shorter Briefings, and Obsessive Cable Coverage." Media Matters, May 30. URL: www.mediamatters.org/blog/2017/05/30/STUDY-Sean-Spicers-first-48-press-briefings/216685

Scacco, Joshua M., and Kevin Coe. 2016. "The Ubiquitous Presidency: Toward a New Paradigm for Studying Presidential Communication." *International Journal of Communication* 10: 2014–2037.

Scheiber, Noam. 2012. *The Escape Artists: How Obama's Team Fumbled the Recovery*. New York: Simon & Schuster.

Schier, Steven E., and Todd E. Eberly. 2017. *The Trump Presidency: Outsider in the Oval Office*. Lanham, MD: Rowman & Littlefield.

Schlesinger, Alexander M. Jr. 1945. *The Age of Jackson*. Boston: Little, Brown.

Schmidt, Susan, and Michael Weisskopf. 2000. *Truth at Any Cost: Ken Starr and the Unmaking of Bill Clinton*. New York: HarperCollins.

Schudson, Michael. 1978. *Discovering the News*. New York: Basic Books.

Scott, Ian. 2000. *American Politics in Hollywood Film*. Chicago: Fitzroy Dearborn.

Sears, David O. 2001. "The Role of Affect in Symbolic Politics." In *Citizens and Politics: Perspectives from Political Psychology*, ed. James H. Kuklinski. New York: Cambridge University Press.

Seelye, Katharine Q., and Ralph Blumenthal. 2004. "Documents Suggest Guard Gave Bush Special Treatment." *New York Times*, September 9: A1.

Sella, Marshall. 2001. "The Red State Network." *New York Times Magazine*, June 24.

Shane, Scott. 2007. "Former Press Secretary Dispels Many Illusions." *New York Times*, January 30.

Shane, Scott, and Adam Liptak. 2006. "Shifting Power to a President." *New York Times*, September 30.

Shane, Scott, and Eric Lipton. 2005. "Storm and Crisis: Federal Response; Government Saw Flood Risk but not Levee Failure." *New York Times*, September 2.

Shane, Scott, and Neil Lewis. 2007. "Bush Commutes Libby Sentence, Saying 30 Months 'Is Excessive.'" *New York Times*, July 3.

Shanker, Thom. 2007. "New Strategy Vindicates Ex—Army Chief Shinseki." *New York Times*, January 12.

Shear, Michael. 2011. "With Document, Obama Seeks to End 'Birther' Issue." *New York Times*, April 27.

Silverman, Craig, Jeremy Singer-Vine, and Lam Thuy Vo. 2017. "In Spite of the Crackdown, Fake News Publishers Are Still Earning Money from Major Ad Networks." *BuzzFeed*, April 4. URL: www.buzzfeed.com/craigsilverman/fake-news-real-ads?utm_term=.qky2P86gQ#.ftvGKLAeb

Sinclair, Barbara. 2000a. "Hostile Partners: The President, Congress and Lawmaking in the Partisan 1990s." In *Polarized Politics: Congress and the President in a Partisan Era*, eds. Jon R. Bond and Richard Fleisher. Washington: CQ Press.

_____. 2000b. "The President as Legislative Leader." In *The Clinton Legacy*, eds. Colin Campbell and Bert A. Rockman. New York: Chatham House.

_____. 2004. "Context, Strategy and Chance: George W. Bush and the 107th Congress." In *The George W. Bush Presidency: Appraisals and Prospects*, eds. Colin Campbell, and Bert A. Rockman. Washington, DC: CQ Press.

_____. 2011. "Congressional Leadership in Obama's First Two Years." In *Obama in Office*, ed. James Thurber. Boulder, CO: Paradigm.

_____. 2012. "Doing Big Things: Obama and the 111th Congress." In *The Obama Presidency: Appraisals and Prospects*, eds. Bert A. Rockman, Andrew Rudalevige, and Colin Campbell. Washington, DC: Sage/CQ Press.

Singh, Robert S. 2012. "Continuity and Change in Obama's Foreign Policy." In *The Obama Presidency: Appraisals and Prospects*, eds. Bert A. Rockman, Andrew Rudalevige, and Colin Campbell. Washington: Sage/CQ Press.

Skocpol, Theda. 1997. *Boomerang: Health Care Reform and the Turn Against Government*. New York: Norton.

Skocpol, Theda, and Vanessa Williamson. 2012. *The Tea Party and the Remaking of Republican Conservatism*. Oxford: Oxford University Press.

Skowronek, Stephen. 2014. "The Development of Presidential Power: Conservative Insurgency and Constitutional Construction." In *The Presidency and the Political System*, ed. Michael Nelson, 10th ed., Thousand Oaks, CA: Sage/CQ Press.

Smith, Culver H. 1977. *The Press, Politics and Patronage*. Athens: University of Georgia Press.

Smith, Gene. 1964. *When the Cheering Stopped: The Last Years of Woodrow Wilson*. New York: William Morrow & Co.

Smith, Hedrick. 1988. *The Power Game: How Washington Works*. New York: Ballantine.

Smith, Richard N. 2001. "'The President Is Fine' and Other Historical Lies." *Columbia Journalism Review*, September–October: 30–32.

Snell, Kelsey. 2016. "Budget Scorekeeper: Obamacare Costs rising as More Enroll in Medicaid." *Washington Post*, March 24. URL: www.washingtonpost.com/news/powerpost/wp/2016/03/24/budget-scorekeepers-obamacare-costs-rising-as-more-enroll-in-medicaid/?utm_term=.787d18da5f0e

Soroka, Stuart N. 2006. "Good News and Bad News: Asymmetric Responses to Economic Information." *Journal of Politics* 68(2): 372–385.

____. 2014. *Negativity in Democratic Politics: Causes and Consequences*. New York: Cambridge University Press.

Stanley, Alessandra, and Maureen Dowd. 2012. "The Dweebs on the Bus." *GQ*, June 26. URL: www.gq.com/story/dweebs-on-bus-alessandra-stanley-maureen-dowd-political-reporters.

Starr, Kenneth W. 1998. *The Starr Report: The Independent Counsel's Complete Report to Congress on the Investigation of President Clinton*. New York: Pocket Books.

Stolberg, Sheryl Gay. 2006. "Buzzwords: The Decider." *New York Times*, December 24.

____. 2017. "Many Politicians Lie. But Trump Has Elevated the Art of Fabrication." *New York Times*, August 7. URL: www.nytimes.com/2017/08/07/us/politics/lies-trump-obama-mislead.html?_r=0

Streitfeld, David. 2017. "'The Internet Is Broken': @ev Is Trying to Salvage It." *New York Times*, May 20. URL: www.nytimes.com/2017/05/20/technology/evan-williams-medium-twitter-internet.html

Stuckey, Mary E. 2010. "Rethinking the Rhetorical Presidency and Presidential Rhetoric." *The Review of Communication* 10: 38–52.

Su, Sara. 2017. "News Feed FYI, New Test with Related Articles." *Facebook*, News release, updated August 3. URL: https://newsroom.fb.com/news/2017/04/news-feed-fyi-new-test-with-related-articles/

Sullivan, Sean, Kelsey Snell, and Ed O'Keefe. 2017. "Republicans Divided on Whom to Blame for Health-Care Defeat, and What to Do Next." *Washington Post*, July 28. URL: www.washingtonpost.com/powerpost/senate-rejects-measure-to-partly-repeal-affordable-care-act-dealing-trump-and-gop-leaders-a-major-setback/2017/07/28/f2865b10-7364-11e7-8f39-eeb7d3a2d304_story.html?utm_term=.044ca1d6923a

Sullivan, Terry. 1991. "A Matter of Fact: The Two Presidencies Thesis Revisited." In *The Two Presidencies: A Quarter Century Assessment*, ed. Steven Shull. Chicago: Nelson-Hall.

Suskind, Ron. 2004. *The Price of Loyalty: George W. Bush, the White House and the Education of Paul O'Neill*. New York: Simon & Schuster.

Swanson, Ana. 2016. "The Myth and the Reality of Donald Trump's Business Empire." *Washington Post*, February 29. URL: www.washingtonpost.com/news/wonk/wp/2016/02/29/the-myth-and-the-reality-of-donald-trumps-business-empire/?utm_term=.16baf08342dc

Swift, Art. 2017. "Trump Approval Highest on Terrorism, Economy." *Gallup*, June 14. URL: www.gallup.com/poll/212237/trump-approval-highest-terrorism-economy.aspx?g_source=Trump+approval&g_medium=search&g_campaign=tiles

Tanter, Raymond, and Stephen Kersting. 2008. "Grand Strategy as National Security Policy: Politics, Rhetoric and the Bush Legacy." In *The Bush Legacy*, eds. Colin Campbell, Bert A. Rockman, and Andrew Rudalevige. Washington: CQ Press.

Tapper, Jake. 2001. *Down and Dirty: The Plot to Steal the Presidency*. Boston, MA: Little, Brown.

_____. 2002. "Down and Dirty, Revisited: A Postscript on Florida and the News Media." In *Overtime: The Election 2000 Thriller*, ed. Larry Sabato. New York: Longman.

Tenpas, Kathryn Dunn, and Stephen Hess. 2002. "The Contemporary Presidency: The Bush White House, First Appraisals." *Presidential Studies Quarterly* 32(3):577–585.

Toobin, Jeffrey. 2001. *Too Close To Call: The 36 Day Battle to Decide the 2000 Election*. New York: Random House.

Trippi, Joe. 2004. *The Revolution Will Not Be Televised: Democracy, the Internet and the Overthrow of Everything*. New York: HarperCollins.

Van Bavel, Jay, and William Brady. 2017. "Twitter's Passion Politics." *New York Times*, July 9. URL: www.nytimes.com/2017/07/08/opinion/sunday/twitters-passion-politics.html

VandeHei, Jim. 2005. "Bush Paints His Goals as 'Crises.'" *Washington Post*, January 8.

Wagner, John. 2017. "Trump signs sweeping tax bill into law." *Washington Post*, December 22. URL: www.washingtonpost.com/news/post-politics/wp/2017/12/22/trump-signs-sweeping-tax-bill-into-law/?utm_term=.974055d84325

Wallace, Tim, and Alicia Parlapiano. 2017. "Crowd Scientists Say Women's March in Washington had 3 Times as Many People as Trump's Inauguration." *New York Times*, January 22. URL: www.nytimes.com/interactive/2017/01/22/us/politics/womens-march-trump-crowd-estimates.html

Walsh, Katherine Cramer. 2012. "Putting Inequality in its Place: Rural Consciousness and the Power of Perspective." *American Political Science Review* 106(3): 517–532.

Wayne, Stephen J. 2012. *Personality and Politics: Obama For and Against Himself*. Washington: CQ/Sage.

Wenner, Jann S., and William Greider. 1993. "President Clinton: The *Rolling Stone* Interview." *Rolling Stone*, December 9: 42–45, 80–81.

West, Darrell M. 2014. *Air Wars: Television Advertising in Election Campaigns, 1952–2012*. 6th ed, Los Angeles: Sage/CQ Press.

White, John Kenneth. 2016. "Sound Work in a Tough Environment." In *Debating the Obama Presidency*, ed. Steven E. Shier. Lanham, MD: Rowman & Littlfield.

White, Theodore H. 1961. *The Making of the President, 1960*. New York: Atheneum.

_____. 1978. *In Search of History*. New York: Warner Books.

Wildavsky, Aaron. 1966. "The Two Presidencies." *Transaction* 4(December): 7–14.

Wilgoren, Jodi. 2004. "Truth Be Told, the Vietnam Crossfire Hurts Kerry More." *New York Times*, September 24: A24.

Williamson, Kevin D. 2017. "Death of a F***ing Salesman." *National Review*, July 30. URL: http://amp.nationalreview.com/article/449988/donald-trump-cant-close-deal-failing-salesman?utm_source=PANTHEON_STRIPPED&utm_medium=PANTHEON_STRIPPED&utm_campaign=PANTHEON_STRIPPED

Williamson, Vanessa, Theda Skocpol, and John Coggin. 2011. "The Tea Party and the Remaking of Republican Conservatism." *Perspectives on Politics* 9(1): 25–43.

Woodward, Bob. 1999. *Shadow: Five Presidents and the Legacy of Watergate.* New York: Simon & Schuster.

_____. 2006. *State of Denial.* New York: Simon & Schuster.

_____. 2013. *Obama's Wars.* New York: Simon & Schuster.

Woodward, Bob, and Carl Bernstein. 1976. *The Final Days.* New York: Simon & Schuster.

Zernike, Kate. 2006. "Bush's Use of Authority Riles Senator." *New York Times*, June 28.

Index

Bold page numbers indicate tables, and italic numbers indicate figures.

O'Reilly, Bill 85, 130, 172
Osnos, Evan 170
Owen, Diana 126

Palin, Sarah 115
passive positive presidents 11
Patriot Act 75
Peele, Jordan 168
Pence, Mike 149
Penny Press 13
Pentagon 4, 52, 81
Perot, Ross 40, 69, 124
Persian Gulf War, 1991 33, 60, 84
Pew Research Center 25–27; on
    Barack Obama 104–105, 112; on
    Bill Clinton 46, 50; on Donald
    Trump 151; on Fox News 64,
    84; on media environment during
    Obama era 92
Philippines, the 176
Phillips 72
pitch to the American people:
    Clinton's 39–41; George W. Bush's
    68–70; Obama's 99–100; Trump's
    137–138
Pizzagate 135
Poindexter, John 24
Poland 80
political humor 35, 71
Politico 34
Politifact 115
Pompeo, Joseph 131
Poor Richard's Almanac 35
presidential character 161–162;
    of Barack Obama 98–102; of
    Bill Clinton 39–44; campaign
    presentations of 2; citizen views on
    5–6; of Donald Trump 141–142;
    foreign policy and 49–51; framing
    of 7–13; of Franklin Roosevelt
    16–17; and the future 177–181;
    general types of 10–12; of George
    W. Bush 66–73; global politics
    and 176–177; of John Kennedy
    17–19; media changes and the
    communication of 165–172;
    ongoing conversations about
    169–171; political concerns and
    scholarly models of 9–13; Trump
    and the future of candidates and
    178–181; value of emphasizing
    162–164; White House staff and
    174–176

Presidential Character (Barber) 10
presidential communication:
    challenges through history 13–25;
    Franklin Delano Roosevelt and the
    rise of radio for 16–17; legacy of
    Barack Obama 119–123; legacy
    of Bill Clinton 55–58; legacy
    of George W. Bush 87–90; new
    communication technologies and
    1–4; presidents' battle for media
    attention and 4–7; "road show"
    events 5; staged events 2, 5; of
    Trump to date 158–160
presidential framing resilience 6–7
presidents: autobiographies by 6,
    91–92; battle for media attention
    4–7; Capitol Hill challenges for
    172–176; citizens opinions of 5–6;
    Framers' vision of limited power
    of 4; impeachment of 1, 51–55;
    medial challenges through history
    13–25; military service by 42, 45;
    and the search for America's moral
    core 171–172
Priebus, Reince 146, 159
Project for Excellence in
    Journalism 98
public opinion: of the Affordable Care
    Act 116–119; of Barack Obama
    104–108, 116–119; of Bill Clinton
    46–49, 55–58, 119; of Donald
    Trump 143–145; of George H. W.
    Bush 56; of George W. Bush 69,
    76–79, 119, 163; of presidents *vs.*
    Congress 4–5; on repealing the
    Affordable Care Act 156–158; of
    Ronald Reagan 56–57, 121; and
    trust in news media 126–128; *see
    also* citizens
Putin, Vladimir 79, 171, 172

racial heritage of Obama 2, 99–100
radio 16–17, 39; conservative talk
    34–35, 55, 63
Reagan, Nancy 22
Reagan, Ronald 8–9, 11, 45, 82, 88,
    166, 171; Iran-Contra and 23–25;
    public opinion of legacy of 56–57,
    121; television and 22–25
Rector, Ricky Ray 41, 69
Reddit 135
Reed, Jack 140
Reeves, Richard 21